For friends

BUNCO

A Comedy About The Drama Of Friendship

EMERGENCY AREA WAITING ROOM - DAWN

The early morning daylight begins to fill the foyer of a hospital waiting room packed with police officers.

ANNE HUTCHINSON, an athletic, petite woman in her early 40s, is sitting dazed and exhausted in bloodstained clothes.

JILL MICHAELS stands behind Anne with her phone to her ear. Over a decade has passed since Jill's tenure as Miss South Carolina ended, but she currently reigns over the local elementary school as parent council president. She masks her anxiety with her polished manners and pleasant southern accent.

JILL

Good morning Miss Lowe, this is Mrs. Michaels. I hope your morning is going well. Would you be a dear and let Mrs. Kaiser know I won't be able to attend today's parent council meeting?

A police officer watches Jill closely as he patrols the room. She reads the judgment on the officer's face.

JILL

Actually, I may not be able to attend tomorrow's fundraiser either. I'll call y'all back as soon as I know. Thank you so much, Miss Lowe.

Jill ends her call, sighs heavily, and takes a seat next to Anne.

RACHEL EASTON, a mid-40s, Midwest-born, and Irish-proud woman, is asleep on the opposite chair. Handcuffs dangle from one of Rachel's wrists. When awake, Rachel harbors a deep and painful secret that manifests itself in belligerent and self-destructive behavior.

A NURSE passes by the three women. The aroma emanating from Rachel's general vicinity stops her in her tracks.

NURSE

How long has this homeless woman been sleeping here?

JILL

She's not homeless. She's with us.

The nurse shakes her head in disgust and continues on her way.

MARY HUESTON approaches the women with coffee in her hands. Now in her early 40s, Mary has traded her Hollywood acting auditions for youth soccer games, and her figure has become less "soap opera star" and more "community bake sale." She hands Jill and Anne the steaming Styrofoam cups.

MARY

Here. Should we wake Rachel?

Mary begins to take a seat next to Rachel but quickly pivots to allow more breathing room. They each deeply inhale the cup's contents to mask the aroma.

JILL

She's been through a lot. Let's let her sleep.

MARY

We've all been through a lot.

Mary notices Anne staring off in the distance.

MARY

How ya doing, Anne?

Anne slowly brings her attention to Mary.

MARY

You okay?

Anne silently examines her bloodstained clothes, contemplates her predicament, and shakes her head in disbelief.

ANNE

(Under her breath)

Fucking bunco.

SIX WEEKS EARLIER...

ROUND 1

Meeting the Players

SUBURBAN CUL-DE-SAC - MORNING

Anne and Mary are nearing the end of a run through their neighborhood. Mary struggles to keep up with the well-conditioned Anne.

MARY
(Labored breathing)
Why... in God's name... did I think... this was a good idea?

ANNE
(Effortlessly)
Last bunco, you made me promise I wouldn't let you back out.

The women continue to run around the corner and up their street. Jill is waiting at the bus stop, along with her three children and Mary's two sons. Anne and Mary end their run in front of Jill.

JILL
How'd y'all do?

MARY
(Panting heavily)
That was... the worst forty-five minutes... of my life.

Mary steps over to her two boys, eight-year-old CHARLIE, and six-year-old ETHAN, as they wait to get on the bus.

MARY
Give your dying mother a kiss goodbye.

Charlie and Ethan both cringe as Mary forcibly plants her sweaty lips upon them. Anne continues her conversation with Jill.

JILL
I didn't see Jack this morning.

ANNE
Megan drove him to school.

Mary rejoins the conversation holding her side.

MARY
I think I'll stay the fat funny one.

ANNE
What?

MARY

You know. Jill's the beautiful sweet one, you're the athletic smart one, and I'm the fat funny one.

Anne waves off Mary's characterizations.

JILL

So, what does that make Rachel?

As Jill finishes her sentence, Rachel pulls up in her top-of-the-line German sports sedan. The car window slides down smoothly as the engine purrs.

RACHEL

(Cigarette in her lips)

Jesus Christ, Mary, I thought you were smarter than to get dragged into this healthy living nonsense.

ANNE

You should give it a try, Rachel. It makes you feel great at the end of the day.

RACHEL

Yeah, so does my vibrator.

Anne shakes her head at Rachel's familiar, unbridled comment.

RACHEL

The Hadley's house sold. I saw the agent taking down the sign.

The women strain to confirm the sign is missing from the front yard.

ANNE

I guess that means we'll have new neighbors soon.

RACHEL

I'd prefer the house stay empty.

ANNE

Come on, Rachel, it'll be nice for you to have someone new to torture in the neighborhood.

Rachel remains silent while giving Anne her trademark smirk.

MARY

Are you going to be at bunco tonight?

RACHEL
Hell yes! Who's hosting?

MARY/JILL
Anne.

ANNE
(Shocked)
Wait, what?!

MARY
Yeah, don't you remember?

ANNE
No. I have to remember the schedule of everyone in my house. Of course, I forget mine.

RACHEL
We can always go to Back Alley Bar.

ANNE
It's okay, I got called off the hospital this morning. I should be fine. Just promise me you'll lower your expectations.

ANNE'S ENTRY HALL - THAT EVENING

The doorbell rings. Anne opens the door to reveal Jill standing outside with two platters of food balanced in her arms.

ANNE
Jill, how many times do I have to tell you? You don't have to ring the bell, just come in.

Jill sheepishly enters Anne's house.

JILL
I know, I'm sorry. I just have trouble bursting into someone's home.

Anne closes the door behind Jill, and gratefully takes one of the plates from her.

ANNE
Let me help you with that.

ANNE'S DINING ROOM - CONTINUOUS

Jill follows Anne to the dining room table and adds her food to the other plates, somehow able to exude hospitality even in someone else's home.

JILL
Since you weren't as prepared as you would have liked, I made a couple extra things to help you out.

ANNE
Thank you so much. I don't know what I'd do without you.

Jill humbly smiles at Anne's sincere sentiment.

JILL
This one is still a bit warm. Do you have a hot pad?

ANNE
Let me go get it.

As Anne disappears into the kitchen, Rachel bursts through the front door with a liter of bourbon in one hand and a six-pack of diet cola in the other. She proceeds to the dining room while barking orders at Anne and Jill.

RACHEL
Get me a glass and some ice!

Anne returns from the kitchen and hands Jill the hot pad.

ANNE
Hey, Rachel. How are you?

Rachel dramatically thumps the liquor and soda on the table.

RACHEL
I'll let you guess.

JILL
Bad day?

Rachel shouts as she heads into the kitchen. Jill rearranges her plates properly on the table for the best presentation.

RACHEL
If only it was limited to just one day!

Jill and Anne exchange knowing glances in the dining room and remain unfazed as yet another of Rachel's rants begin.

RACHEL
(From the kitchen)
Kevin is a self-absorbed ass! I'm starting to think his first wife didn't die, she ran away! My oldest stepdaughter is a money-grubbing snot whose sole purpose in life is to out-spend and out-bitch me! News flash, she's winning! And, my mother's calling me to find out why the chickens won't stay in the bathtub!

Rachel returns to the dining room and begins to fill her glass with bourbon.

JILL
Why does your mother have chickens in her bathtub?

Rachel looks at her half-full glass of bourbon, then the unopened can of soda. She neglects to open the soda and just throws half of what's in the glass down her throat.

RACHEL
She doesn't have chickens OR a bathtub.

Rachel opens the soda and adds it to what's left in the glass.

RACHEL
She doesn't understand why her Irish Catholic guilt is ineffective on imaginary poultry.

ANNE
How long has she been this bad?

Rachel continues to drink more.

RACHEL
Oh, she's always been bat-shit crazy. Now there's just a diagnosis from a doctor.

Mary enters the front door with a store-bought cake in her hand and continues to the dining room.

MARY

Hello, ladies!

Anne takes the cake from Mary.

ANNE

That looks delicious.

MARY

It was the most fattening looking one in the case. I figured I deserved it after the misery you put me through this morning.

Mary notices Rachel's almost-empty glass.

MARY

Am I late?

JILL

(Whispers to Mary)

She just got here.

MARY

Well, it looks like you've initiated your warp drive, Rachel.

Rachel raises her drink to acknowledge Mary, then takes a seat in front of the buffet and begins loading a plate.

ANNE

So, anyone know anything about our new neighbors?

Rachel keeps her attention on her food.

RACHEL

Nothing.

MARY

Will we be extending an invitation to a new player?

JILL

I think it would be nice to have someone new in the group.

Rachel looks up from her plate.

RACHEL

We aren't enough for you, Jill?

JILL

Of course, y'all are enough. It's just that I remember when I moved here from South Carolina. I knew no one in this state, and I was terrified I'd be lonely forever. Then y'all invited me to bunco and I found my best friends.

Mary and Anne are moved by Jill's kind words.

RACHEL

But, what if she's an insufferable bore?

Mary's gratitude toward Jill shifts to irritation toward Rachel.

MARY

We took YOU.

ANNE'S FAMILY ROOM - LATER THAT EVENING

The ladies are sprawled out on the couch and floor. Wine and liquor glasses are in varying states of empty, as are the plates of food. The alcohol has imbued a very comfortable, uninhibited atmosphere.

ANNE

I was so bad at oral sex when Bill and I first started dating, he actually asked me to stop.

MARY

When you first started dating?! My God, Anne, you need to reserve that for big purchases and speeding tickets.

ANNE

Oh honey, trust me. I'm accused of the bait-and-switch all the time.

RACHEL

(Very inebriated)

It's a dick in your mouth, how hard can it be?

Rachel drunkenly laughs at her own pun as she finishes off another drink.

ANNE

Let's just say, I wasn't aware of the topography of my oral cavity back then.

MARY

So, you've gotten better?

ANNE
(Confidently)
I got the bathroom remodeled last fall, didn't I?

The women share a round of laughter.

MARY
(Emboldened)
Okay, here's a question I just heard on the radio. Have any of you ever thought about someone else while having sex with your husband?

RACHEL
I can't remember.

ANNE
No way. What if I called out the wrong name?

MARY
That's why you should only scream, "Oh God!"

JILL
(Mildly judgmental)
Scream?

MARY
Okay, maybe not scream, but you know what I mean.

Jill tilts her head away from Mary.

JILL
I'm not having this conversation.

Mary playfully teases Jill.

MARY
Come on, Jill. Your pastor is not here. You don't have to pretend to be innocent with us.

Jill pleasantly smiles and refuses to give Mary the reaction she's looking for.

ANNE
Leave her alone. You know she doesn't talk about this.

Rachel takes her empty glass and moves toward the kitchen.

RACHEL
(Under her breath)
Let's all adopt that policy.

ANNE
I can barely touch Bill without him thinking it's a green light for sex. Sometimes I just want to kiss or cuddle, not sign up for the full pregame, postgame, and halftime show.

MARY
Craig is the same way. I have to take off my bra in the closet or he thinks I'm sending him "signals." I so wish he was a butt guy.

JILL
What's a "butt guy?"

MARY
All men prefer either a woman's butt or boobs. Craig is all about boobs. I swear the man would bring a snorkel to bed if I let him.

Rachel re-enters the room, sipping her refreshed cocktail.

ANNE
Hey, Rachel, is Kevin a butt man?

Rachel chokes dramatically on the liquor in her mouth and is forced to spit most of it back into her glass. She continues to cough violently as she tries to regain her composure. Jill gets up to assist Rachel by patting her forcefully on the back.

RACHEL
(Through coughs)
I'm not choking, it just went down the wrong pipe.

JILL
You okay?

RACHEL
I'm fine.

Rachel grabs a napkin as Jill returns to her seat.

ANNE
How 'bout it, Rachel? Is Kevin a butt man or a boob guy?

Rachel, now beyond inebriated, does her best to wipe herself off.

RACHEL
God, I wish you knew how absurd you sound.

MARY
Oh, come on.

RACHEL
How many times do we have to have these sex discussions? Can't we talk about something less depressing like exploited children or tortured lab animals?

Rachel lets out another cough, but there's something behind it. She raises her hand to her mouth and sets down her drink. She looks toward the front door, then bolts through the kitchen. Anne, Jill, and Mary jump up and follow behind her.

ANNE
(Panicking)
Wait! Are you throwing up?! Where are you going?!

ANNE'S LAUNDRY ROOM - CONTINUOUS

Anne, Jill, and Mary scramble into the doorway just in time to see Rachel throw up in the utility sink. Jill and Mary cringe as Anne becomes outraged.

ANNE
Are you kidding me?! You just ran past the front door where you could have puked outside, past the bathroom where I could have flushed it, past the kitchen sink with a garbage disposal, and into my utility sink! That thing has a drain the size of a nickel!

Rachel keeps her head in the sink and deflates into a miserable state of drunkenness.

MARY
And that's the end of bunco.

Rachel pulls her head up from the sink.

RACHEL
Don't touch it. I'll clean it tomorrow.

ANNE
Tomorrow?! You think I'm going to let that sit in there and stink up my house all night?!

Rachel slumps along the wall and slides down into a pathetic ball. Mary makes her way through the doorway.

MARY
Come on, Rachel. Let's get you home. Jill, can you help me?

Jill and Mary pick up Rachel and begin to guide her out of the laundry room.

MARY
We'll be back to help you.

Anne stares at the vomit-filled sink.

ANNE
(Under her breath)
She's going to pay for this.

OUTSIDE ANNE'S HOUSE - MOMENTS LATER

Mary and Jill support Rachel as they walk her outside the house and down the driveway. As they approach the street, Mary's eyebrows rise as she notices a large moving van outside the vacant home. Movers are quickly and efficiently moving furniture inside the house.

MARY
Hey, check it out. Looks like the new neighbors can't wait to move in.

JILL
That's quite the moving company to be working at this hour.

Their attention snaps back to Rachel, who is now requiring even more assistance as the alcohol's effects sink deeper into her bloodstream. The women struggle to keep her walking upright.

RACHEL
(Mumbling)
Stop spinning me around.

MARY
We aren't spinning you, that's your brain cells doing the backstroke in all the bourbon you drank.

JILL
(To Mary)
Why does she always have to drink so much?

RACHEL
(Slurring)
I can hear you! I'm drunk, not deaf. We all can't be as perfect as you, Jill.

Mary nervously quickens the pace.

MARY
A few more yards and you can pass out around your own toilet.

RACHEL'S FRONT PORCH - CONTINUOUS

Mary and Jill support Rachel as they knock on the door. KEVIN EASTON, a distinguished, greying gentleman in his early 50s, answers the door. He looks over the all-too-familiar post-bunco situation on his front porch.

KEVIN
I already bought cookies from the sober girl scouts.

MARY
Ha, ha, you're hysterical. Let us in, Kevin. She's not getting any lighter.

Kevin pushes the door wide and takes Rachel into his arms.

KEVIN
Another successful bunco. Thanks for bringing her home.

Kevin turns to take Rachel inside.

MARY
You may want to flush her out with some mouthwash.

Jill grabs the door to pull it shut.

JILL
Good night, Kevin.

NEIGHBORHOOD STREET - CONTINUOUS

Jill and Mary walk back toward Anne's house.

MARY
You go home. I'll help Anne clean up.

JILL
No, I'll help.

MARY
You've got a sitter, and between the dog and the boys, I've got more experience cleaning up vomit than I'd like to admit.

JILL
Are you sure?

MARY
Yeah. I'll bring your stuff over tomorrow.

JILL
Thanks, Mary.

Jill and Mary finish their goodbye, and Jill turns toward her home. Mary pauses in the street and watches the movers more closely.

ANNE'S LAUNDRY ROOM - MOMENTS LATER

Mary enters the laundry room where Anne is elbow-deep in the sink with a bucket. Anne fishes out a large chunk of undigested food. Anne turns to see Mary standing behind her, then continues her work.

ANNE
What the hell did she eat tonight?

MARY
They're moving in now.

Anne lifts her head from the sink.

ANNE
What?

MARY
The new neighbors are moving in now.

ANNE

Now?

MARY

RIGHT now.

ANNE

Why would they be moving in at this hour?

Mary dramatically shrugs her shoulders.

MARY

I have no idea.

NEIGHBORHOOD STREET - NEXT MORNING

Anne runs around the corner, down the street, and past Rachel's house. Rachel is clearly hungover as she gingerly bends over to fetch the newspaper from her driveway.

RACHEL

(Shouts to Anne)

Do I owe you an apology?!

Anne continues to run past Rachel.

ANNE

I'm not talking to you!

Rachel lowers her head and turns back to her house. Anne stops in her driveway and takes notice of the previously vacant home next door. Through the front windows, she sees an interior that looks surprisingly settled and fully furnished. Her mouth unconsciously pops open.

COLLEEN YOUNG, an athletic, beautiful, blonde woman in her late 20s, runs up behind Anne and takes her by surprise.

COLLEEN

(Perky and upbeat)

Hi!

Fully engrossed in the expediency of the moving company, Anne jumps back and almost trips over her feet.

COLLEEN

(Concerned)

Oh my gosh, I am so sorry. I didn't mean to scare you.

Anne holds her now pounding chest.

ANNE
That's okay. I just wasn't expecting anyone behind me.

COLLEEN
I'm Colleen Young. I'm living next door.

Colleen extends her hand and Anne shakes it.

ANNE
Hi, Colleen. I'm Anne Hutchinson.

COLLEEN
Nice to meet you. Do you run every morning?

ANNE
When I can.

COLLEEN
We should run together sometime.

Anne, clearly intimidated by Colleen's appearance, looks her up and down.

ANNE
(Hesitant)
Something tells me you'd be hard to keep up with.

Colleen laughs at the notion and Anne awkwardly smiles.

COLLEEN
I'll see you around.

Colleen continues her run down the street.

ANNE
(Insincerely)
Yeah, see ya.

Anne cranes her neck to evaluate Colleen as she walks up her driveway.

ANNE'S KITCHEN - CONTINUOUS

Anne enters through her garage door and greets her husband in the kitchen. BILL HUTCHINSON is a former college linebacker whose youthful muscles have fallen victim to gravity, and who now leaves more of a Santa Claus impression than an elite athlete.

ANNE
I met one of our new neighbors.

Bill remains preoccupied with his phone.

BILL
Oh yeah, which one?

ANNE
(Mockingly)
Colleen.

BILL
What's wrong with "Colleen?"

ANNE
Nothing. She seems wonderful. She's young, pleasant, and beautiful.

Bill looks up from his phone.

BILL
So, great.

ANNE
Great? Really? Like I need a specimen of perfection staring at me from next door. Having Jill, the former beauty queen, across the driveway is intimidating enough.

Bill grabs Anne around the waist and pulls her toward him.

BILL
You've got a specimen of perfection staring at you right here, baby.

ANNE
(Playfully)
You think so, huh?

They kiss.

BILL
(Amorously)
Should I be late for work?

Anne pulls away from his embrace and moves to the coffee pot.

ANNE
(Dismissive)
This is why we can't kiss.

Bill sighs but moves on from disappointment quickly and shouts at the kitchen ceiling.

BILL
Jack! I'm leaving!

ANNE
Make sure he has lunch money today, okay?

BILL
Sure. Oh, hey, what happened in the laundry room?

Anne closes her eyes, holds up her hand and shakes her head. Bill figures she is sparing him a story and moves toward the garage.

BILL
Jack! I'm walking out the door!

JACK HUTCHINSON, their 13-year-old son, enters the kitchen disheveled and fumbling with his backpack. Anne puts a banana in his hand as he runs to follow Bill out of the door.

THE NEIGHBORHOOD - LATER THAT DAY

Jill comes out of her house, armed with a freshly baked pie. She crosses the street to where Anne has just pulled into her driveway. Anne, still in hospital scrubs, opens her car door and is immediately greeted by Jill.

ANNE
Hey, Jill! How are you?

JILL
(Nervously)
Well, I'm not sure I went with the right pie. Derby pie is local, but I would have felt so much more confident going with a chess pie or simple pecan.

Anne exits her car and smells the pie.

ANNE
Jill, are you capable of making a bad dessert? Besides, if they don't eat it, I will.

JILL

Oh, I know these are your favorites, so I made you one too. It's my way of apologizing for not helping you deal with Rachel's mess last night.

ANNE

She pukes and you apologize. Yep, that's about right.

Anne puts her keys in her purse.

ANNE

I'm not sure the new neighbor will have any interest in pie.

Jill's face reflects concern for possibly preparing an unwanted dessert.

JILL

What do you mean?

ANNE

I met her this morning, and I would be incredibly surprised if she ever EATS, let alone indulges in pie.

JILL

What's she like? Is she nice?

ANNE

(Sardonically)

Very. She's nice, young, beautiful, blonde... I hate her.

JILL

(Confused)

What?

ANNE

(Reassuring)

I'm kidding, Jill.

Mary approaches Jill and Anne on the driveway.

MARY

Are you talking to Rachel yet?

ANNE

Why? Is she waiting for your signal that it's okay to come over?

Mary holds up her cell phone.

MARY

No, my call.

Anne sighs, knowing a grudge is pointless.

ANNE

Go ahead and call her.

Mary hits a speed dial number and holds the phone to her ear.

MARY

Okay, you can come over.

Mary ends her call and Anne shuts the car door. The three women walk through Anne's garage.

ANNE'S KITCHEN - MOMENTS LATER

Anne sets her purse and other belongings on her kitchen table. Mary detects the lingering stench as they pass through the laundry room.

MARY

Wow. That smell isn't going away is it?

ANNE

Don't remind me. I'm going upstairs to change. I'll be right back.

Mary and Jill are left in the kitchen. Mary bends to sniff the pie in Jill's hands, looking for olfactory relief.

MARY

What'd you make?

JILL

Derby pie. I thought I'd give 'em a taste of Kentucky.

MARY

Do we know where they're from?

JILL

No, but Anne said she met the woman this morning, and I guess she's young and quite attractive.

MARY

(Wary)

Really? How young? How attractive?

Rachel enters the kitchen through the garage door and drops two dice into Anne's purse.

RACHEL
Look, I'm sorry about last night, I'll pay any amount of money to have it cleaned.

MARY
Save it. She's upstairs.

RACHEL
Is she still mad?

Mary folds her arms.

MARY
Did you eat anything before you came to bunco, Rachel?

Rachel contorts her face with disgust as she remembers her meal.

RACHEL
Soup.

MARY
Soup? What kind of soup?

RACHEL
(Ashamed)
Seafood gumbo.

Mary patronizingly nods.

MARY
Imagine dealing with a mixture of THAT, everything you inhaled when you got here, the hundred proof bourbon you consumed, and your stomach bile. How long would you stay mad?

Anne re-enters the kitchen in casual attire.

ANNE
Okay, we ready?

RACHEL
(Sincerely)
Listen, I know I was wrong to leave four gallons of vomit in your sink last night.

ANNE

Ya think? Rachel, I did an internship at a New Orleans hospital during Mardi Gras and your mess was, without question, the worst thing I've ever had to deal with.

RACHEL

I will hire a disaster restoration crew, a hazmat team, AND an exorcist to come here and clean your house.

ANNE

No, thank you. That won't be necessary. But you are not allowed to be surprised when the day comes, and I get even with you.

RACHEL

(Apprehensively)

What are you planning to do?

Anne takes a deep, contemplative breath.

ANNE

I don't know yet.

JILL

Come on, this pie is getting heavy.

NEW NEIGHBOR'S HOUSE - MOMENTS LATER

The women are huddled on the porch.

MARY

(Quietly)

So, we agree. If she's quasi-normal, we invite her to bunco.

RACHEL

Quasi-normal? Are we raising our standards?

Jill hushes the ladies as she rings the doorbell. The door opens, and Jill extends her arms, offering the pie.

JILL

Hi, y'all! Welcome to the neighborhood.

Standing at the open door is LEIGH MCMILLAN, a mid-30s, soft-spoken, homely-looking woman. Her husband, TREVOR MCMILLAN, a strong, fit, incredibly attractive man in his 30s, quickly joins Leigh at the door as she accepts the pie from Jill.

LEIGH

Thank you.

Trevor quickly swoops in to take over the conversation. The women are dumbstruck by the disparity in Leigh and Trevor's appearances.

TREVOR

Hi. I'm Trevor, Trevor McMillan.

Mary accidentally lets her thoughts spill out of her mouth.

MARY

I'm perplexed... I mean I'm puh...leasured to meet you.

Mary offers an enthusiastic smile to try and sell her verbal correction. Jill speaks up quickly.

JILL

We're your neighbors, and we wanted to come by and welcome you both.

TREVOR

Well, thank you. This is my wife, Leigh.

Trevor seems suspiciously enthusiastic and overbearing while Leigh is shy and noticeably uncomfortable.

LEIGH

Hi.

Anne and Mary share a quick, puzzled glance.

ANNE

I'm sorry, I met a young woman this morning named Colleen. She said she lives here.

TREVOR

Oh, that's Colleen Young. She's a friend of Leigh's. She's in the process of a divorce, so we're letting her stay in the spare bedroom until she finds a place.

Colleen quietly approaches the porch from behind the women and interrupts.

COLLEEN

Talking about me again, Trevor?

The women are all startled by the interruption. Anne turns around and Colleen recognizes her.

COLLEEN

Hello, Anne.

ANNE

Hi! Everyone, THIS is Colleen.

Colleen throws her hand up in a coy wave before moving next to Trevor and Leigh. The sight of all three standing beside each other adds to the shared confusion.

COLLEEN

Hi!

JILL

Welcome to our neighborhood. I'm Jill, and I live over there.

Jill indicates she lives across the street.

JILL

I made y'all a Derby pie. It's a pecan base with chocolate chips and Kentucky bourbon.

Rachel cringes at the mention of bourbon.

COLLEEN

Sounds amazing. Thank you so much. There may be a fight for it after dinner, right guys?

TREVOR

Yeah!

Rachel silently evaluates the body language between Colleen and Trevor while Anne continues with introductions.

ANNE

This is Mary. She lives next to Jill.

MARY

Don't concern yourself with the screaming and yelling coming from my house. I have two boys... or my husband is balancing the checkbook.

COLLEEN
(Through a laugh)
Nice to meet you.

ANNE
This is Rachel. She's at the end of the cul-de-sac.

Rachel half-heartedly smiles.

ANNE
And as Colleen knows, I'm next door.

COLLEEN
It's so nice to meet all of you. Trevor and Leigh have moved to such a great neighborhood.

Jill speaks with her perfect mixture of refined poise and sincere geniality.

JILL
We women have a friendly get together every other week where we eat, drink, and play a dice game called bunco.

ANNE
We haven't actually played bunco in years. Most of our members quit or moved away, but we still like the eating and drinking part.

JILL
We'd love to have you join us. Both of you, of course.

Leigh seems to liven up a bit.

LEIGH
That sounds like fun.

TREVOR
Maybe we should wait til we're settled in?

COLLEEN
Yeah, Leigh. You have a lot of unpacking to do.

Leigh ignores Colleen and addresses Trevor pleadingly.

LEIGH
I know, but I think I need to get out of this house, Trevor.

Trevor's overly friendly demeanor dissolves as he forces a pleasant response.

TREVOR

Of course, honey.

Colleen tries to deflect the tension between Trevor and Leigh.

COLLEEN

Why don't we start digging into the boxes and do our best to make it?

JILL

Great! Our next bunco night is on the 15th. It'll be at my house at 7:30. Y'all don't need to worry about bringing a thing, we'll take care of it all.

COLLEEN

We'll be looking forward to it!

TREVOR

Thanks again for the pie.

JILL

You are most welcome. We'll see y'all on the 15th, if not sooner.

Trevor and Colleen lead Leigh back into the house and close the door.

TREVOR AND LEIGH'S FOYER - CONTINUOUS

Trevor's pleasant demeanor quickly morphs into anger and frustration. He locks the door, removes the key from the deadbolt, and secures it in his pocket. His teeth clench as he confronts Leigh.

TREVOR

Which of my instructions were unclear to you?

Leigh cowers as Trevor hovers over her.

LEIGH

I'm sorry.

Trevor backs down and addresses Colleen.

TREVOR

Keep her from doing anything else stupid.

NEIGHBORHOOD STREET - CONTINUOUS

The women head back over to Anne's house.

RACHEL
Did anyone else feel the sexual tension between Trevor and Colleen?

Jill uses her smile to hush Rachel.

ANNE
I've got to put a bell on that Colleen. That's twice now she's snuck up on me like a member of Seal Team Six.

ANNE'S KITCHEN - MOMENTS LATER

Mary, Jill, and Rachel follow Anne into the kitchen. Mary is about to burst from holding in her comments.

MARY
What the hell is going on over there?!

RACHEL
Trevor is definitely banging Colleen!

JILL
Stop it!

MARY
I agree with Rachel. There is no way that... guy isn't finding a way to get into bed with that... woman.

ANNE
How can they be having an affair? She's his wife's friend, for crying out loud.

RACHEL
Like that means anything! Their whole affair probably started when he comforted her during her divorce.

Rachel plays out a scene between Trevor and Colleen, complete with dramatic imitations.

RACHEL

-Oh, Trevor, I'm just so sad and lonely.

-You know what will make it all better, Colleen? My penis!

Mary raises her fingers to make air quotes.

MARY

What if they're all "together?"

Anne imitates Mary's gesture.

ANNE

What do you mean "together?"

MARY

I'm just saying... I watch a lot of reality TV and there are quite a few "alternative" living arrangements out there.

Jill mocks them both by using air quotes.

JILL

I think all y'all are "horrible." They are delightful people who complimented my pie and accepted our invitation.

RACHEL

Leigh accepted the invitation. The other two were obviously trying to get out of it.

Mary becomes horrified at a revelation.

MARY

What if they're traffickers?

ANNE

Drugs?

MARY

I was thinking humans, but yeah, it could be humans or drugs.

Rachel interrupts.

RACHEL

It could easily be human trafficking.

ANNE

Oh, you're an expert now?

RACHEL

I'm just saying, let's see what happens next week. If Leigh shows up, Colleen is taking the opportunity to bang Trevor. If they both show up, Leigh is probably being pimped out at truck stops.

ANNE

And if neither shows up?

RACHEL

Then Mary's swinger theory is probably right.

Anne facetiously entertains Mary and Rachel's assumptions.

ANNE

So, just to recap... after a five-minute encounter, you've decided these people are either human traffickers, cheaters, or swingers.

RACHEL

Don't forget the drug possibility.

ANNE

Right, or drug dealers.

Jill is disgusted by the suggestions.

JILL

Unbelievable. How can you two be so suspicious and nasty?

RACHEL

It's a gift.

ANNE'S HOUSE - A WEEK LATER

Anne is standing at her front window, watching Trevor take out the trash. She shouts upstairs.

ANNE

Bill!

No response forces Anne to raise her voice.

ANNE

BILL!

BILL

(From upstairs)

What?!

ANNE

Come here!

BILL

(From upstairs)

Why?!

Anne begins to insistently shout.

ANNE

Just come down here! I need you to do me a favor!

Bill reluctantly comes downstairs.

BILL

(From the staircase)

This better be a sexual favor.

ANNE

No, but I'll owe you one if you do this for me.

Bill quickens his step down to the front window alongside Anne.

BILL

You have my attention.

Anne takes Bill by the arm and leads him to the door.

ANNE

I need you to go talk to the new neighbor.

Bill pulls his arm away.

BILL

What?! No.

ANNE

Come on, Bill. I have to get a second opinion here. There are some pretty crazy rumors going around.

BILL

That YOUR friends started!

ANNE

Just help me out here! I want to know what you think.

BILL

I think - no wait - I KNOW I don't care.

ANNE

Bill! Come on!

BILL

(Whiny)

Oh God, don't make me do this.

ANNE

Look, get me some answers and I'll make it worth your while.

Bill considers for a moment.

BILL

Like, "bathroom remodel," worth my while?

Anne begins to push Bill out of the front door.

ANNE

Yes. Fine. But the duration will be contingent upon the quality of the information you get.

Bill feigns shame as he reluctantly exits.

BILL

You make me feel like such a whore.

ANNE

Don't forget to ask why they moved in so late.

Bill goes out of the door, and Anne pulls out her phone to call Mary.

ANNE

Mary. Bill just went out to talk to Trevor. Send Craig over.

Anne ends her call and watches Bill start to interact with Trevor. Her attention shifts to Mary's garage door going up and CRAIG HUESTON, a tall man in his 40s, being shoved out of the door. Anne continues to watch the scene unfold as Craig approaches the guys.

Anne is so preoccupied with watching the men that she fails to notice Mary walk across the street and enter her house. Mary joins Anne at the window watching the men.

MARY
What's happening?

ANNE
(Startled)
Jesus, you scared me. I didn't hear you come in.

MARY
Sorry. What's going on?

ANNE
I'm not really sure. Bill met Trevor out at the trash cans, they talked for a bit, and then Craig showed up. I see them laughing and talking, so I hope they're getting us some answers.

Mary points out Colleen running up the street.

MARY
Look. Here comes Colleen.

ANNE
(Shocked)
Seriously? She already went running this morning. Is she training for the Boston Marathon?

Anne and Mary watch silently as Colleen approaches the three men. Although they can't hear a thing, Anne and Mary can see both of their husbands enthusiastically engaging Colleen in the conversation. After a few moments of watching the four, Anne and Mary witness Colleen flirtatiously toss her hair back and laugh at something the men said.

Anne and Mary imitate Colleen's behavior.

ANNE
Are you kidding me?

MARY
I'm surprised she didn't just take her top off!

Anne and Mary continue to watch as the foursome breaks up and Trevor and Colleen return up their driveway. Craig and Bill congenially walk back to his house.

ANNE'S KITCHEN - CONTINUOUS

Bill and Craig unknowingly advance into a waiting ambush.

BILL
I'm free Friday afternoon if we can get a tee time at Eagle Ridge.

CRAIG
I'll just have to reschedule my two o'clock.

Anne and Mary stand eager for a report.

ANNE
Well?!

BILL
Well, what?

ANNE
What did you find out, Bill? What does he do for a living? Why did they move in during the middle of the night? Did he offer you drugs? What city did they come from? Did he seem weird when Colleen came up? Do you think he's the cheating type? What about the swinger theory? You were over there for ten minutes! You must have some information or formed some impression!

Bill stands wide-eyed and open-mouthed for a moment, then turns to Craig who shares the same expression. Bill returns his attention to Anne.

BILL
He's an eight handicap.

Anne's posture deflates with disappointment.

ANNE
Golf.

CRAIG
AND, he's played Augusta.

MARY
You have got to be kidding us.

Bill walks to the refrigerator and pulls out two beers for himself and Craig.

BILL

Look, I'm sorry I'm not TMZ. You told me to go talk to the guy and I did.

ANNE

No, I told you to go get ANSWERS.

BILL

What am I supposed to do, Anne? Interrogate the poor guy only days after he moves into a new neighborhood?

MARY/ANNE

Yes.

Bill opens the beers and hands one to Craig.

BILL

I know what you four gossip girls are theorizing, and I don't buy any of it.

ANNE

Did you notice anything about his demeanor change when Colleen joined you?

BILL

Like what? Did he get an instant boner when he saw her?

ANNE

No, smart ass. Did he alter his eye contact? Did his body language shift or become agitated? Did he seem preoccupied or distracted?

BILL

Wow. No more Nancy Grace for you.

ANNE

I'm serious, Bill. Now, I know you think this guy is going to be a great addition to your golfing foursome, but he left us with a very weird feeling and I'm not terribly comfortable with him living next door without some serious questions getting answered.

BILL

(Defeated)

Fine. Next time he's out, I'll go talk to him again. But in my opinion, you ladies are just looking for something to get all worked up about.

Anne folds her arms.

ANNE

Well, in my opinion, the bathroom doesn't need to be remodeled.

Bill shows obvious signs of disappointment as Anne grabs Mary by the arm and leads her into the other room. The men decide to enjoy their beers, shaking their heads over the suspicions of their wives.

JILL'S HOUSE - A WEEK LATER, EVENING

Jill scampers through her Martha Stewart-inspired home, applying the finishing touches for her bunco night. Jill's husband, JOHN MICHAELS, a handsome, confident man in his late 30s, comes downstairs with their three kids: six-year-old WIL, and four-year-old twins, GRACE and EMMA, all in their pajamas.

JOHN

All right. Let's give mommy a kiss and go upstairs for nighttime.

Jill stops in the middle of her preparations and affectionately kisses each child as well as her husband.

JILL

I'll bring you up a plate of food.

JOHN

(Suggestively)

Don't be too late tonight.

John takes the kids upstairs as Jill continues to create her culinary masterpieces. A knock at the door interrupts her. Mary and Anne enter the house carrying trays of food.

ANNE

Sorry, we're early.

JILL

You're fine. Come on in.

Mary adds her tray of plain sugar cookies to the already overflowing table of handmade appetizers, desserts, decorations, and beverages.

MARY

What's all this?

JILL

With us having new players, I just wanted to make them feel welcome by doing a little something special.

Anne squeezes in her tray of cut vegetables.

ANNE

A little something?

JILL

It's just a few extras. Besides, I like doing it.

MARY

And you're very good at it.

Jill sheepishly accepts the compliment.

JILL'S HOUSE - CONTINUOUS

Rachel is standing on the front porch, sucking the last few drags off her forbidden cigarette. She notices Colleen and Leigh step out of their front door. Trevor stands on his porch and watches the women as they approach Jill's house. Rachel throws her cigarette to the ground and crushes it.

Colleen and Leigh step onto Jill's porch.

COLLEEN

Hello, Rachel.

Rachel throws her head back slightly to acknowledge Trevor on his porch.

RACHEL

Why the watchful eye?

Colleen turns to see that Rachel is referring to Trevor.

COLLEEN

Oh, he's just making sure we're safe.

RACHEL

(Condescendingly)

I was talking to Leigh.

Rachel and Colleen share a challenging look. Leigh tries to lighten the mood.

LEIGH

He watches too many horror movies.

Colleen nervously giggles at Leigh's response. Rachel smiles reluctantly. Their tense exchange is interrupted as Jill opens the front door.

JILL

I thought I heard voices out here. Y'all come on inside.

Rachel watches Colleen and Leigh enter the house. Jill steps onto her porch, pulls the front door shut, and has a private word with Rachel.

JILL

You've been smoking.

RACHEL

No, I haven't.

Jill looks down and sees the cigarette butt on the ground. She bends down, picks up the evidence, and presents it to Rachel.

JILL

Really?

RACHEL

You got me, Nancy Drew.

Jill takes a deep breath and channels her inner "parent council president."

JILL

Can I trust you to behave yourself tonight, remembering that we have new members to the group, and we don't want to say or do anything that may make them feel uncomfortable or embarrassed in any way?

RACHEL

(Annoyed)

Yes.

JILL

Good. Now, go inside, step into my vanity, and spray some perfume on yourself. You smell like an ashtray.

RACHEL

(Under her breath)

I should have stayed at home and smoked in my garage.

Rachel enters the house and Jill follows.

JILL'S LIVING ROOM - LATER

The evening progresses as usual. Food is eaten, beverages are consumed, and conversation is flowing. Jill circles her seated guests, ready to tend to any request. Leigh lifts a sugar-lined, brightly colored martini glass to her lips.

LEIGH
What is this called again?

JILL
Damnation on the Plantation. It's just a little something from back home. Do you like it?

LEIGH
A little too much.

Mary sips her own cocktail.

MARY
Oh, enjoy yourself Leigh, that's what these nights are for.

JILL
I'll go get dessert.

ANNE
Let me help you.

Anne and Jill gather up dirty dishes and glasses and head into the kitchen.

JILL'S KITCHEN - CONTINUOUS

ANNE
(Keeping a low tone)
Leigh seems to be having a good time. I think we can safely abandon the human trafficking theory.

JILL
I can't believe those two and their outrageous imaginations.

Anne looks into the glass she collected from Colleen.

ANNE
What's in here?

Jill inspects the glass Anne is asking about.

JILL

Water.

ANNE

Colleen has been drinking water all night?

JILL

Yes.

ANNE

That's weird, isn't it? Not drinking at a girl's night?

JILL

Maybe she's not a drinker.

ANNE

Leigh certainly is.

Anne pauses.

ANNE

She's enjoying herself so much she'll probably pass out as soon as she gets home. You don't think...

Jill sighs at the same unfounded suspicions.

JILL

What?

Anne realizes Jill wants no part of her theories.

ANNE

Nothing. What can I take back?

JILL

Why don't you take the cake, and I'll bring out some fresh plates and forks.

JILL'S LIVING ROOM - CONTINUOUS

Anne walks into the room carrying the decorative cake, sets it down on the table, and sinks into a chair to rejoin the conversation.

COLLEEN

So, Mary, you have two boys?

MARY

Three, if you count Craig.

LEIGH

They're so cute. I saw them riding their bikes down the street the other day.

ANNE

Do you and Trevor want to start a family?

Leigh lowers her head.

LEIGH

No.

ANNE

(Facetiously)

Really? Bringing aloof, disrespectful tech-zombies into your home doesn't interest you?

Anne throws up her hands to stop herself.

ANNE

Sorry, I have teenagers.

Leigh smiles through a sigh at Anne.

LEIGH

I'd love to have kids one day. I just don't know if that's going to work out.

ANNE

You're still young. You've got plenty of time.

RACHEL

Yeah, not like Mary here and her antiquated uterus. What did they call you during your pregnancy with Ethan?

MARY

"A woman of advanced maternal age." And thank you for bringing THAT up.

Jill enters the room with fresh plates and forks in hand.

JILL

Who wants some dessert?

Jill begins to cut and distribute cake without waiting for an answer.

JILL
What are we talking about?

ANNE
Mary's age-defying reproductive system.

Jill smiles.

JILL
And how are Ethan and Charlie?

MARY
Ethan's fine. I think his teacher moonlights as an underwear model, so he's never been more focused on classroom instruction. Charlie's okay.

JILL
Just okay?

MARY
He complains about being bullied by a kid at school. I've offered to go have a talk with the teacher, but he won't hear of it. I see him hanging his head when he gets off the bus and I want to help, but at the same time, I don't want to make things worse.

ANNE
Jack went through some of that. I think boys feel like they need to deal with it on their own. If their mom gets involved, they're mortified. Whereas girls are so hormonal that moods shift almost hourly. I've learned not to get too upset over Megan being in tears. If I wait twelve hours, she'll recover and move onto a new manufactured drama.

JILL
I'd be happy to say something to his teacher.

MARY
Oh, I know you would, but don't. I'm going to let this play out a bit before I get involved. Hopefully, this kid will get bored with Charlie and move on to someone else.

RACHEL
He won't stop until someone pushes back. If I were you, I'd put Charlie in karate lessons and tell him to let loose on the kid if he gives him any more trouble.

JILL
That's no way to handle it, Rachel.

RACHEL
You're right, Jill. What was I thinking?

Rachel looks at Mary behind Jill's back.

RACHEL
(Mouthing the words)
I'll pay for it.

ANNE
Colleen, are you originally from the Cincinnati area?

COLLEEN
I spent summers with my dad in the Midwest and the school year with my mom in California.

MARY
I lived out there for a while.

COLLEEN
Really, where?

MARY
North Hollywood. I worked in the entertainment industry.

COLLEEN
Really? What did you do?

MARY
I was an actress.

Rachel rolls her eyes.

RACHEL
(Quietly)
Here we go.

COLLEEN
Wow! Have you done anything I might have seen?

RACHEL
You've still got some headshots with you, don't you, Mary?

Mary gives Rachel a dirty look.

ANNE
Mary was on a soap opera back in the nineties.

COLLEEN
(Genuinely impressed)
Really? Very cool.

MARY
(Humbly)
Thanks.

RACHEL
Maybe you could reprise your dramatic role as bartender number two and get me another drink?

Mary watches with distaste as Rachel laughs at herself.

LEIGH
I bet you have a lot of interesting stories.

MARY
Not really. I wasn't in the same circle as the A-listers. It was before married life. After a few years and several not-so-memorable roles, I met Craig. We moved back here, and kids followed.

Rachel shifts the attention to Leigh.

RACHEL
Where are you and Trevor from?

Leigh is caught off guard by the question.

LEIGH
We, uh, met in New York.

JILL
Are you originally from there?

LEIGH
No, I'm not from anywhere that exciting.

ANNE

Well, Cincinnati certainly isn't the thrill capital of the world.

Rachel is not distracted from her line of questioning.

RACHEL

Seriously, where are you from?

Jill watches Leigh uncomfortably fidget and interrupts to save her from Rachel's interrogation tactics.

JILL

Can I get anyone anything? More cake or something to drink, perhaps?

Anne aids in Jill's attempt.

ANNE

I don't know if I can take another one of your Plantation Damnations, but I'd love a water.

RACHEL

I'm going outside for some fresh air.

Rachel grabs her purse and heads out of the front door.

COLLEEN

(Concerned)

Is everything all right with her?

ANNE

Yeah, she's just going outside for a cigarette. We give her a hard time for smoking, so she sneaks away to avoid a lecture.

LEIGH

Did I offend her? She seems angry.

ANNE

That's just Rachel. She seems angry all the time. Don't take it personally.

MARY

We think her time in jail hardened her.

Jill shakes her head.

JILL

Stop telling people that. She has not been to jail. She's just a complicated person who has a different way of communicating.

MARY

Different way of communicating? That's a nice way to phrase contempt and sarcasm.

Jill continues to make excuses for Rachel.

JILL

She's just not as soft around the edges as most.

MARY

Jill always defends Rachel since they have a history of starting fights together.

Jill uncharacteristically raises her voice.

JILL

I had nothing to do with starting that fight!

Jill stifles her outburst and shrinks with embarrassment. Colleen snickers at the thought.

COLLEEN

Like a fist fight?

ANNE

No, like a chair-throwing, nose-breaking, pay-for-damages bar brawl.

LEIGH

You're kidding! What happened?

Anne hesitates until Jill reluctantly approves of sharing the story.

ANNE

This was several years ago. We're all at this crowded bar somewhere downtown, and Rachel gets up to go to the bathroom. Suddenly, some drunk college girl starts accusing Jill of hitting on her boyfriend.

Jill blushes with embarrassment.

JILL

Can you imagine?

ANNE

So, we try to calm the situation down when Rachel comes out of the bathroom. She sees the girl pushing Jill, and without even asking what's going on, she tackles the girl to the ground.

COLLEEN

(Jestingly)

Jill, you're such a troublemaker.

JILL

The ladies of Fiddle De Dee Finishing School would have been mortified.

ANNE

Then the bar kind of splits into the college crowd and, I'll use this term loosely... mature crowd, and a full-out rumble starts.

Leigh and Colleen are amused, impressed, and intimidated all at the same time.

LEIGH

How did it end?

MARY

Let's just say Rachel's bank account recovered quickly, but that girl will, forever, have to explain a rather detailed bite mark on her forehead.

NEIGHBORHOOD IN FRONT OF JILL'S HOUSE - SIMULTANEOUSLY

Rachel is enjoying her cigarette on Jill's porch. A faint conversation catches her attention. She leaves the porch and quietly proceeds down Jill's driveway. She notices a car out front of Trevor and Leigh's house.

Someone is bending their head into the driver-side window and speaking with the driver. The person pulls back from the car to check the street when Rachel realizes it is Trevor. They make eye contact, and Trevor motions for the car to drive away. Trevor walks toward Rachel.

RACHEL

Who was that?

TREVOR

Who?

The two meet at the end of the driveway.

RACHEL
(Bothered)
The person you were just talking to.

Trevor looks down the street, stalling in thought.

TREVOR
Nobody. A guy asking for directions.

RACHEL
(Skeptically)
Directions? No one has asked for directions in a decade.

TREVOR
I guess his GPS directed him into a cornfield one too many times.

Trevor tries to change the topic of conversation.

TREVOR
I didn't know you smoked. Mind if I bum one off you?

Rachel pulls out her cigarette box and lighter.

RACHEL
I don't do a very good job hiding this dirty little secret.

Rachel takes a long drag as Trevor fires up his cigarette.

TREVOR
Are you better at hiding other secrets?

Rachel violently chokes on the smoke in her lungs.

TREVOR
(Smugly)
Are you ladies having fun tonight?

Rachel clears her throat.

RACHEL
Yeah, but your wife doesn't say much.

Trevor hesitates for a moment before sharing.

TREVOR
That doesn't surprise me. She's pretty quiet.

RACHEL

I get quiet, but we're having trouble just learning where she grew up.

TREVOR

She had an ugly childhood and hates talking about it.

RACHEL

(Unimpressed)

Who didn't?

TREVOR

Yeah, but her parents weren't the most responsible people. They made a lot of bad decisions, got into trouble with the law, spent some time in jail.

RACHEL

I get it. We all have family members we're ashamed of. Hell, some of us are the ones our family is ashamed of.

TREVOR

(Condescendingly)

You can understand why she doesn't want to share things in her past she's not proud of.

Rachel and Trevor lock in a mutual stare of distrust. Rachel takes a drag off her cigarette, then fills the air between them with a smoky cloud.

RACHEL

Sure.

Trevor de-escalates the intensity of the conversation with a lighter tone.

TREVOR

It really meant a lot to her that you invited her over tonight. She needs some friends right now.

RACHEL

Moving to a new neighborhood can be quite overwhelming.

TREVOR

Yeah, but... Leigh is going through a rough time right now. She recently lost a baby.

RACHEL

What?

TREVOR

A miscarriage, I mean. She lost it just before the move. She's been quite distant and withdrawn. I was hoping the new surroundings would help her move forward.

Rachel remains skeptical of his sincerity.

RACHEL

I'm so sorry... for both of you.

Trevor fails to acknowledge Rachel's sympathy.

TREVOR

Do me a favor, don't mention any of this to her. She'd probably deny the stuff about her family, and the pregnancy might trigger her depression.

RACHEL

Of course.

Rachel changes the subject.

RACHEL

How long have you known Colleen?

TREVOR

A long time, why?

RACHEL

She's very attractive.

TREVOR

I guess.

RACHEL

Lines ever get blurred?

TREVOR

Lines?

RACHEL

You know. The line between the caring friend's husband and the lonely guy looking for some attention.

TREVOR

(Nervously)

I never thought about it.

RACHEL
Why did you move in so late?

TREVOR
Excuse me?

RACHEL
From what I understand, you moved in after midnight.

TREVOR
And from what I understand, you were practically unconscious and being carried home at the time.

RACHEL
How do you know about that?

TREVOR
It's a small cul-de-sac.

Rachel takes a moment to ponder all the answers Trevor has provided.

TREVOR
Shouldn't you get back in there before they start to miss you?

Rachel takes a long final drag off her cigarette and drops it to the ground. She turns and heads back up to Jill's house. Trevor continues smoking as he watches her walk away. He drops his cigarette and blows smoke into the air.

JILL'S LIVING ROOM - CONTINUOUS

As Rachel comes through the front door and joins the other women still engaged in conversation, Colleen's cell phone rings.

COLLEEN
Yes. Hi. Sure, hold on a second. Jill, it's my boss. Do you mind if I take this in the other room?

JILL
Not at all, you can go in the kitchen.

Colleen gets up and exits the room. Mary leans over to Rachel.

MARY
(Quietly)
Did you enjoy your tobacco respite?

Rachel sits down next to Anne.

RACHEL
(Equally quiet)
Can't let one go, can you?

Anne starts to get up to leave.

ANNE
I hate to cut the night short, but I have an early shift tomorrow.

Rachel abruptly grabs her by the hand and pulls her back down.

RACHEL
(Whispering urgently)
Sit down.

Mary doesn't see what happened between Rachel and Anne.

MARY
I should go too.

Rachel makes eye contact with Mary and subtly signals for her to stay put. Colleen re-enters the room.

COLLEEN
I've got to go. My boss needs some information I have on my computer at home.

Colleen taps Leigh on the shoulder as her cue that it is time to leave.

RACHEL
What's your job, exactly?

COLLEEN
I research and analyze sales, marketing, and service data for a global communication company.

RACHEL
Sounds important.

COLLEEN
It's not, but at least I can work from home.

JILL
Let me make you a plate of food to take home to Trevor.

LEIGH
That's so nice of you, thank you.

MARY
It's been so much fun getting to know you both. I hope we didn't scare you away for next time.

COLLEEN
Not at all. I had a wonderful time.

LEIGH
(Inexplicably melancholy)
You all have a special friendship. Thank you for letting me be a part of it.

Jill returns.

JILL
Aww, well you're welcome, Leigh. And I'm sure I speak for all of us when I say that we are so happy to have y'all join us.

Jill hands her the prepared plate, neatly covered in plastic wrap.

MARY
Is it my turn to host next?

ANNE
No, I think it's Rachel's turn.

RACHEL
Field trip.

COLLEEN
Field trip?

Rachel motions around to all of Jill's preparations.

RACHEL
I don't do all of this... stuff. I let Back Alley Bar do it.

LEIGH
(Enthusiastically)
Sounds fun.

COLLEEN
(Hesitant)
I'll just have to check my calendar.

JILL

We can always change the date and time to make sure you both can make it.

COLLEEN

I wouldn't want everyone to change just for me.

JILL

Don't be silly. Nothing is carved in stone. We change things all the time.

Colleen forces a smile.

COLLEEN

Thank you again for a really fun evening.

LEIGH

Yes, this was a needed break.

The women share good nights, and Jill escorts Leigh and Colleen out of the front door. Rachel motions for Mary and Anne to come closer.

ANNE

(Agitated)

What?!

RACHEL

Guess who I saw outside...

MARY

Officials from the mental institution?

RACHEL

No, smart-ass, Trevor.

Jill rejoins the group.

MARY

Did you talk to him?

Rachel dramatically nods her head.

JILL

What are you three whispering about?

ANNE

(To Jill)

Rachel saw Trevor when she went outside.

MARY

What was he doing out there?

RACHEL

He was talking to someone driving through the neighborhood.

ANNE

Who does he know in the neighborhood?

RACHEL

(Indignant)

Right?! He claimed he was helping a guy with directions, but I don't buy it.

ANNE

So... what did you say to him?

The women lean in with their full attention.

RACHEL

Okay, so first I catch him with his head in some random car window, probably finalizing a drug deal...

Mary listens intently while Anne and Jill collectively roll their eyes.

RACHEL

...when he recognizes me and walks over. We start casually talking and I said Leigh was really shy and he said it's because she comes from a family of white trash. I'm thinking that's a weak reason because everyone comes from white trash if you dig deep enough. Then he tells me that the reason she seems so distant and withdrawn is because SHE just lost a baby.

Jill gasps and places her hand to her chest.

JILL

Oh my gosh, that poor thing.

RACHEL

No, no, didn't you hear me? He said SHE lost a baby. Not WE lost a baby.

JILL

Rachel, he probably just misspoke.

RACHEL

No way, I call bullshit. When your wife has a miscarriage, you BOTH lose a child.

MARY

I know I'm guilty of trying to root out some covert conspiracy, but Jill's right on this one. He probably didn't give much thought to what he was saying.

Rachel continues to try to convince them.

RACHEL

Okay, okay, it wasn't just WHAT he said. It was the WAY he said it. No emotion, no empathy.

MARY

I'm sorry, Rachel, I can't encourage this anymore. Now we're talking about serious loss. It actually makes sense that Colleen is here. I mean, wouldn't any of us run to the aid of the other if something like that happened?

RACHEL

Jesus. You pick now to become righteous! Anne, you think I'm right, right?

Anne's face grimaces, and her shoulders slowly shrug as she raises her eyebrows and blankly stares at Rachel.

RACHEL

OH, COME ON!

ANNE

Look, Rachel, is his choice of pronouns odd? Yes. Is he devoid of all emotional attachment? Maybe. Is he lying or hiding something? Possibly. But most likely, it's the boredom from our uneventful lives fueling these crazy scenarios.

Jill and Mary shamefully remain quiet while Rachel indignantly shakes her head.

ANNE

You realize, of course, the more we try to convince ourselves they're involved in some diabolical scheme, the more ridiculous we're going to look when it turns out they're just three regular people living lives as dull as the rest of us!

Anne's speech doesn't move Rachel.

RACHEL
What about Jill?! She clearly doesn't trust Colleen!

JILL
What?! I never said that!

RACHEL
You jumped in pretty quick to accommodate her!

Jill shifts her eyes between the women.

RACHEL
You didn't want to give her an opportunity to be left alone with Trevor.

Jill cannot contain her discomfort.

JILL
All right, yes! It crossed my mind! But now that I know all this, I feel terrible thinking that.

Rachel gets up and gathers her things.

RACHEL
You all want to pretend like they're just a harmless trio of weirdos, but I'm telling you this right now - I trust those people about as much as I trust the turbo setting on my vibrator.

Rachel turns on her heel and heads for the door. Mary shouts to her back.

MARY
I worry about you with that thing!

Rachel dramatically slams the door.

MARY
(Concerned)
She's going to sprain her vagina.

NEIGHBORHOOD STREET - A WEEK LATER, MORNING

Anne is nearing the end of her neighborhood run. Colleen briskly runs up alongside her.

COLLEEN
(Effortlessly)
Hey!

Anne breathes heavily as she finishes her run with maximum effort.

ANNE
Oh, hey!

COLLEEN
How long are you going?

ANNE
I'm just about done.

COLLEEN
Lucky you. I'm just getting started.

Anne notices Colleen's faster pace and speeds up to try to stay with her.

COLLEEN
I wanted to thank you again for the invitation last week.

Anne pants heavily and is only able to get a word or two out every couple of strides.

ANNE
Oh...it was...fun...I'm glad...you could...come.

COLLEEN
Leigh really needed a night like that.

ANNE
I...hope...we...didn't...scare her.

COLLEEN
Not at all. She's looking forward to next time. We both are.

Colleen and Anne continue to run together with Colleen setting the pace. Anne strains to keep up. They run around the corner to where Jill and Mary are putting their kids on the bus. Anne pulls up from an all-out sprint and stops behind Mary and Jill, who turn to watch Colleen run by. Anne has trouble catching her breath.

JILL
It's like watching a jungle cat.

MARY
Running down its prey.

Anne puts her hands on her hips and stands straight up as she continues to try to breathe. Jill turns around and sees Anne laboring.

JILL

Are you okay?

Mary also turns to see Anne having trouble. Anne shakes her head violently as she reaches for Mary to steady her.

MARY'S KITCHEN - MOMENTS LATER

Mary, Jill, and Anne walk into the kitchen from the garage. Anne is still panting.

MARY

Tell me again how great running is.

Mary goes to the refrigerator and removes a water bottle. Anne begins to breathe a bit easier.

ANNE

It was like she was running from the police.

JILL

Do I have to remind you she's practically half your age?

ANNE

No, watching her ass remain motionless during an all-out sprint reminded me.

Mary gives Anne the bottle of water.

ANNE

Thank you. Did either of you notice if Bill took Jack to school?

JILL

Yes, I saw them.

ANNE

Good.

Anne opens the water and gulps down half the bottle.

MARY

You could have killed yourself trying to keep up with her.

ANNE

Trust me, I won't try it again.

JILL

Now that I know you're okay, I'm going to head out.

MARY

Are you going to the school?

JILL

Yes, parent council meeting this morning.

MARY

I'll see you there.

JILL

Oh, are you coming to the meeting?

MARY

No, I have an appointment with Mrs. Kaiser.

JILL

Really? Why?

MARY

Remember the other night when I told you about Charlie getting bullied? I can't wait any longer, it's become physical.

ANNE

What? Is he okay?

MARY

He's fine. He had some red marks on his arm, and they were bad enough for him to finally tell me who it is. A kid named Carter Baumann.

JILL

Oh, Mary, I didn't know it was Carter giving him trouble. You may have a tough fight on your hands. He's quite the troublemaker. His mother is a big shot attorney and the only person who intimidates Mrs. Kaiser. She overlooks a lot of his behavior.

MARY

(Sarcastically)

Great.

JILL

I should warn you. Mrs. Kaiser is a great administrator, but she is horrible with public relations. Many parents walk out of her office angrier than when they walked in. I tread very lightly around her.

MARY

So, I should kiss her ass?

JILL

It wouldn't hurt.

LOBBY OF PRINCIPAL'S OFFICE - LATER

Mary is sitting outside, waiting for her appointment. She looks curiously at a series of security monitors, including one coming from the principal's office, in a cabinet behind the secretaries. An exchange is taking place between the stern and unsympathetic MRS. KAISER and a second-grade girl, LIZZIE.

Mary eavesdrops on their conversation through the open office door.

MRS. KAISER

You understand I removed you from class because you were being disruptive, don't you, Lizzie?

LIZZIE

(Confused)

I guess.

MRS. KAISER

Do you understand that behavior won't be tolerated?

Lizzie begins to cry at Mrs. Kaiser's unjust accusation.

LIZZIE

Mrs. Kaiser, all I did was accidentally tap my pencil on the desk.

MRS. KAISER

Yes, but it was during a test and that is considered disruptive. You know what the rules are. I'm afraid you'll be spending next week in my office during lunch. Hopefully, that will help remind you how to keep yourself from being troublesome.

Mary's jaw drops at the severity of the punishment.

MRS. KAISER

Now, return to your classroom.

Lizzie dries her eyes as she exits. Mrs. Kaiser comes out to meet Mary.

MRS. KAISER

Mrs. Hueston?

Mary stands.

MARY

Yes.

Mrs. Kaiser extends her arm, allowing Mary to enter her office.

MRS. KAISER

Please, come in.

MRS. KAISER'S OFFICE - CONTINUOUS

Mrs. Kaiser shuts the door behind Mary. Mary takes a seat across the desk as Mrs. Kaiser settles into her chair. Her office is cold and sterile, with a sleek modern desk without drawers. Everything on her desk and walls is carefully curated in a detached, minimalist style.

MRS. KAISER

What brings you here today?

Mary feels intimidated and shifts in her chair.

MARY

Well, my son Charlie has been having some trouble lately.

Mrs. Kaiser nods her head slightly.

MRS. KAISER

I'm very familiar with Charlie.

MARY

(Surprised)

You are?

MRS. KAISER

Yes, he has come to me a couple of times this year.

MARY
Oh really? About what?

MRS. KAISER
He's had some stories about his classmates misbehaving.

Mary is surprised to learn Mrs. Kaiser is aware of the situation.

MARY
And what have you done about it?

MRS. KAISER
I looked into the claims and found them to be... exaggerations.

MARY
Exaggerations? What makes you think Charlie is exaggerating?

MRS. KAISER
Mrs. Hueston, I get these kinds of stories all day long. My job is to sort out the facts from the different versions I hear. And the truth is, the boy he named isn't the kind of student that causes trouble.

Mary starts to show irritation.

MARY
Doesn't cause trouble or doesn't get caught causing trouble?

Mrs. Kaiser changes the subject in an effort to redirect the conversation.

MRS. KAISER
What is it about Charlie that you wanted to talk to me about?

MARY
I wanted to talk about this. About the bullying that's going on at your school.

MRS. KAISER
Mrs. Hueston, I assure you, we have a zero-tolerance policy.

MARY

Zero-tolerance? Sounds like you're pretty tolerant of some kids around here.

Mrs. Kaiser shifts almost imperceptibly in her desk chair, but her tone clearly turns quiet and condescending.

MRS. KAISER

The truth is, Mrs. Hueston, I think Charlie can be a little sensitive.

MARY

(Increasingly agitated)

Sensitive? A classmate is shoving him in the lunch line, calling him names during recess, and twisting his arm to get him off the swings, and you label THAT sensitive?

MRS. KAISER

There will always be some degree of "boys will be boys."

MARY

(Becoming outraged)

Well, which is it, Mrs. Kaiser? Zero-tolerance or "boys will be boys?!"

Mrs. Kaiser continues to patronize Mary with her inside voice.

MRS. KAISER

Mrs. Hueston, I think Charlie will have a much easier time throughout his school career, if he gets a little thicker skin.

MARY

(Defiantly)

How about I put him in karate classes and tell him to unload on anyone who pushes him around?

Mrs. Kaiser sternly continues her condescension.

MRS. KAISER

Then he'd be considered the one bullying and treated as such.

Mary becomes angrier and more animated.

MARY

Hey, "boys will be boys!" Sorry my boy's going to be a black belt!

MRS. KAISER
Mrs. Hueston, this kind of attitude will only lead to Charlie getting into more trouble later on.

MARY
I'd rather have him get into trouble sticking up for himself than be someone's playground bitch.

Mrs. Kaiser becomes offended by Mary's use of profanity.

MRS. KAISER
(Haughtily)
I will not tolerate that kind of language in my office, Mrs. Hueston. Your overbearing attitude is obviously contributing to Charlie's inability to deal with conflict.

Mary leans forward and holds the arms of the chair to contain her rage.

MARY
MY overbearing attitude? Fuck you.

Mrs. Kaiser stands, tense with anger.

MRS. KAISER
I am now convinced that no good can come from continuing this conversation. Why don't we reschedule for another time when you are able to control yourself.

Mary stands.

MARY
Fine! In the meantime, I'm instructing Charlie to defend himself if he feels threatened by anyone at this school.

MRS. KAISER
If he does, he'll be suspended.

MARY
You aren't protecting him!

MRS. KAISER
Mrs. Hueston, with the attitude and language you've displayed here today, it's clear to me that Charlie needs protection more from YOU than from any student at this school.

With this last statement, Mary loses all rational thought. She grabs Mrs. Kaiser's desk and throws it upward, causing it to topple over. Mrs. Kaiser jumps back to avoid the falling furniture and desk debris.

Mary opens the door and storms out of the office. Administrators and children in the lobby look into Mrs. Kaiser's office and see her standing in disbelief at what just took place.

MARY'S HOUSE - MOMENTS LATER

Mary frantically pulls into her driveway, jumps out of her car, and rushes into her kitchen. She holds her trembling hand to her mouth, still shocked at her own behavior. The phone rings.

Her hand shakes as she picks up the handset. Her voice quivers.

MARY

Hello?

SCHOOL OFFICE

JILL

What on Earth happened?!

MARY

I don't want to talk about it!

JILL

This is bad, Mary.

MARY

I know, Jill!

JILL

I hate to tell you this, but Mrs. Kaiser called the police.
They're on their way to your house.

Mary nervously places her hand on her forehead.

MARY

Oh, dear God.

JILL

Mrs. Kaiser is livid! What got into you?

Mary nervously peers out of the front window.

MARY

That woman! She was so smug and condescending. She was blaming me and calling Charlie sensitive. I just totally lost control of myself.

JILL

(Sympathetically)

Oh, honey.

MARY

What should I do? Should I call and apologize?

JILL

I'm afraid it's way past that. Right now, you should just focus on not getting arrested.

MARY

Arrested? Oh God. Craig is going to kill me. And I've made it so much worse for Charlie. He's going to be known as the kid with the crazy mom. They will tease him mercilessly now! And Ethan is going to be mortified when this gets around school. I won't be surprised if they never want to go back! I won't be surprised if she doesn't let them back!

JILL

You might want to consider a large donation to the parent council.

Mary looks out her front window and sees two police cars approach her house.

MARY

Oh my God! The police are here.

JILL

Think of something, quick!

MARY'S DRIVEWAY - CONTINUOUS

Mary steps out on her front porch and adopts the most contrite face she can muster. She meets OFFICER 1 and OFFICER 2 halfway up her driveway.

MARY

Good afternoon, officers.

OFFICER 1

Good afternoon, ma'am. We understand you had a little trouble down at the school.

Mary notices Colleen running up the street but stays focused on her ad-lib alibi.

MARY

Yes, that was all my fault, officer. I should have rescheduled my appointment. I was recently prescribed some new medication and I haven't gotten the dosage quite right.

OFFICER 1

What's the medication for?

MARY

I suffer from... uh... Tourette syndrome. It's a condition where I have uncontrollable impulses to shout horrible words and throw things.

Mary sees the officer's skepticism and begins to dramatically exhibit symptoms.

MARY

Hamster fart!

Mary removes the watch she's wearing and throws it across her yard.

MARY

See. I can't control myself. Hairy nipple sucker!

OFFICER 1

Look ma'am, if this is a medical issue, perhaps we should call a doctor.

MARY

Oh, that won't be necessary, officer. I think I realized where I went wrong. See, the label on the bottle said take one pill every two hours, and I read twelve hours. I wasn't getting nearly the amount needed. Castrated virgin snot!

Mary smiles with shrugged shoulders.

MARY

Obviously.

After trading nonverbal expressions of uncertainty, the officers relent.

OFFICER 1

Do us a favor and stay away from the school for a while, okay?

MARY

Not a problem, officer.

OFFICER 1

All right, go back inside and take care of yourself.

MARY

I will. Thank you again, officer.

Mary turns toward the house and lets out a sigh of relief as she drops her head and shakes it in shame.

MARY'S LIVING ROOM - LATER

Mary is pacing her front room while waiting for Charlie and Ethan to arrive. After several peeks out of the front window, the bus pulls up and kids tumble out. Mary fights to hold in tears as she watches Charlie race ahead of Ethan and up to the house. She nervously wrings her hands together as the front door flies open. Mary opens her mouth to speak but is quickly interrupted by Charlie. He throws his backpack down, rushes toward his mom, and begins shouting.

CHARLIE

Mom! You did it!

MARY

(Surprised and wary)

What did I do?

Charlie can barely contain his excitement, with his arms gesturing wildly and his explanation punctuated with laughter.

CHARLIE

You totally scared the pants off Carter! He thinks I've got this crazy mom who will freak out and kill him if he comes near me. He bought me an ice cream at lunch!

Mary slowly realizes that her fears may not actually transpire.

MARY

He did?

CHARLIE

Yeah! And everybody thinks you are the coolest mom ever! Everybody was talking about it all day. Mrs. Kaiser even told me she felt sorry for me. I'm not sure why, but it was the first time she's ever been nice to me!

Ethan enters the house.

MARY

(Overwhelmingly relieved)

I'm so happy!

Ethan tosses his backpack down like usual. Mary scans Ethan's face for any sign of his state of mind.

ETHAN

Can I have a snack?

MARY

(Leery)

Sure, honey.

Ethan goes to the kitchen and starts digging in the pantry.

MARY

(Quietly to Charlie)

Does Ethan know what happened?

CHARLIE

(Gleefully)

Everyone knows what happened.

MARY

Is he upset?

CHARLIE

Why would he be upset? We're like rock stars now. Seriously, mom, you might want my autograph.

Mary throws her arms around Charlie.

MARY

Oh, I'm so happy this worked out like this. I was really scared you'd be labeled the kid with the crazy mom!

CHARLIE

I am. But crazy is cool!

Mary releases her hug as her mind leaps to the next potential situation.

MARY
Hey, look, we don't need to tell your dad about this. I don't think he understands that whole "crazy is cool" thing, okay?

CHARLIE
Okay.

The phone rings. Mary, now pleased with herself, picks up the phone with a renewed confidence.

MARY
Hello?

SCHOOL OFFICE

JILL
Have you checked your phone or computer lately?

MARY
No, why?

JILL
This morning's incident was captured by the school security camera. Once the high school cyber security club found out, they hacked into the system and uploaded the footage to every social media outlet imaginable.

MARY
(Mortified)
Are you kidding me?

JILL
I wish. I've seen twelve different versions of the video.

Mary covers her forehead and eyes with her hand.

MARY
Oh God! Just when I thought everything was going to be okay.

JILL
Oh, here's one set to music...

Mary can hear Wagner's "The Ride of the Valkyries" over the phone.

JILL

And another one in slow motion...

MARY

Don't tell me anymore.

JILL

And another one in slow motion AND set to music...

MARY

Enough!

JILL

The good news is you aren't identified in the clip. It's titled, "And you thought your mom was psycho."

MARY

(Sarcastically)

Fabulous.

JILL

You've hit eight thousand views so far.

MARY

THIS is how I finally attain fame.

JILL

I'm going to call our district IT department and see if they can do anything.

MARY

Thank you.

JILL

Do Charlie and Ethan know?

MARY

Yeah, apparently, they're celebrities now.

JILL

How did you handle the police?

MARY

I exploited a serious medical condition and insulted thousands of people afflicted with it.

JILL

I worry about your soul, Mary.

MARY

Oh Jill, my ticket to Hell was punched a long time ago. I'm just relieved I don't have to call Craig from a jail cell.

JILL

I better make that call before IT leaves.

MARY

Thanks.

BACK ALLEY BAR - ONE WEEK LATER, EVENING

Mary and Anne enter the restaurant. The atmosphere is rowdy and loud. Cincinnati sports memorabilia, local team photos, and neon beer signs fill the space on the walls between giant flat screen televisions.

Rachel interrupts her conversation with CALEB SHAUGHNESSY, a charming, ginger bartender in his mid-30s, as the women approach her.

Caleb turns to wait on other patrons.

RACHEL

Finally!

Rachel nudges Mary in the side.

RACHEL

Oh, hey! Loved your viral meltdown medley! My favorite was the one where they auto-tuned you.

Mary prepares herself for a barrage of ridicule.

MARY

Go ahead. Get it all out of your system. I was expecting this.

RACHEL

No, I won't torture you. But I do want to make sure you've added it to your resume and highlight reel.

MARY

(Sarcastically)

You are truly hilarious.

RACHEL

Seriously, I'm proud of you. You know how many times I've wanted to throw a desk at someone?

MARY
And yet, you haven't. So, in a contest of patience and sanity, I lose... to you.

ANNE
Where is everybody?

RACHEL
Jill just called and said she'd be late, and Colleen is bringing Leigh. Let's get a table.

Rachel gets the attention of the hostess, LISA.

RACHEL
Lisa, three more will be joining us, but you can seat us now.

LISA
Yes, Mrs. Easton. We have the table in the back room reserved for you and your party, just as you requested.

RACHEL
I didn't request that, but we'll take it.

Rachel takes her drink from the bar and the women follow Lisa, winding between packed tables and rowdy patrons along the way.

RACHEL
Remind Caleb he still owes me five bucks from the Notre Dame game.

LISA
Sure, Mrs. Easton.

BACK ALLEY BAR BACK ROOM - CONTINUOUS

Lisa escorts the women to an area in the back of the restaurant. Tinted glass surrounds the room, helping to provide privacy and block some of the noise.

Lisa turns on the light as the women enter. They situate themselves as Lisa distributes menus before returning to the hostess stand. Anne sees Colleen and Leigh approach the back entrance to the restaurant, which opens directly into their room. She gets up and unlocks the door.

ANNE
Hey, you two!

COLLEEN

Hi! Are we late?

MARY

No, we just sat down.

Colleen and Leigh take seats next to each other.

COLLEEN

We noticed you sitting here as we were walking up.
Saved us a trip around the restaurant.

ANNE

How are you both?

LEIGH

Good. How about you?

ANNE

Work is killing me, but what else is new?

The friends exchange greetings all around as the group settles in for another bunco night. Mary leans across the table to Colleen.

MARY

I'm sure you're wondering why the police were outside
my house the other day.

COLLEEN

Actually, I heard what happened at the supermarket. I
realized it was you when I put two and two together.

RACHEL

What two and two? What happened?

Mary hesitates, but gives in quickly.

MARY

After my... altercation with the principal, she called the
police and they came by to have a little chat with me.

RACHEL

Why am I just now finding out about this?

MARY

Because, although I'm not proud of how, I was able to
get myself out of it.

RACHEL
What'd you do? Fondle their nightsticks?

Mary plays along.

MARY
Yes, and I was so good they let me play with their sirens.

The women share a laugh.

COLLEEN
Hey, we do what we have to.

ANNE
What did Craig say?

MARY
(Adamantly)
He doesn't know, and I'd like to keep it that way.

RACHEL
You had a visit from the police, and you've managed to keep it from him. Wow! You're a much better actress than I give you credit for.

Caleb comes to the table and stands closest to Rachel.

RACHEL
(To Caleb)
They let you out from behind the bar?

Mary watches Caleb interact with Rachel.

CALEB
I wanted to make sure you were taken care of.

Caleb addresses the entire table.

CALEB
Can I get you ladies something to drink?

RACHEL
(To Caleb)
They'll probably need a minute.

Caleb displays his familiarity with Rachel by putting his hand on her back and leaning down to her ear.

CALEB
(Under his breath)
I'll get you another one.

RACHEL
Thanks.

Caleb leaves the table while Mary silently assesses the exchange.

MARY
(Quietly to Rachel)
You realize he's flirting with you, right?

RACHEL
(Dismissive)
He's seen my huge tips.

A flustered Jill rushes into the back room and throws her coat and purse down at the empty seat.

JILL
I am so sorry, John had a meeting run late, and I got stuck waiting for a train that was a mile long...

Rachel interrupts Jill.

RACHEL
You're fine. Relax.

Mary changes the subject as Jill takes a breath and gets situated.

MARY
Now that we're all here, I have an announcement to make.

RACHEL
You're entering an international furniture-hurling competition...

Rachel thumps the table as she laughs at herself.

MARY
You're not as funny as you think you are, Rachel.

RACHEL
Yes, I am!

Jill brings the table's attention back to Mary.

JILL

What's your announcement?

MARY

Craig's parents have a house on Elk Lake down in Kentucky, and they left for Europe yesterday. So, what do you think of doing a bunco weekend down there? Now, I know you have to ask the guys and make arrangements for the kids...

ANNE

I'm in!

JILL

John has been working late a lot lately. I think it's fair if I ask for a little vacation.

RACHEL

You know I look for any excuse to sleep anywhere but my own bed.

Colleen becomes very uncomfortable.

COLLEEN

I'm not sure...

Rachel interrupts.

RACHEL

What do you mean, you're not sure? You, of all of us, have the most freedom. No husband, no kids.

COLLEEN

You're right. I'm just not sure I can get the time away from work.

RACHEL

You said you worked from home.

COLLEEN

I do. It's just that...

MARY

Look, you can come down on Friday and decide whether to stay one night or two, okay?

COLLEEN
(Uncomfortably)
Okay.

JILL
How about you, Leigh. Will Trevor let you out of his sight for a weekend?

Leigh allows a subtle smile to cross her face.

LEIGH
I hope so.

MARY
Great! I'm thinking maybe the weekend after next.

COLLEEN
Weekend after next?

MARY
Yes, will that work?

The ladies confer among themselves about the date while Colleen becomes preoccupied with concern.

BACK ALLEY BAR BACK ROOM - LATER

Half-eaten appetizer dishes and empty glasses litter the table. The ladies are in varying states of inebriation, with Rachel leading the pack. Mary dramatically thumps her finished cocktail glass on the table.

MARY
Okay, Craig wants me to get boobs. What do you think?

RACHEL
You have boobs. What does he want, two more?

MARY
Not more, just new and improved boobs. Bigger, better, and positioned where nature intended.

ANNE
That's a major surgery with weeks of recovery.

JILL
Do YOU want them?

MARY

In the past, yes. I think when I was younger it was more important to me. Now I feel like, if I get new boobs, I'd have to have the tummy tuck and ass lift as well or it would look like flashy chrome rims on a broken-down jalopy.

ANNE

You don't need a tummy tuck or ass lift.

MARY

Keep drinking, Anne.

Jill enthusiastically turns the conversation into a game.

JILL

Alright y'all, if you could change one thing about yourself, what would you pick?

RACHEL

Just one thing?

JILL

Yep, only one thing.

ANNE

Stomach. Definitely my stomach.

MARY

Please! What's wrong with your stomach?

ANNE

Childbirth was not kind to me. My midsection looks like my children carved their way out using a broken Swiss Army knife.

As the women share a laugh, Mary notices someone inside the main restaurant with his phone aimed at them. She begins to get embarrassed.

MARY

I think there's a guy trying to take a picture of me.

Everyone turns to see the photographer in question.

ANNE

What?

MARY
There's a guy out there with his phone pointed in here. He's been snapping pictures in this direction for a couple of minutes now.

RACHEL
That's ridiculous. He's probably taking pictures of something in the other room.

Mary is convinced she is on the verge of humiliation.

MARY
No, he's not.

RACHEL
We're in the private room. The windows are tinted.

Mary drops her head into the palm of her hand.

MARY
He knows I'm "psycho mom."

Rachel jumps up from her chair and goes to the window.

RACHEL
Stop thinking everything is about you, Mary! No one wants your picture! Besides, he couldn't see through these windows if he wanted to! Here, I'll prove it to you!

The women cringe as Rachel lifts her shirt and presses her bare breasts against the glass.

RACHEL
See! No one can see through the tint!

She drops her shirt and returns to her seat.

ANNE
(Mortified)
Christ, Rachel.

RACHEL
Comfortable now?

MARY
(Sarcastically)
Yes! You've put me completely at ease.

RACHEL
What were we talking about?

JILL
Before your public display of nudity? I believe Leigh was going to tell us what she'd like to change.

LEIGH
Honestly, I'd just like to be twenty-five again.

JILL
Why twenty-five?

LEIGH
That's when I should have paid more attention to the choices I was making.

Leigh's comment quiets the table. Rachel, on the other hand, becomes visibly agitated.

JILL
Uh, what about you, Colleen?

RACHEL
No! She doesn't get to answer.

COLLEEN
Why not?

RACHEL
Because you're young, gorgeous, and you have the body fat of a hummingbird. And any manufactured complaint you may come up with is just going to make me want to puke.

COLLEEN
(Apprehensively)
Uh... thank you, I guess?

Mary rolls her eyes at Rachel's comment, signaling Colleen to ignore her.

MARY
So, Jill. Your question comes back to you.

Jill hesitates before bashfully confessing.

JILL
Honestly... I wish I had the courage to get a tattoo.

Rachel scoffs and becomes irrationally irritated by Jill's statement.

ANNE
Really?!

RACHEL
I'll buy. I know a place. Get in the car!

JILL
No, I could never.

MARY
You've obviously given this some thought. What would you get?

Jill playfully considers her hypothetical tattoo, raising her finger to her chin in debate.

JILL
I don't know. Maybe a symbol of South Carolina, like the wren or yellow jessamine.

RACHEL
(Sardonically)
I got it, I got it! Shave your crotch curls and tattoo "Martha Stewart Living" right in the middle. That way your twat will match the rest of the decor in your life.

The women are visibly taken back by Rachel's mean-spirited comment, shifting uncomfortably in their chairs. Jill's jaw pops open in surprise.

MARY
Wow, Rachel.

Jill closes her mouth, straightens her shoulders, and calls upon her etiquette training.

JILL
I don't think John would appreciate that.

Rachel continues to bait Jill.

RACHEL
If you shaved your lady-fro, I bet he'd go for anything!

Fed up, Jill shows her irritation with Rachel's tone.

JILL
Maybe my... lady area... is already shaved.

RACHEL
(Dismissive)
It's not.

JILL
(Insulted)
It's funny you're so sure you know.

Rachel starts to become belligerent with Jill.

RACHEL
Oh, I know. Pruning your fun box is wild and crazy, and there are lots of words to describe you, Jill, but wild and crazy are not two of them.

Jill quickly grows intolerant.

JILL
Really? What words would you use to describe me?

Rachel gets nasty as she enunciates each descriptive word.

RACHEL
Let's see, I'd use words like impeccable, and uptight, and PERFECT.

JILL
I don't know where you get this idea that I'm perfect. I'm far from it.

RACHEL
Are you kidding me?! You're the picture of perfection with your PERFECT house and your PERFECT family and your whole PERFECT God damn life.

Mary attempts to thwart Rachel's needless attack on Jill.

MARY
(Forcefully)
Rachel, relax.

Jill uncharacteristically goes on the offensive.

JILL

One might say you have a pretty perfect life yourself. None of us drive around a hundred thousand dollar car.

The combination of comments enrages Rachel.

RACHEL

That car is Kevin's restitution!

JILL

Restitution?! What are you talking about? All he does is provide you with everything you could ever want.

RACHEL

Everything I could ever want?! You really are blissfully ignorant. I wish you knew how ridiculous you sound. PLEASE do everyone a favor and exercise better control over the colossally stupid remarks tumbling out of your boiled peanut hole!

Jill knows Rachel's idiosyncrasies well but still shakes her head and struggles with her insult.

JILL

I don't know why this deep-seated resentment towards me surfaces at the end of every evening.

Anne looks over and sees Colleen again uncomfortably shift in her chair while Leigh shakes her head in disgust.

RACHEL

Don't kid yourself, Jill, I don't just resent YOU...

Anne leans over to Mary and whispers in her ear.

ANNE

Stop her, please.

Rachel finishes her sentence aggressively leaning toward Jill.

RACHEL

I resent EVERYTHING about your unblemished EXISTENCE!

Mary deliberately knocks over a cocktail glass. The syrupy beverage and ice cubes flood onto Rachel. Rachel jumps back from the table but is unsuccessful in avoiding the mess. Mary jumps up with a napkin and tries to clean up the area.

MARY

Oh, no. I'm so sorry.

Rachel's anger grows as she examines her wet and sticky hands. Colleen tries to hand Rachel a napkin, but her kind gesture is rudely rejected. Rachel turns from the table and heads for the bathroom. Leigh jumps up and chases behind Rachel. Mary, Anne, and Jill sit bewildered at Rachel's behavior.

Colleen fidgets in her chair as she strains to see what happens near the bathroom.

BACK ALLEY BAR BATHROOM - CONTINUOUS

Rachel washes her hands in the sink. Leigh bursts into the bathroom in an aggressive manner unlike anything she has displayed before. She begins a conversation with Rachel's reflection in the mirror.

LEIGH
(Outraged)

Why are you so mean?!

Rachel addresses Leigh's reflection.

RACHEL

Excuse me?

LEIGH

You heard me! You were horrible to Jill, and for what? Because she wants a tattoo? Because YOU think she's perfect? Please tell me there's some other heinous act she's committed to make you think you can treat her like that!

Rachel is taken back by Leigh's sudden audaciousness.

RACHEL

Look, Leigh, don't think you can come to a couple of buncos and understand our relationship.

Rachel takes paper towels from the dispenser and dries her hands.

LEIGH

In a million years, I could never understand your relationships! I can't imagine what you have to offer that would keep these women friends with you!

Rachel silently dries her hands.

LEIGH
My life has been ruined by callous assholes like you!

Rachel turns to face Leigh head-on for the first time in their conversation.

RACHEL
(Irritated)
You have to know me better before you get to call me that.

LEIGH
I would NEVER want to know you better! Just being around you the past MONTH has been horrendous!

Rachel remains silently stunned at Leigh's tirade.

LEIGH
You need to figure out what the hell your problem is and quit taking it out on your friends. They won't take it forever, and from what I can gather, you don't have much else.

Leigh turns and grabs the door handle. As Leigh pulls the door to exit, Anne is pulled from the other side while simultaneously trying to enter. Leigh abruptly continues on her path, exiting the bathroom. Anne watches Leigh storm out before she cautiously moves closer to Rachel.

ANNE
Hey. You okay?

Rachel hangs her head with newly recognized shame.

RACHEL
I shouldn't have snapped at Jill. Did she leave?

Anne speaks through a smile.

ANNE
Of course not. She's used to your tantrums.

BACK ALLEY BAR BACKROOM - CONTINUOUS

Mary, Jill, and Colleen are still sitting at the table as Leigh begins to gather up her belongings.

LEIGH
(To Colleen)
Take me back.

Colleen obediently jumps up and prepares to leave. Rachel and Anne return to the table before Leigh and Colleen have made their exit out of the back door.

RACHEL
Leigh, Colleen, please, sit back down.

Colleen waits for a cue from Leigh.

RACHEL
(Sincerely)
Please.

Leigh reluctantly puts her purse and jacket back over her chair and sits down. Colleen follows.

Rachel and Anne take their seats.

MARY
(Quietly to Anne)
What happened in there?

ANNE
(Quietly to Mary)
I have no idea.

Jill tries to initiate a reconciliation.

JILL
Rachel, I'm sorry if I've...

Rachel extends her hand to interrupt Jill.

RACHEL
Don't, Jill. Don't you apologize for me being...

Rachel looks at Leigh to acknowledge her earlier characterization.

RACHEL
...a callous asshole. There's no excuse for lashing out at you like I did.

Rachel faces Jill as she takes a deep breath and continues.

RACHEL

My problem has nothing to do with you, and I'm wrong for treating you like it does.

The women are all taken aback by Rachel's apologetic words.

JILL

Is there anything we can do to help?

Rachel quietly shakes her head.

MARY

Maybe just sharing what you're going through would be helpful.

RACHEL

I really don't think you want to go there.

Anne softly chuckles with surprise.

ANNE

Rachel, I administered your hepatitis screen after you bit that homeless guy. Mary fished you out of a fountain when Crowley's Pub barred you from using their bathroom. You told Jill her fried chicken tasted like it had been stored inside Paula Dean's fat folds. I don't think there's anything you can tell us that's going to shock us.

Rachel takes a deep breath as if to accept the challenge.

RACHEL

Kevin's in love with someone else.

The mouths around the table collectively drop.

RACHEL

And...

Rachel surveys the facial expressions around the table.

RACHEL

...his name is Jason.

The information slowly processes across the table. After an excruciatingly uncomfortable period, Jill musters the courage to break the silence.

JILL

How did this happen?

Rachel slowly turns and stares at Jill with complete disbelief.

JILL

What I meant to say was, how'd you find out?

RACHEL

My first suspicion rose when he went to play golf every Thursday.

MARY

Why was that suspicious?

RACHEL

He doesn't own golf clubs.

A paralyzing silence blankets the women for a few moments.

ANNE

Are you one hundred percent sure?

RACHEL

Yes, Anne. I'm one hundred percent sure. The love letters he hid in his dead wife's jewelry box left no room for doubt. They've been together since college.

Rachel drops her guard.

RACHEL

I always thought he was incapable of intimacy. I felt pretty stupid reading how he passionately displayed it to someone else.

The women trade looks of uncertainty between themselves. No one knows what to say or how to say it. Mary feels forced to offer something.

MARY

If he's in love with someone else and you're unhappy, why are you still married?

RACHEL

It's complicated.

Rachel drops her head, heavy with her tormenting secret.

MARY

You deserve better, Rachel.

Rachel softly snickers.

RACHEL

No. I don't.

Jill reaches over and grabs Rachel's hand.

JILL

Yes, you do.

A moment is shared between the women before Rachel halts any chance of becoming more vulnerable.

RACHEL

You can let go of my hand. Kevin's the gay one, not me.

Jill lets go of Rachel's hand.

RACHEL

Please don't try to make me feel better or give me words of advice. I accepted this life a long time ago knowing exactly what to expect, or, what not to expect, to be more accurate.

JILL

I'm very sorry, Rachel.

RACHEL

Don't be. I realized quickly this was divine justice.

Jill is puzzled by Rachel's comment but doesn't inquire further. Rachel checks her watch.

RACHEL

It's getting late. You all have family waiting for you at home and I have two brand new D batteries in my nightstand. I'll pay the check.

Everyone welcomes the levity with subtle laughter and prepares to leave. Rachel makes eye contact with Leigh and appreciatively smiles. The women gather their things and prepare to head out of the back room.

COLLEEN

Leigh and I will go on ahead since my car is right out here.

MARY
(Quietly to Colleen)
You've probably been eyeing that exit door all night.

The women share goodbyes as Leigh and Colleen exit using the back door. Rachel and Jill continue their reconciliation, exiting side by side out of the back room while Anne and Mary follow through the restaurant. Mary turns back to look through the windows and sees they are undoubtedly transparent.

MARY
Those windows may be tinted, but you can see right through them when the lights are on.

ANNE
So, Rachel exposed herself to the entire restaurant?

MARY
Looks like it. But, hey, if her picture ends up on the internet, it'll take the heat off me.

Mary steps in front of Anne to exit.

ANNE
(To herself)
Let's form a bunco group, they said. It'll be fun, they said.

Anne follows Mary out of the restaurant.

ANNE'S BEDROOM - LATER

Anne enters her dark bedroom. She goes to the closet, turns on the light and changes out of her clothes into pajamas. Bill stirs.

BILL
Have fun?

Anne finishes putting on her sleep clothes and steps out of the closet.

ANNE
I'm sorry, did I wake you?

BILL
Not really. Megan's not home yet, and Jack's not feeling well.

ANNE

Is he okay?

BILL

He's fine. I thought I may have felt a fever, so I gave him some ibuprofen. That seemed to help him sleep.

Anne crawls into bed next to Bill and hugs him tight.

BILL

This isn't the treatment I usually get after one of your buncos.

ANNE

This wasn't the usual bunco.

BILL

Everything okay?

ANNE

Yeah. It's just that... I should... I should tell you I appreciate you more often.

Bill smiles as he tightens his embrace. Anne's eyes widen as she feels something rise under the sheets.

ANNE

Bill.

BILL

(Amorously)

It appreciates your appreciation.

Anne becomes frustrated and rolls over.

ANNE

This is why we can't cuddle.

ANNE'S BEDROOM - LATER

The bedroom door slowly creaks open.

JACK

Mom?

Anne wakes up and sees Jack standing at the door. She reads the clock at 3:10 a.m. and sits up.

ANNE

What is it, honey?

JACK

I'm shivering.

ANNE

Come here.

Jack walks to the bedside as Anne gets up. She kisses his forehead.

ANNE

Let's get you some more ibuprofen.

Anne guides Jack into his bathroom, finds the medicine, and gives him the dose.

ANNE

Did you hear your sister come home?

JACK

No.

ANNE

Try to go back to sleep, honey.

As Jack heads back to his bedroom, Anne proceeds down the hall to check on Megan.

MEGAN'S BEDROOM - CONTINUOUS

Anne opens the door and finds her seventeen-old daughter, MEGAN sleeping. She looks across the room and sees the window open. She crosses the room to shut the window.

MEGAN'S BEDROOM/NEIGHBORHOOD STREET

Anne notices the light of a cigarette on the side of Trevor and Leigh's house. There are two people in the shadows, talking expressively. Anne continues to watch as the couple makes their way back up to the house. The porch light illuminates the faces of Trevor and Colleen. Anne strains to hear bits of the whispered conversation.

COLLEEN

We can use this to our advantage.

TREVOR
I don't like it. We're taking too many chances.

Trevor nervously smokes.

TREVOR
Coming here was a mistake. I just want to be done with her.

Colleen moves closer to Trevor and takes his hand.

COLLEEN
Trust me, the drama that surrounds these women is the perfect distraction. She'll be so preoccupied, she won't realize it's coming. Then...

Colleen snaps her fingers.

COLLEEN
...we're done with her.

MEGAN'S BEDROOM - CONTINUOUS

Megan stirs in her sleep and begins to unconsciously moan.

MEGAN
Oh, Drew...

Anne's attention is pulled toward her fantasizing daughter. Concerned she may hear more than she should, she quickly exits the room.

RACHEL'S DRIVEWAY - TWO WEEKS LATER, AFTERNOON

Jill and Anne are loading travel bags into Rachel's car. Once finished, Rachel closes the trunk.

RACHEL
Why did Mary go down early?

ANNE
She said Craig's parents leave the place empty. She wanted to do some shopping and stock the kitchen.

JILL
How far away is it?

ANNE

About an hour and a half.

RACHEL

Let's get going if we want to beat traffic.

RACHEL'S CAR - CONTINUOUS

Rachel gets behind the wheel, Jill in the passenger seat, and Anne in the back. Jill is very impressed with Rachel's car, admiring the supple leather seats and futuristic instrument panel.

JILL

This might be the prettiest form of transportation I've ever been in.

RACHEL

Let your husband sleep with men and this too can be yours.

Jill apprehensively chuckles. Rachel starts to back the car down the driveway.

JILL

We have to wait for Colleen and Leigh.

RACHEL

Why did they need to take a separate car?

ANNE

I stopped asking questions.

Rachel looks up to her rear-view mirror. Anne shifts nervously and appears to be hiding something.

RACHEL

What?!

Anne looks up and makes eye contact with Rachel in the mirror.

ANNE

What?

Rachel turns around and looks Anne directly in the eyes.

RACHEL

You are the worst liar. What do you know?

ANNE

I'm not sure. I really shouldn't say anything.

Jill turns around to look at Anne as well.

JILL

Don't let her bully you.

RACHEL

Shut up, Jill! Tell us what you know, Anne, or I'll drag you out of the backseat and kick your ass!

Anne takes a deep breath and reluctantly begins.

ANNE

Who can resist your charms, Rachel? After bunco at the Back Alley, I got up to check and see if Megan had gotten home yet, and...

Anne pauses and shifts in her seat.

RACHEL

And...

ANNE

I saw Trevor and Colleen outside talking.

JILL

That's not bad.

ANNE

Just after three a.m.

Rachel turns and looks at Jill.

RACHEL

That's bad.

JILL

What were they doing?

ANNE

Just talking, but...

RACHEL

(Impatiently)

But what?!

ANNE

It didn't sound good.

RACHEL

Well, what did they say?

ANNE

I'm not a hundred percent certain, but...

Rachel runs out of patience.

RACHEL

BUT WHAT?!

Anne takes a deep breath and shifts her eyes from Rachel to Jill.

ANNE

(To Jill)

If I heard what I think I heard...

Anne addresses both of them.

ANNE

...I'm worried about Leigh.

A loud honk from Colleen's car breaks up their huddle.

RACHEL

(Startled)

Damn it!

Colleen and Leigh signal they are ready to leave. Rachel slips the car in reverse using the luxury model's sophisticated auto-shift transmission. The car backs effortlessly down the driveway.

RACHEL

Still sticking with your "harmless trio of weirdos" theory?

She starts down the street as Colleen and Leigh follow. A few moments pass before Trevor's garage door opens and his car's brake lights illuminate.

KENTUCKY LAKE HOUSE - LATER THAT AFTERNOON

Rachel and Colleen pull their cars into the driveway. Mary comes from the house to greet them.

MARY
Thank goodness, you found the place.

Anne, Jill, and Rachel climb out of the car.

ANNE
Sorry we're late. Baby Bladder over there had to stop twice on the way down.

RACHEL
What can I say? What my vagina lacks in bedroom amusement, it makes up for in urine production.

The rest of the women get out of their cars and grab their bags. Colleen and Leigh enter the house first and set down their bags. Colleen continues straight to the balcony, opens the door and walks out. She looks around, notices the light on and comes back inside. Mary sees Colleen looking at the walls.

MARY
What can I get you, Colleen?

COLLEEN
Where is the light switch for the balcony?

MARY
It's over here in the kitchen. Brilliant design, huh?

COLLEEN
Do you mind if I turn it off? It's attracting quite a few bugs.

MARY
(Obliviously)
No, not at all.

Colleen turns off the light.

Jill points out a spread of liquor and mixers on the table.

JILL
What's all this?

MARY
I thought we'd experiment with some stuff I found in a bartending book.

RACHEL
I remember the last time we experimented. Mojitos, I think it was.

ANNE
Ah, yes, the mojitos. We started with spiced rum, fresh lime, grated sugar cane, and homegrown mint. Three hours later, we were using light beer, lime Jell-O powder, and crushed breath mints.

MARY
Why doesn't everyone just grab a bedroom, stick your luggage in it, and then we'll go grab some dinner.

COLLEEN
(Nervously)
Oh, I thought we were eating here.

MARY
I thought we'd make dinner tomorrow night when we can start earlier. Besides, you guys HAVE to eat at The Boat House. They have the best onion rings.

COLLEEN
Where's The Boat House?

MARY
It's on the other side of the lake. It takes about twenty minutes in the car.

Colleen becomes visibly agitated.

ANNE
Is there a problem, Colleen?

Colleen bites her upper lip and shakes her head.

COLLEEN
No. No problem.

JILL
Are you sure?

COLLEEN
I'm sure. It's fine. Let's go.

RACHEL
I'll drive.

JILL

Your car only seats five.

RACHEL

Colleen and Anne only have half an ass each. We can fit four in the back.

ROAD TO THE BOAT HOUSE - 10 MINUTES LATER

Rachel drives around the lake toward The Boat House. They pass a few homes under construction on their way to the restaurant.

THE BOAT HOUSE RESTAURANT PARKING LOT - 10 MINUTES LATER

Rachel's car pulls into The Boat House's parking lot. A sign reads, "Karaoke Night." The women get out of the car.

MARY

(Sarcastically)

Oh great. It's karaoke night. I can't wait to be serenaded by a bunch of tone-deaf drunks.

BOAT HOUSE RESTAURANT - LATER

Rachel, Mary, Jill, Anne, and Leigh are drunk, sweaty, and huddled around a microphone mumbling incoherent lyrics to the 80's hit, "Come On Eileen." The bar patrons exercise great patience as the ladies exhibit no knowledge of the actual lyrics and just shout nonsense words to the beat of the music. Colleen sits at a table, arms folded, with a soda in front of her. The song ends and the women stumble back to their table.

JILL

I love that song. I have no idea what it's about.

Anne notices Colleen's disinterest.

ANNE

Not a Dexys Midnight Runners fan, Colleen?

COLLEEN

Who?

RACHEL

Oh my God! Try not to get any afterbirth on the table.

MARY

It's getting late. We should probably head back. Let's pay the check.

RACHEL

I'll get it.

MARY

No, Rachel, it's my bunco. I'll get it.

While Rachel and Mary argue over the check, Anne notices a bar patron who is attentively watching their group. The patron realizes he has been seen and quickly leaves.

THE BOAT HOUSE RESTAURANT PARKING LOT - MOMENTS LATER

COLLEEN

How about I drive back?

RACHEL

Probably a good idea.

Colleen gets into the driver's seat, Rachel in the passenger, while the rest stuff themselves in the backseat.

COLLEEN

Keys?

Rachel reaches over and pushes the keyless ignition to start the car. Colleen looks over the interior and is very impressed. She slides her hand over the polished wood dashboard and admires the craftsmanship.

COLLEEN

Wow. I can see where this could be more satisfying than sex.

RACHEL

And it doesn't require any cleanup.

Colleen backs the car out and starts the drive back.

The women are halfway back to the house when Rachel has an intense urge.

RACHEL

I've got to pee.

COLLEEN

Can't you hold it?

RACHEL

No, I have to pee now.

ANNE

Why didn't you go back at The Boat House?

RACHEL

(Sarcastically)

Thank you, Anne. Nothing makes the sensation in a bladder disappear quite like a lecture.

COLLEEN

Do you want to go in the woods?

RACHEL

No, I can't go in the woods.

COLLEEN

Then where do you want me to go?

RACHEL

Turn around.

MARY

We can be back at the house in the same amount of time.

ANNE

Just go in the woods.

RACHEL

Look, I'm not going in the woods! I haven't had anything slither between my legs in years, and as much as I'd love to break that streak, I'm willing to keep it intact until we are out of the dark, creepy forest!

Rachel notices a port-a-potty at one of the home construction sites.

RACHEL

Oh, stop there.

COLLEEN

Seriously? You won't go in the woods, but you'll go in that?

RACHEL
(Very uncomfortable)
Yes, and drive fast, I'm going to explode.

HOME CONSTRUCTION SITE - CONTINUOUS

Colleen pulls the car into the dirt driveway. Rachel leaps out of the car and runs to the side of the property where the closest port-a-potty is perched high above the water's edge. After a brief second to admire the view wasted on the portable toilet, she throws open the door and disappears from view. Colleen leaves the lights on, puts the car in park, and gets out of the car.

COLLEEN
I'm going to make a phone call.

MARY
Who the hell do you have to call right now?!

Colleen shuts the car door without answering and walks away from the car, leaving the four drunken women in the backseat. Anne wriggles free from the sardine-like seating arrangement and climbs into the driver's seat.

ANNE
It's payback time.

JILL
(Nervously)
What are you doing, Anne?

ANNE
Remember the seafood & bourbon stomach chowder I sifted out of my sink?

Anne inspects the car for the gear shift.

JILL
I don't think this is a good idea. Why don't you come back here?

Anne continues to touch controls as she turns around to answer Jill.

ANNE
Relax, I'm just going to pin the door shut so she thinks she's stuck.

As the words come out of Anne's mouth, she accidentally hits the transmission shifter on the steering wheel. The car lurches forward and violently hits the port-a-potty.

Anne quickly stomps the brake pedal. The women watch in horror from the inside of the car as the enclosure tips off balance, goes bottom over top, and slides down the embankment of the lake.

Colleen hears the commotion, ends her call, and runs to the edge of the embankment.

The women scramble out of the car and join Colleen at the edge. The port-a-potty is now upside down, twenty feet down the hillside, wedged between a tree and the lake bottom.

JILL

You killed her!

The women stand motionless as they watch the door to the port-a-potty open slowly, and gallons of solid and liquid human waste pour out. Colleen hurries down the embankment and into waist-deep water to help.

ANNE

(In disbelief)

What did I do?

MARY

(Stunned)

If she's not dead, she's going to be a kind of pissed we've never seen before. Pun intended.

The women keep their eyes fixed on the swirling feces and urine pouring from the enclosure. Mary shows visible signs of repulsion.

MARY

I'm going to be sick.

Colleen tries to help Rachel out of the port-a-potty.

COLLEEN

A little help!

The women make their way down to the water. Rachel slowly crawls out of the enclosure. She is covered in feces and urine. Mary positions herself behind Rachel to conceal her disgust. She dramatically strains her face to keep from getting sick. Rachel stands furiously speechless as she eyeballs Anne.

Mary struggles to keep her stomach contents settled.

ANNE

Are you okay?

Rachel remains silent and looks over her condition.

Mary begins to lose her bile retention battle.

ANNE
(Humbly)

I am so sorry.

Mary violently throws up all over the back of Rachel. Anne and Jill simultaneously bring their hands to their mouths in horror. Rachel just stands there covered in yet another body fluid. After several awkward moments, Mary manages to compose herself.

JILL
(Gently)

I would say it could be worse, but I can't imagine how.

Rachel takes a few deep breaths in an attempt to calm herself down. She shifts her attention between Anne and Mary.

RACHEL

I can't decide which one of you to kill first.

Anne sheepishly smiles. Rachel lunges at Anne's throat and they both fall into the water. The rest follow into the water to separate them.

KENTUCKY LAKE HOUSE - 20 MINUTES LATER

The front door opens, and the soaking-wet women slowly make their way into the house. Mary directs Rachel.

MARY

You can have the first shower.

Rachel turns to Mary and looks at her intensely. Mary yields to Rachel's hostility.

MARY

You can have ALL the showers.

Rachel silently sloshes down the hall to the bathroom. The other women are left standing in the main room. Colleen walks to the balcony and draws the curtains closed. Mary grabs all of the towels she can find and hands them out.

JILL
(To Anne)
You are officially the irretrievably stupid one.

ANNE
I had no intention of knocking the thing over. I just wanted to block the door so she couldn't get out. If that God damn car of hers wasn't so fancy... besides, it was Mary who made matters worse by puking all over her. You couldn't have aimed somewhere else?

MARY
I had no control. I honestly think I lost consciousness for a few seconds.

COLLEEN
I suggest we all give Rachel a lot of space this evening.

A reflective pause hangs over the women.

JILL
I have never felt so sorry for anyone in my entire life, and yet at the same time, it was all I could do to keep from laughing hysterically.

All the women let out the laughs they have been holding in the entire ride back.

ANNE
I thought I killed her. I really did.

JILL
I'm freezing. I'm going to go change out of these clothes.

MARY
Let's all shower and get cleaned up. There's a shower downstairs and another one up here we can use.

KENTUCKY LAKE HOUSE LIVING ROOM - LATER

Except for Rachel, the women have showered, put on fresh clothes, and are in the main room.

LEIGH
Should we check on her?

Mary goes to the kitchen and begins opening cupboards.

MARY

You wanna go in there? Be my guest.

Everyone shakes their heads.

Mary holds up bags of snacks.

MARY

Is it just me or is anyone else starving?

The women eagerly join Mary in the kitchen for food. After a few moments of snack sorting, silence falls over the room as they hear the bedroom door open. Rachel emerges with a carton of cigarettes under her arm and proceeds to the group in the kitchen.

MARY

(Cautiously)

All clean?

Rachel struggles to contain her anger.

RACHEL

There isn't enough anti-bacterial cleanser in the world.

ANNE

(Sincerely)

Rachel, I am so sorry, I...

Rachel holds up her hand to interrupt Anne.

RACHEL

Save it. There is nothing you can say that will make me stop hating you right now.

ANNE

Rachel, I was just trying to get even with your bourbon mess.

Rachel unleashes her anger.

RACHEL

I'd like to survey everyone here! Show of hands! She had to clean up a little regurgitated alcohol from someone she's known for a decade, and I was covered in crap and piss from countless disgusting strangers! Hmmmm, let's see, who thinks those two scenarios are remotely even?!

Jill slowly starts to raise her hand.

RACHEL
Put your God damn hand down, Jill!

MARY
Rachel, you did start this whole thing.

RACHEL
Really puker?! Don't you think enough has come out of your mouth tonight?!

Mary retreats and accepts the insult under the circumstances.

RACHEL
Anyone else have something brilliant to say?!

No one moves or says a word.

RACHEL
Good! Now, I'm going to go sit in my car, listen to angry rap music, and smoke as many of these as I want. Anyone who feels the need to offer me healthy living commentary can direct it here.

Rachel holds up both fists, extends her middle fingers to the group, then turns and walks out of the front door.

MARY
I think she's handling this pretty well.

The women continue to eat and talk. Leigh begins to withdraw. She creeps away from the group and exits to the balcony. Colleen quickly follows her through the sliding glass doors.

DARK BALCONY, KENTUCKY LAKE HOUSE - CONTINUOUS

COLLEEN
(Whispering)
Mrs. Barton. Mrs. Barton. I can't have you outside.

After a moment of being ignored, Colleen approaches Leigh, who is softly crying to herself.

LEIGH
This is so hard. I thought getting away would help take my mind off everything, but it just reminds me of how much I'm going to miss everyone back home. I just want my silly, ordinary life back.

COLLEEN
(Sympathetically)
We know. We took an unprecedented risk placing you where you could have a sense of normalcy until the trial. Not that this group is close to normal. Things will become better once you permanently enter the program.

LEIGH
No, they won't. I'm never going to get over watching Danny executed in front of me. I'm never going to be able to trust anyone or go out without wondering who's behind me. My life is completely ruined because of choices I wasn't even consulted on.

COLLEEN
You're right, Joann, Danny picked the worst people to do business with, and you're paying the price.

Colleen puts her hands on Leigh's shoulders.

COLLEEN
But right now, it's my job to make sure you stay safe and make it to testify. I need you back in the house.

KENTUCKY LAKE HOUSE KITCHEN - SIMULTANEOUSLY

JILL
Is there a switch for more light in here?

MARY
Yeah, it's over there.

Mary motions toward the wall. Jill begins to flip switches, one of which illuminates the balcony.

LAKE HOUSE BALCONY - CONTINUOUS

Colleen panics as the light comes on.

COLLEEN
(Sternly)
Get inside!

As Leigh turns to go inside, Colleen spots a red dot of light on Leigh's back. Colleen springs into action, and tackles Leigh to the balcony floor to shield Leigh with her body. Their momentum sends them crashing through the sliding glass door.

LAKE HOUSE KITCHEN - CONTINUOUS

The women are startled by the crash of bodies and shattered glass.

COLLEEN (FROM THE BALCONY)
Get down! Get down!

Confused but stunned by the scattering debris, they quickly follow Colleen's instruction. Leigh crawls back into the house.

LEIGH
Anne!

Anne stays close to the ground as chaos continues to explode around her. She crawls over to the shattered door of the balcony. Colleen struggles to crawl back into the house and slumps on the ground near Anne.

ANNE
What happened?

LEIGH
Someone is shooting at us.

ANNE
Shooting?!

The scene quiets as Anne goes to Colleen and turns her over. Colleen labors to breathe.

COLLEEN
My phone.

ANNE
What?

COLLEEN
Get my phone. It's in my pocket.

Anne starts feeling Colleen's clothes for her phone. She draws back her hand and sees blood.

ANNE
Mary! Jill! Get over here!

Mary and Jill crawl over to Anne.

JILL
Is that blood?

Anne hushes Jill.

ANNE

Find her phone.

Mary and Jill grope Colleen's clothing while Anne tries to find her wound. Jill reaches behind Colleen's back and pulls out a gun.

JILL

This is not a phone.

Mary looks at Leigh.

MARY

Who the hell are you?

Leigh ignores Mary and addresses Anne.

LEIGH

Anne, please. I can't watch anyone else die.

Anne feverishly works to stop the bleeding.

MARY

Anyone ELSE?!

Jill pulls out Colleen's phone.

JILL

Found it!

Colleen struggles to breathe and speak.

COLLEEN

Call Trevor. My passcode is zero, six, zero, five.

JILL

I don't have this kind of phone! I don't know how to use it!

MARY

Give it to me!

Mary grabs the phone, finds Trevor's number, and dials.

ANNE

Why Trevor? What good will he do us?

LEIGH

He's FBI.

Jill points to Colleen.

JILL

Who's she?

LEIGH

She's FBI.

ANNE

Who are you?

LEIGH

I'm the one they're protecting.

MARY

Trevor! Colleen's been shot!

COLLEEN

(Labored)

Tell him shots came from the southwest. Near Lakeshore Drive and Hilltop.

MARY

She said shots came from the southwest! Near Lakeshore Drive and Hilltop!

LEIGH

Is she going to be okay?

Anne takes off her sweatshirt, balls it up, and holds it to Colleen's bleeding exit wound.

ANNE

(To Leigh)

Hold this here, as tight as you can.

MARY

Hurry!

Mary ends the call.

MARY

He's on his way.

ANNE

What good will that do us? He's in Cincinnati. We need to get her to a hospital now!

LEIGH

No, he's close.

LAKE HOUSE DRIVEWAY - CONTINUOUS

Rachel is sitting in her car with the radio blasting while self-soothing with her carton of cigarettes. She is oblivious to the drama unfolding inside. Her attention is drawn to blue and red lights coming around the corner. She gets out of the car and watches a dozen unmarked federal cars race toward her.

RACHEL

(Under her breath)

It was just a plastic container of shit. Who do I make the check out to?

The cars screech to a halt just short of her, spraying gravel. Agents exit their vehicles, guns drawn, as a helicopter approaches over the ridge.

RACHEL

Jesus, they take vandalism really serious in this state.

Rachel drops the cigarette from her mouth and the box in her hand as she exits the vehicle and puts both hands in the air. An agent approaches Rachel, holsters his gun, and places handcuffs around her wrists. He bends her over the hood of her car and forces her head down to immobilize her. The helicopter lands. Trevor, along with several other agents, hop out and run into the house.

LAKE HOUSE LIVING ROOM - CONTINUOUS

Trevor sees Anne administering CPR to Colleen. He points to Leigh and instructs the other agents.

TREVOR

Secure her.

The two agents pick Leigh up off the ground and escort her out of the house. Trevor bends down next to Anne.

TREVOR

Let me take her.

ANNE
She's in arrest. She needs an emergency room now.

Trevor stops Anne and picks up Colleen.

TREVOR
(To Anne)
Come with me.

LAKE HOUSE DRIVEWAY - CONTINUOUS

Rachel remains in custody as she watches Trevor carry Colleen out to the helicopter. Anne follows them aboard and continues CPR.

As the helicopter takes off, Mary and Jill exit the house. An AGENT approaches the officer holding down Rachel.

AGENT
The witness is secure. You can release her.

As the agent frees one wrist from the handcuffs, Rachel pulls away in disgust and hurries over to Mary and Jill.

RACHEL
Nice weekend getaway, Mary! Mind telling me what the hell is going on?

MARY
The neighbors aren't who they say they are.

RACHEL
No shit! Who the hell are they?!

MARY
I think Leigh may be in witness protection.

Jill grabs the arm of AGENT #2 to get his attention.

JILL
Excuse me. Our friend just flew away in that helicopter. Do you know where they are going?

AGENT #2
University of Louisville Medical Center.

HOSPITAL LOBBY - LATER THAT EVENING

Jill, Mary, and Rachel enter the lobby and head for the RECEPTIONIST.

MARY
Can you tell us if Colleen Young was brought here?

The receptionist checks her computer records.

RECEPTIONIST
I don't have a Colleen Young. Was she brought into emergency?

MARY
You know, that's probably not even her real name...

Anne, covered in bloodstains, exits the ER doors. The women race over to her.

JILL
Dear God, are you okay?

MARY
How's Colleen?

RACHEL
Where's that lying douche nozzle, Trevor?

ANNE
(Exhausted)
I'm fine, Colleen is with doctors, and I don't know where Trevor went. He told me not to leave, then he disappeared.

JILL
Where's Leigh?

ANNE
I have no idea. I haven't seen her since the house.

HOSPITAL LOBBY WAITING ROOM - LATER

Hours have passed, and early morning sunlight fills the foyer of the hospital. Police officers mill around the waiting room while awaiting further orders. Jill and Rachel are asleep on a couch. Rachel still has the handcuffs dangling from her wrist. Anne and Mary are seated across from them, trying to stay awake.

MARY

How ya doing?

Anne takes a minute to think.

ANNE

I think next time I'll skip the onion rings. They gave me a little heartburn.

The women share a smile.

MARY

You know, seeing you every day in the suburban mom role makes me forget you have this whole other life outside the neighborhood.

ANNE

What do you mean?

MARY

I mean, you're a skilled professional. I forget to give you credit for that.

ANNE

To be fair, it's usually not this dramatic.

MARY

Regardless, you saved someone's life tonight.

ANNE

I don't know about that.

MARY

You did. And I'm incredibly impressed.

The main hospital doors open. Trevor enters with a folder under his arm. He's flanked by FBI agents. Anne gently pats Jill on the shoulder to wake her while Mary violently smacks Rachel's midsection.

Trevor summons the women to him.

TREVOR

Mrs. Hutchinson, I didn't want to leave without thanking you for what you did tonight.

ANNE

How's Colleen?

TREVOR
I'm sorry. I can't comment on that.

MARY
You can't comment? Where's Leigh?

TREVOR
I can't comment on that either.

RACHEL
This is bullshit! These three were shot at! I was forced to make out with a hood ornament...

Trevor interrupts Rachel's attack with one of his own.

TREVOR
Mrs. Easton, I'm sorry if you were inconvenienced tonight, but understand that you jeopardized a federal prosecution and endangered the life of my partner because of your total lack of self-control!

Trevor pulls out a print of the picture taken at the Back Alley Bar. The photograph shows Rachel's topless breasts pressed against the window with Leigh clearly seen in the background. Various "Back Alley Bar" and "Cincinnati" signs make it easy to identify their location.

Jill places her hand on her mouth, Anne shakes her head, and Mary smirks.

TREVOR
I know this may come as a shock to you, but it turns out salami-nipples-dot-com is a website frequently visited by organized crime members.

Trevor returns the picture to his folder.

TREVOR
I would have expected someone with your background to know careless actions come with serious consequences, Mrs. Easton.

Trevor steps away to leave.

JILL
So, this is it? Y'all just disappear into the night?

Trevor returns to answer Jill.

TREVOR
Mrs. Michaels, if this had all gone as planned, we would have just disappeared into the night.

Trevor leaves the women, exits the hospital lobby, and gets into the back of a waiting car. The shooter is sitting cuffed in the back of the car.

Anne recognizes him.

ANNE
That guy was at The Boat House.

JILL
Was he the one shooting at us?

The women silently watch as the agents and cars drive away. After a few silent moments, Rachel speaks.

RACHEL
So, who's hosting next?

NEIGHBORHOOD STREET - SEVERAL WEEKS LATER, MORNING

Anne is finishing up her run. She turns the corner to her street and sees a moving van parked in front of the house once occupied by Leigh and Trevor. As Anne stops at her driveway, her presence attracts the attention of her new neighbors LARRY and MISSY. After the last neighbor debacle, she is reluctant to introduce herself.

Larry crosses his yard and his wife follows. He extends his hand.

LARRY
Hi! I'm Larry, and this is my wife Missy.

ANNE'S KITCHEN - MOMENTS LATER

Bill is sitting at the table, reading his laptop.

Anne enters from the garage, goes to the cabinet, pulls out a mug, and prepares her morning coffee.

ANNE
(Nonchalantly)
I met our new neighbors.

Bill is preoccupied and keeps his eyes on his laptop.

BILL

Oh yeah. Do I have to worry about either of them being secret agents?

Anne sits down next to Bill and casually begins to drink her coffee.

ANNE

Nah. They're just swingers.

END OF ROUND 1

ROUND 2

Establishing the Rules

SPRING, THE FOLLOWING YEAR

JOHN MICHAELS' CAR - EVENING

John is driving home when his text notification sounds. He pulls over and stops before reaching his street. He picks up his phone and reads the message. A smile spreads across his face while he enthusiastically types a response. John ends his messaging and continues to his driveway.

He steps out and turns to admire his immaculately kept vehicle. He rubs a watermark off the hood with his shirt tail before closing the door and heading into his house.

MICHAELS' HOME - MOMENTS LATER

Jill is in the middle of preparing dinner. The children, Wil, Emma, and Grace jump up to greet their father with hugs. Jill interrupts her preparations to welcome John home.

JILL

I hadn't heard from you all day, so I didn't know when to expect you.

Jill completes her welcome with a kiss on John's cheek.

JOHN

I was in meetings all day.

Jill goes back to fixing dinner.

JILL

I know you're busy. Dinner will be a little late, I hope you don’t mind.

JOHN

No, I don't mind. I'm going to go upstairs and change. Do you have bunco tonight?

JILL

Yes, I have to leave in about twenty minutes.

JOHN

So soon?

JILL

I told you I had to leave at seven.

JOHN

I know. I just thought you could be a little late.

John smiles as he gives Jill a suggestive gesture to go upstairs.

JILL

John...

Jill motions toward the kids and her dinner preparations. John pouts as he exits the kitchen. Jill just shakes her head at his silly behavior and continues with dinner.

JILL

Girls, help your brother set the table.

ANNE'S LIVING ROOM - LATER

Bunco night is "in progress." Jill helps Anne clear plates and refresh drinks. Mary stands at the base of Anne's staircase, sipping a glass of wine. Mary glances upstairs and sees Rachel sneaking down the hall. Rachel remains under Mary's heavy surveillance as she makes her way down to the first level.

MARY

I'm going to be called to testify about this, aren't I?

Rachel raises her index finger to her lips to suggest her actions should remain secret. She walks past Mary and into the living room. Mary rolls her eyes, knowing she has just witnessed some mischievous act.

All of the women make their way to the living room, gather drinks, and sit down.

JILL

Have you heard anything else from the neighbor next door?

ANNE

Since she invited me to a threesome? No.

RACHEL

If I'm denied sex with one person, I certainly don't want to hear about someone who's getting it from two at a time.

ANNE
It's a shame. She was really nice.

MARY
Of course she was nice, she wanted to tag team husbands.

JILL
I still can't believe they came out and told you.

ANNE
I would rather they'd kept that extracurricular activity to themselves.

MARY
Why couldn't someone normal have moved in?

RACHEL
Right, normal. Like us. I'm married to a closet homosexual, you've gained fame for throwing a desk at a school official, Anne's super-nurse, and Jill... Jill is as close to normal as we can hope for.

MARY
Hey, I thought we agreed never to speak of my mental lapse in judgment again.

Jill rescues Mary with a change in topics.

JILL
How's your mom, Rachel?

RACHEL
She remembers just enough to make me regret every visit.

ANNE
Is she responding to any treatment?

RACHEL
Not unless you count sponge baths as treatment.

JILL
I'm sorry to hear that.

RACHEL
(Frustrated)
Thanks.

MARY
Where's your brother during all this?

RACHEL
(Bitterly)
How should I know? I haven't seen that useless butt plug in years.

MARY
Sorry, Rachel. I foolishly thought you might have reached out for help.

RACHEL
I wouldn't ask that guy to piss on me if I was on fire.

MARY
Why would you? The last time you were on fire, you pissed on yourself.

RACHEL
Well, when you want something done right...

Anne gets up and heads toward the kitchen.

ANNE
All right, enough you two. Anyone need anything?

JILL
I'll have another water.

MARY
I just realized... it's been two whole hours and you haven't gone outside for a cigarette, Rachel.

RACHEL
Yes, believe it or not, all your annoying health facts and buzzkill statistics are making me think it's time I try to quit.

JILL
Good for you. What method are you using?

Rachel takes a dramatic, deep breath.

RACHEL
Cold turkey.

MARY
Really? How's that working?

RACHEL
Every night I dream I'm quilting myself into a blanket of nicotine patches, if that tells you anything.

Anne returns and places wine, beer, and water on the table.

ANNE
Wouldn't it be amazing to have a wife?

Anne takes her seat.

MARY
Are you switching teams on us?

ANNE
No, I mean, someone who takes care of everything. I'd ask for a personal assistant, but there are things they'd flat out refuse to do.

MARY
Like pull dead frogs out of pant pockets, clean month-old bananas out of backpacks, or pick dog vomit from shag carpet.

ANNE
Exactly. And simple stuff, like making sure the refrigerator is stocked with cold pop, emptying the overflowing trash cans, and knowing the house is almost out of toilet paper.

MARY
They think it's the housekeeping fairy. I swear, one of these days we should just let them drown in their own filth.

Jill smiles tenderly.

JILL
I enjoy taking care of everything.

MARY
You do?

JILL

Yeah. Being a wife and mother is all I ever wanted. I love taking care of the house and kids. It lets me show them how much I love them.

Mary and Anne shamefully regret the harsh criticisms of their families. Rachel leans in to whisper to them both.

RACHEL

(Quietly)

I wouldn't bother submitting those mother-of-the-year applications.

The reflective lull in conversation is broken, with Mary eagerly changing the subject.

MARY

I'm reading a book about relationships. It claims the traits we are drawn to during the dating process become the things that grow into intolerable resentment years later.

RACHEL

I was attracted to Kevin's devotion to Catholicism.

Rachel shakes her head and rolls her eyes.

MARY

Craig says he fell in love with my sense of humor. He claims he couldn't get enough of my sarcastic wit. Now, I can see he's disgusted with himself if he laughs at anything that comes out of my mouth.

ANNE

I never thought about it, but that book may be right. I loved Bill's sensitivity, and just last week we got into a fight because I thought he was acting like a baby.

JILL

What happened?

ANNE

Okay, for the record, I know I was wrong.

Rachel repositions herself and settles in for a story.

RACHEL

Go on.

ANNE
We were... together... and ESPN happened to be on. Right in the middle of some intense intimacy, they reported a key player was in a labor dispute with his team. I was surprised and said something. Then he got all hurt because I wasn't paying attention to him and left in a pout.

MARY
You should have focused less on the strike and more on his balls.

ANNE
I know. Like I said, I was wrong. But if he wants my advice about his fantasy baseball team, I have to keep up on this stuff. Most men would love a wife who knows so much about sports.

JILL
Why don't you turn off the television?

ANNE
God, no. That has to be on.

JILL
Why?

ANNE
Because the kids are too old to fall for the "we're wrapping Christmas presents" excuse.

JILL
That works?

ANNE
Oh yeah. You mention Christmas presents, even in March, and they leave you alone for hours.

MARY
We tell the kids we're taking a nap and they're welcome to join us. They scatter like an open bag of Skittles left on a dashboard.

ANNE
I accidentally walked in on my parents once. THAT was an awkward winter.

MARY
That's my worst nightmare. Once the boys realize how things work, I'll never have sex in my house again.

Jill checks her watch.

JILL
I should get going.

ANNE
What? It's still early.

JILL
I know, but John's been working late an awful lot lately, and he was disappointed when I left. I should go spend some time with him.

Jill gets up and gathers her things.

JILL
Rachel, are you still hosting at your pool Friday?

RACHEL
Yeah. Tell the kids to come around back when they get off the bus.

JILL
They always love your last day of school party. I'll see all y'all later.

The women say their goodbyes as Jill heads home.

MEGAN'S BATHROOM - NEXT MORNING

Anne is collecting trash in her daughter's bathroom. Her husband, Bill, comes to the door.

BILL
I'm leaving.

ANNE
Okay, I work late tonight, so feed the kids, will you?

BILL
Sure. Anyone need a ride this morning?

ANNE

No, Megan took Jack.

BILL

All right. Have a good day at work.

Bill kisses Anne and exits. Anne continues dumping trash into a collection bag. Something catches her attention and she starts to dig through the trash liner. After a moment of study, she pulls out a used pregnancy test. Anne sits wide-eyed and stunned on the edge of the bathtub as she studies the positive indicator.

HOSPITAL NURSE STATION - LATER THAT NIGHT

Anne is sitting at a desk, resting her chin in her hand, and staring blankly at the wall. She has an untouched meal in front of her. TANYA, a heavyset, no-nonsense co-worker notices her angst.

TANYA

Anne?

Anne remains deep in thought, so Tanya raises her voice.

TANYA

Anne!

Anne turns her attention.

TANYA

Hey. You okay?

Anne allows her hand to fall to the desk.

ANNE

Do you have teenagers?

TANYA

If they haven't killed each other by the time I get home, yeah.

ANNE

How do you bring up a topic that's extremely difficult to discuss?

TANYA

I've got boys. They have no interest in any topic unless it's what I can buy them or where I can take them.

ANNE

What I would give for it to be one of those two things.

TANYA

What's going on?

Anne pushes her untouched food into the trash can.

ANNE

Nothing.

DR. MACDONALD, a bossy, grey-haired woman, runs up to Anne and Tanya.

DR. MACDONALD

Break's over, multi-car accident on seventy-one. We're getting two criticals.

Anne and Tanya jump up and follow Dr. MacDonald.

ANNE'S KITCHEN - TWO DAYS LATER

Anne is cutting fruit to take to Rachel's pool. She's still in a state of preoccupation and distress. Megan enters from the garage.

MEGAN

I'm officially a senior!

Megan continues through the kitchen and up to her room. Anne drops what she is doing and follows her upstairs.

MEGAN'S BEDROOM - MOMENTS LATER

Megan throws her bag down on her bed and kicks off her shoes. As she begins to change into more comfortable clothes, Anne hovers by the bedroom door, trying to muster the courage to bring up the touchy subject.

ANNE

You don't want to come over to Mrs. Easton's?

MEGAN

No offense mom, but "The Real Housewives of Cincinnati" pool party is NOT how I want to spend my first afternoon of summer vacation. I'm going over to Abby's house.

ANNE

When will you be home?

MEGAN

I don't know. Tonight sometime. I'll text you.

Anne apprehensively enters Megan's room and turns the conversation serious.

ANNE

Megan, is there anything you want to talk about?

Megan doesn't give Anne much attention as she continues to carelessly flit around the room.

MEGAN

What do you mean?

Anne goes to Megan, takes her hand, and leads her to the bed. They both sit down. Megan becomes suspicious of Anne's odd behavior.

ANNE

You know that I will always love you, and if you've made a mistake, I will do everything in my power to help you through it.

MEGAN

(Confused)

Yeah.

ANNE

I don't want to mention anything to your dad until we have a chance to discuss this.

MEGAN

Is this about my chemistry grade?

Anne struggles to continue with the discussion.

ANNE

No, it's not about your chemistry grade.

MEGAN

Good, because Mrs. Koslov gave us this pop quiz two days before the final that might as well have been written in Russian and I totally...

Anne interrupts.

ANNE

Megan, I'm not talking about chemistry.

Megan can feel the seriousness of Anne's tone, but doesn't understand it.

MEGAN

Okay. What ARE you talking about?

Anne fuels her courage to continue with a deep breath.

ANNE

I'm talking about the choices you're going to have to make pretty soon.

MEGAN

Like college?

Anne nods.

ANNE

College is something you're going to have to consider. I don't think you should make any quick decisions. You need to know all of your options and discuss them with the father.

MEGAN

(Confused)

Father?

Anne closes her eyes and shakes her head.

ANNE

Please, Megan, don't make this harder for me than it already is.

Megan straightens up.

MEGAN

Mom, what are you talking about? It sounds like you think I'm pregnant.

Anne dramatically sighs.

ANNE

I know you are.

MEGAN
(Flabbergasted)
Really?! This is news to me. What makes you think I'm pregnant?

Anne reaches into her pocket and pulls out the pregnancy test.

MEGAN
What's that?

ANNE
It's your pregnancy test.

MEGAN
No, it's not!

ANNE
Megan, I found it in your bathroom.

MEGAN
In MY bathroom? I don't know what to tell you, it's not mine!

ANNE
(Relieved)
Are you sure?

MEGAN
Yeah, mom, I'm sure! Something needs to happen before I would NEED a pregnancy test!

Anne grabs Megan and gives her an unreciprocated embrace. Megan's emotionless demeanor doesn't change as Anne releases her.

ANNE
Then how did it get there?

MEGAN
I don't know!

Anne takes a moment to think.

ANNE
Could it be one of your friends?

MEGAN
(Insulted)
Could it be one of yours?

Anne thinks a moment then realizes how it must have mysteriously appeared. Anne gets up quickly and leaves Megan's room. Megan follows Anne to her doorway and shouts out to her.

MEGAN
Thanks for assuming I'm an irresponsible slut, mom!

RACHEL'S POOL - MOMENTS LATER

Mary and Jill are sitting at a patio table on Rachel's deck. Rachel is standing with a drink in her hand at the edge of the pool. Anne silently enters the backyard and walks deliberately toward Rachel.

Mary notices Anne.

MARY
Hey, Anne! What can we get you to drink?

Rachel turns around just in time to see Anne coming straight toward her. Anne thrusts her arms forward and aggressively shoves Rachel into the pool.

ANNE
Bitch!

Mary and Jill get up and hurry to the edge of the pool. Rachel comes up out of the water and looks at her now empty glass.

RACHEL
Damn it, Anne! I just poured that!

Anne continues to shout at Rachel.

ANNE
I haven't slept in three days! I've lost four pounds! And I'm pretty sure I've developed an ulcer!

Rachel moves to the steps of the pool and gets out.

MARY
What did she do?

Anne addresses Mary and Jill.

ANNE
She put a positive pregnancy test in Megan's trash can!

Mary is unable to stop the smirk that spreads across her face.

MARY
(To Rachel)
I knew you were up to something the other night.

Anne confronts Mary.

ANNE
You knew about this?!

Mary backtracks her comment.

MARY
No! I mean, I saw her upstairs, but...

Anne interrupts Mary and turns back to the drenched Rachel.

ANNE
How long am I going to have to pay for last fall's mishap?!

RACHEL
You're seriously going to call what you did to me a "mishap?!" Serving an animal rights activist veal is a "mishap!" Letting the dog you're pet sitting get hit by a car is a "mishap!" Driving through a crowded playground is a "mishap!"

Mary leans closer to Jill.

MARY
(To Jill)
There is something wrong with the way her brain works.

Anne invades Rachel's personal space.

ANNE
Do you have any idea the emotional turmoil I've been in the past few days?!

Rachel aggressively leans inches from Anne's face.

RACHEL
Do you have any idea the side effects of the antibiotic cocktail I was prescribed?! I couldn't be more than fifty feet from a toilet for six weeks!

Rachel backs down, grabs a towel, and wraps it around herself.

ANNE
Where the hell did you get this thing?

Rachel looks over at Jill.

RACHEL
I found it.

ANNE
Found it? Right! What poor unsuspecting pregnant woman did you knock over the head and steal this from?!

Jill lowers her head and a quiet moment passes.

RACHEL
For your information, she gave it to me willingly.

Anne and Mary turn to the now blushing Jill.

JILL
I never would've let you have it if I knew what you were going to do with it.

Mary takes a step closer to Jill and takes hold of her arm.

MARY
Wait a minute, you're pregnant?

Jill takes a deep breath and shrugs her shoulders.

JILL
Yes.

The anger of the moment turns to celebration as Anne and Mary surround Jill and smother her with congratulations.

ANNE
Now that it's not my teenage daughter having a baby, I'm thrilled!

MARY
Do the kids know?

JILL
No. We want to wait a few months before we tell them.

ANNE

How far along are you?

JILL

Just weeks. I haven't even been to the doctor yet. Rachel just happened to come over the day I took the test. She said she had a fun way to tell y'all.

Anne shoots Rachel a dirty look.

RACHEL

I had fun.

ANNE

Okay, Rachel. Are we even now? Can we end this?

Rachel thinks for a moment.

RACHEL

I think you've been adequately punished the last few days.

ANNE

Good. You're all witnesses. This is officially over.

Rachel and Anne shake hands but both have a distrustful look in their eye.

JILL'S HOUSE - 10 DAYS LATER, EVENING

Jill is hosting her bunco with the usual extravagant spread of food and beverages. Rachel and Anne are in the living room. Wil walks in, sits on the couch, and strikes up a conversation with Rachel.

WIL

Your car is super cool.

RACHEL

Thanks, Wil.

WIL

Does it go fast?

Rachel raises her eyebrows and smiles.

RACHEL

Real fast.

WIL

My mom says it costs a lot.

RACHEL

All my dignity.

Wil squeezes his forehead with confusion.

RACHEL

Want to go for a ride sometime?

WIL

(Enthusiastically)

Yeah!

RACHEL

Okay, just promise you won't tell your mom how fast we go.

Jill enters the living room and sees Wil talking to Rachel.

JILL

What are you doing downstairs, Wil?

RACHEL

He's fine, Jill. We're just talking about school and stuff.

Rachel winks at Wil and he attempts to wink back.

JILL

I'm so sorry. John called last minute and said he had to stay late.

ANNE

Do you want me to call Megan over? She can entertain them upstairs.

JILL

Is she busy?

ANNE

No, she's at home on her phone. Let me give her a call.

Anne steps away and pulls out her phone. Jill turns her attention to Wil.

JILL

Miss Megan is going to come over and play with you for a little bit before bed, okay?

WIL

Can we play video games?

JILL

How about some reading instead?

Anne finishes her call and returns to Jill.

ANNE

She's on her way over.

Mary, wearing a very low-cut shirt, dramatically comes through the door and enters the living room.

MARY

Jill, John has a gun, doesn't he? I need someone to shoot me!

Jill directs Wil.

JILL

Wil, go upstairs, Miss Megan will be here in a minute.

Wil heads upstairs as Mary takes his place on the couch.

MARY

Craig's mother is coming to stay for an entire month.

ANNE

How did you let THAT happen?

MARY

I didn't have a choice. She just called and announced it.

RACHEL

Wait, Craig's mother? Isn't she the one who offered to pay for your nose job?

MARY

Yes, unsolicited and across the Thanksgiving dinner table.

Rachel nods and smiles.

RACHEL

I miss her.

Rachel exits to the kitchen.

JILL

She's always been delightful to me.

MARY

That's because you're the proper doting wife and mother. Whereas, I'm the narcissistic, self-centered, theater trash her son settled for.

ANNE

When does she arrive?

MARY

Week after next.

Megan knocks and opens the door.

MEGAN

Hello?

JILL

Hello, Megan. The kids are upstairs. I really appreciate this.

MEGAN

No problem, Mrs. Michaels.

Megan proceeds upstairs.

JILL

Look at it this way, you'll get a little help with the boys for a while.

Rachel returns to the living room with a glass of wine and hands it to Mary. As Mary accepts the beverage, calm descends over her.

MARY

That's true. They love it when she rides her credit card into town.

The evening progresses as usual, with the drinks flowing freely. Mary is now VERY relaxed.

MARY

(Slurring)

Ya know what I remember most about my wedding? That bitch asking what happened to my weight loss plan during the rehearsal dinner.

ANNE

She didn't.

MARY

Oh, yeah she did. When I was getting fitted for my wedding dress, I was surprised my busty friend and I had the same bra size. She proclaims, in front of everyone, "Oh, that's because they're measuring your back fat."

The women can't contain their laughter.

MARY

That woman is a vicious cunt.

Anne and Rachel cringe at the sound of Mary's scathing comment. Jill becomes incensed at the use of such language in her home.

JILL

Mary!

MARY

(Shamefully)

Sorry, Jill.

RACHEL

I don't know what the problem is. Just give it back to her.

MARY

Right! Then she goes off and pouts, whines to Craig, and we get into a huge fight.

JILL

Doesn't he ever say anything to her?

MARY

No. He's such a wimp when it comes to her. He's always asking me to just ignore her. Okay, I'll ignore her, as long as I can ignore him when he wants his pecker pampered!

Mary tries to pour more wine into her glass but has trouble. Anne reaches over and steadies her hand.

ANNE

Let me help you.

RACHEL

You can't let this woman get to you. You're an insult ninja. Don't hold back and just deny anything she accuses you of.

MARY

Oh, I wish I could, but she's SO much better at it than me. She criticizes so fast and so harshly that I'm left speechless.

RACHEL

Nonsense. Let's practice. I'll say something really insulting and you hit me with a comeback. You ready?

Jill becomes worried Rachel's exercise will end badly.

JILL

Nothing about this is a good idea.

Rachel waves off Jill's warning. Mary prepares for the exercise by taking a deep breath.

MARY

Ready.

RACHEL

Mary, did you at least tip the prostitute you pulled that shirt off of?

Mary looks down at her shirt.

MARY

What?

RACHEL

No, you need to come back with something. Here, try it again. Mary, you should keep in mind, airlines now charge you for two seats after you get a certain size.

MARY

I changed my mind. I don't like this game.

RACHEL

I'm helping you. It's better if you're prepared. One more time. Mary, I saw your same hairstyle on an unattractive homosexual woman I met at the hardware store.

MARY

Stop “helping” me.

Rachel smiles as Jill interjects.

JILL

Might I suggest, killing her with kindness.

MARY

Is "kindness" slang for some lethal street drug?

Jill shakes her head as if she’s dealing with incorrigible school children.

JILL

You will completely disarm her if you just laugh everything off. Don't give her the satisfaction of knowing she's getting to you.

ANNE

That is the mature thing to do.

RACHEL

Who said anything about being mature? This woman needs a big fat serving of "Shut the hell up!" With a side of "Go screw yourself!”

Mary sighs through a smile.

MARY

Rachel, as wonderful a fantasy as that is, it's never going to happen. Not if I want to keep peace in my house. I think I should take Jill's advice here and try to be as pleasant as possible.

RACHEL

(Sarcastically)

Good luck with that.

JILL

The first few days will be the hardest. Just remember to keep your head high and let every insult bounce off you.

Megan comes downstairs and approaches the women.

MEGAN

Mrs. Michaels, the kids are asleep, so I'll go ahead and head home, if that's okay?

JILL
Yes, thank you so much, Megan. Can I pay you tomorrow?

MEGAN
Don't worry about it. I enjoy playing with them. Have a nice night.

Megan leaves as the women say their goodbyes.

MARY
She's a good kid.

ANNE
Yeah. I think she's still a bit upset with me for thinking she was pregnant.

Rachel giggles wickedly. Anne smacks her on the leg.

ANNE
I still can't believe you thought that was funny.

RACHEL
You're right, it wasn't funny. It was HILARIOUS!

MARY
Did you really think she might have been pregnant? Boys aren't really her priority.

ANNE
Oh, like that matters. I know I was wrong to think the worst of her, but how much stuff did we do behind our parents' backs?

JILL
I snuck into "R" rated movies.

MARY
You snuck into "R" rated movies?

JILL
(Shamefully)
Quite a few, actually.

MARY
I snuck into Mexico.

RACHEL
Everyone tries to sneak out of Mexico, why the hell did you sneak in?

MARY
Drinking age was eighteen.

ANNE
What if something would have happened to you?

MARY
I know. It was so dangerous. I get sick to my stomach thinking about Charlie or Ethan doing something like that.

RACHEL
Well, the scariest place they can sneak into is Kentucky and really, how much damage can they do down there?

Mary sarcastically smiles.

MARY
We managed to put their entire FBI field office on tactical alert.

Rachel raises her eyebrows and nods.

HOSPITAL CORRIDOR - ONE WEEK LATER

Jill walks out of her doctor's appointment with her three children in tow. All four walk to the elevator.

JILL
Y'all were so good at my doctor's appointment. What do you say we get some ice cream on the way home?

WIL
Can I get a waffle cone?

The group reaches the elevator and Jill pushes the call button.

JILL
Sure, you can. What are you going to get, girls?

GRACE
I want a chocolate shake.

EMMA
I want a waffle cone like Wil.

WIL
You can't eat a whole waffle cone.

JILL
Don't worry, Wil. I'll help her if she needs it.

The elevator arrives, the doors open, and the group loads in.

ELEVATOR - CONTINUOUS

JILL
Did y'all know Miss Anne works here?

GRACE
Can we go see her?

JILL
She's probably really busy. We'll see her at home.

The elevator doors open. Jill and Wil step out, but Grace and Emma hesitate. Jill turns around just in time to see the terrified faces of her twins disappear between the closing elevator doors. Jill throws herself against the closed doors.

JILL
No!

Jill begins to panic. She frantically hits the buttons on the elevator call panel and looks around for any help.

JILL
What do I do?! What do I do?!

WIL
I'll go in the other elevator and look for them.

JILL
No! Don't move!

Jill notices the elevator coming back down. She waits nervously as she watches the floor indicator slowly tick down to her location.

The elevator arrives.

The doors open.

The elevator is empty.

Jill dramatically screams in distress.

HOSPITAL NURSE STATION - MOMENTS LATER

Anne interrupts her rounds to answer her ringing phone.

ANNE
This better not be Jack with fifty reasons why he can't mow the lawn.

Anne sees the caller ID and answers her phone.

ANNE
Hey, Jill. What's up?

HOSPITAL CORRIDOR

JILL
I lost the girls!

ANNE
What?!

JILL
We're here for my doctor's appointment, and they didn't get off the elevator! The doors closed, and now they're gone!

ANNE
Okay. Don't panic. I'll call security.

JILL
Please hurry! I'm about to have a complete nervous breakdown!

Anne grabs a two-way radio from the nurse's station.

ANNE
Security. We have a code "L." Two four-year-old girls last seen in the west end elevator.

SECURITY

We just got a call from the eleventh floor. They have them.

ANNE

We have the mother here. Can you bring them to the ER nurse station?

SECURITY

On our way.

Anne puts down the radio and raises her phone back to her ear.

ANNE

Jill, they're safe.

HOSPITAL CORRIDOR

Jill raises her hand to her chest.

JILL

(Relieved)

Oh, thank you so much.

ANNE

Security is bringing them to me.

JILL

Okay, I'll be right there.

HOSPITAL EMERGENCY AREA - MOMENTS LATER

Jill and Wil exit the elevator and rush to the nurse station. Anne stands with the twins. Jill rushes over, bends down, and hugs her girls.

JILL

Thank God y'all are all right.

ANNE

Apparently, a nice homeless man found them in the elevator and took them to security.

Jill stands upright.

JILL

A homeless man?

ANNE

We have our regulars. You're lucky Crazy Frank didn't find them.

Jill's voice cracks with apprehension.

JILL

Who's Crazy Frank?

Anne gently pats Jill on the shoulder.

ANNE

It's better I don't tell you.

Jill has a sick feeling come over her.

JILL

As much as I hate to admit it, I think I need some help.

ANNE

There's nothing wrong with asking for help, Jill.

JILL

Would Megan be interested in a daily babysitting job?

ANNE

Actually, she's been looking for a way to make some money. I'm sure she'd love it.

MARY'S FAMILY ROOM - 3 DAYS LATER, EVENING

Mary puts the finishing touches on her home as Ethan and Charlie run down the stairs.

ETHAN

She's here!

Both boys race for the door, open it and run outside. Mary takes a deep breath, looks to the ceiling, and prays to herself.

MARY

Please God, give me the strength to ignore every nasty insult that comes out of this woman's mouth... and while you're at it, help me resist the urge to smother her while she sleeps too.

Mary manufactures a pleasant smile and heads out of the front door.

MARY'S DRIVEWAY - CONTINUOUS

Mary walks out and greets the rest of her family in the driveway. PATRICIA HUESTON is a petite woman in her early 70s, with tidy grey hair, and an uptight manner. The boys embrace their grandmother as Craig takes luggage out of the trunk.

MARY
Hello, Patricia!

PATRICIA
Hello, Mary.

Patricia looks Mary up and down.

PATRICIA
I thought you were dieting.

Mary mumbles to herself through a smile.

MARY
(Through clenched teeth)
Why can't you come down with some disease?

Craig closes the trunk of the car.

CRAIG
Come on boys, help me get grandma's stuff inside.

MARY'S FAMILY ROOM - CONTINUOUS

Craig and the boys bring in luggage as Mary invites Patricia to sit down on the couch.

As Craig takes the luggage to the guest room, Mary joins Patricia.

MARY
So, what brings you down to Cincinnati for an entire month?

PATRICIA
Besides spending time with my underfed grandsons?

Mary forcibly smiles, with a tightening jaw.

MARY
Yes, besides that.

PATRICIA
Well, we've sold the lake house, and I need to be available to sign closing documents.

MARY
You sold the lake house? Hasn't it been in your family for generations?

PATRICIA
Yes, but after the FBI treated it like a common crime scene, I lost all affinity for it.

Mary becomes uncomfortable in her seat.

MARY
I'm sorry to hear that. I always thought it would be fun to teach the boys to water ski down there.

PATRICIA
Oh, we're buying another place. Craig and the boys will be welcome any time they'd like.

Mary bites her upper lip to keep quiet, a small vein rising in her forehead. Craig re-enters the room.

CRAIG
Mom, do you want anything to drink?

PATRICIA
Do you have any good scotch?

Mary stands.

MARY
Let me get that for her, Craig.

PATRICIA
I did say, GOOD scotch, Mary. You know the difference, don't you?

Mary's artificial smile complements her swelling forehead vein.

MARY
I'm not sure. Craig, will you help me pick the good scotch?

Craig gets up to help Mary. The boys sit closer to their grandmother.

CRAIG
Can I get you anything to eat, mom?

PATRICIA
Oh no, I had something earlier on the plane.

Patricia makes eye contact with Mary.

PATRICIA
I eat little to stay little.

Mary feels the sting of another insult as she escapes to the kitchen. Craig follows close behind. He appears painfully clueless to the hailstorm of insults. Mary goes to the cabinet and pulls out a glass.

CRAIG
She'll want it in a low ball.

MARY
How about I shove the bottle up her ass?!

Craig hushes Mary.

CRAIG
She'll hear you.

Mary returns the glass, goes to the liquor cabinet, and grabs the appropriate barware.

MARY
I don't know how I'm going to make it, Craig. She's been here five minutes and she's insulted me four times.

CRAIG
To be fair, there was more truth than insult to the FBI comment.

Mary pulls out a bottle of scotch and pours it into the glass.

MARY
I wasn't even counting that one.

CRAIG
It's only for a month.

MARY

You say that like it's not that long. We go without having sex for a week, and you act like you're an escapee from seminary school.

CRAIG

Look, you're going about this all wrong. Take advantage of her being here. Let her watch the boys. Let her cook every night. She loves to do that stuff.

MARY

Yeah, then I get to hear how deficient I am.

CRAIG

Who cares? It's getting done, and you don't have to do it.

Mary takes a deep breath as she considers his statement.

MARY

I wouldn't mind taking Rachel up on her offer to hang out at her pool.

CRAIG

Exactly, and we could go out on an actual date.

MARY

What's that?

Craig puts his hands around Mary's waist.

CRAIG

It's a meal where we don't unwrap our food, and there's not one mention of dump trucks, weapons, or boogers.

Craig amorously cradles Mary in his arms.

MARY

I don't know, I can get into some pretty riveting conversations about boogers.

Craig kisses Mary.

MARY

All right. I can get through this.

Craig releases Mary.

CRAIG

Look on the bright side, she can't live forever.

Craig takes the drink Mary has prepared and leaves the room.

MARY

That's the thought that gets me up every morning.

Mary takes a swig of scotch directly from the bottle.

NEIGHBORHOOD STREET - 4 DAYS LATER, EVENING

Rachel backs her car out of her driveway and parks in front of Mary's house. She gets out and meets Anne and Jill in the street. Jill's arms support a large plate of prepared food.

ANNE

Was it really necessary to drive here?

Rachel motions to the sky.

RACHEL

There's supposed to be a storm later.

Anne points to Jill's plate.

ANNE

Mary called and told me not to bother bringing anything.

JILL

I know, but I already made it.

RACHEL

This will come as a shock to both of you, but I had nothing prepared.

The women proceed up to Mary's porch. Mary bursts out of her front door and closes it behind her as the women walk up the steps.

MARY

Save yourself.

ANNE

From what?

Patricia opens the front door. Mary cringes at the sound of her mother-in-law's voice.

PATRICIA

Where are you sneaking off to?

Mary turns around to address Patricia.

MARY

I'm not sneaking off, it's bunco night.

PATRICIA

You're still playing childish games at your age?

Mary fights to hold her tongue. Her jaw muscles are becoming quite toned.

MARY

Patricia, you remember my friends.

PATRICIA

Of course, I do. I'm not senile, Mary.

Mary forcibly smiles to display maturity in front of her friends.

PATRICIA

Rachel, I'm surprised to see you, what with it being happy hour.

Rachel doesn't pretend to be mature.

RACHEL

Oh, Patricia, it's the first place I intend to go after our visit.

Patricia insincerely laughs, and Rachel responds with a fake grin.

PATRICIA

Anne, you look a decade older. When was the last time I saw you?

ANNE

Christmas.

PATRICIA

Well, that goes to show the toll working takes on a woman.

Anne is dumbstruck and nods her head numbly.

PATRICIA

And Jill, looking as beautiful and vibrant as ever.

Jill displays her pageant-winning smile and grace.

JILL

Thank you, Mrs. Hueston.

MARY

Jill's pregnant.

PATRICIA

Oh, your mother must be thrilled knowing another grandchild is on the way.

JILL

My mother passed away several years ago.

PATRICIA

Well, take it from me, she would have been thrilled having so many grandchildren to love. I wish Mary hadn't waited so long...

Mary interrupts.

MARY

Patricia, we really should be going.

PATRICIA

You're just going to leave without feeding your family?

MARY

They'll be fine. Craig is bringing home a pizza.

PATRICIA

A pizza. I wish dinner was such an afterthought when I was...

Mary takes the plate from Jill's hands.

MARY

Here. Start on this.

Mary puts the plate in Patricia's hands and gently pushes her back into the house.

MARY

Good night!

Mary closes the front door and directs everyone away from the house like a highly motivated border collie herding its sheep to safety.

MARY'S DRIVEWAY - CONTINUOUS

ANNE
Where are we going?

MARY
Anywhere. I just can't stay in that house any longer.

RACHEL
Back Alley?

ANNE
We always go there.

JILL
I've been wanting to check out The Riverview.

MARY
Perfect. It's downtown and twenty minutes away. Let's go.

The women load into Rachel's car, looking forward to a fun, relaxing evening.

RIVERVIEW RESTAURANT ENTRANCE - 20 MINUTES LATER

A heavy rain blankets the area. Rachel pulls up to the door of the restaurant, and the women run for the door, avoiding puddles on the city streets. Rachel drives off to park the car.

RIVERVIEW RESTAURANT LOBBY - CONTINUOUS

The women enter and shake the water off themselves.

ANNE
Why didn't she let the valet park it?

MARY
After the lake house, she's become more protective of that car than I was of my hymen.

Mary spots the host and approaches him about a table. As Jill and Anne wait near the door, Jill glances across the room and is surprised to see her husband sitting at a table. She's more surprised at the presence of a young woman sitting across from him. She watches as the two engage in a passionate kiss. Their level of intimacy is painfully obvious.

ANNE
(Obliviously)
Bill and I have been meaning to come here for months. I hope she can sweet talk her way to a table.

Anne notices Jill is preoccupied.

ANNE
Jill?

Anne turns her attention to the focus of Jill's stare.

ANNE
(Under her breath)
Oh shit.

Mary gleefully approaches.

MARY
You may now tell me how fabulous I am. I got us in.

Jill steps away from the women and moves toward her husband's table. Anne rubs her forehead nervously.

MARY
I didn't expect you to fall on your knees with gratitude, but a "thank you" would be nice.

Anne uses her eyes to direct Mary's attention.

MARY
Is that...?

JOHN'S TABLE - CONTINUOUS

Jill approaches John and his much younger dinner guest.

JILL
John?

John looks up and discovers Jill standing above him. His eyes widen as he takes a deep breath but says nothing. Jill turns her attention to his female companion.

JILL
I'm Jill Michaels. John's wife.

The female companion sits speechless, trading looks between Jill and John.

RIVERVIEW RESTAURANT LOBBY - CONTINUOUS

Rachel enters the restaurant and joins Anne and Mary.

RACHEL
I'm parked two blocks away, so I hope we plan on being here until the rain lets up.

MARY
We're leaving.

RACHEL
What?!

Mary points out John and his companion to Rachel.

RACHEL
That fornicating wad of pubic lint.

JOHN'S TABLE - CONTINUOUS

Jill stiffens to prevent herself from breaking down.

JILL
If y'all will excuse me, I'm going to go home and check on our children.

RIVERVIEW RESTAURANT LOBBY - CONTINUOUS

Jill turns and quietly walks past the women and out of the door. Mary and Anne follow her. John stands up to follow Jill, but Rachel stops him.

RACHEL
You have a babysitting job to finish.

JOHN
Stay out of this, Rachel.

Rachel punches John in the crotch. John collapses onto a seated restaurant patron as he doubles over in pain. Rachel flashes his companion a dirty look and turns to exit.

OUTSIDE RIVERVIEW RESTAURANT - CONTINUOUS

Heavy rain continues to fall. Jill stands without direction as Mary and Anne approach.

ANNE

Jill, I'm so sorry.

JILL

I want to go home.

MARY

We don't know where Rachel parked.

JILL

Please, just take me home.

Anne puts her arm around Jill.

ANNE

Okay.

Anne looks over her shoulder and directs Mary to find Rachel.

JILL

I feel sick.

ANNE

I don't know what to say.

JILL

There's nothing to say.

Mary rushes to meet up with Rachel as she comes out of the restaurant.

RACHEL

Where is she?

Mary motions down the street.

MARY

Just down here. She's devastated, Rachel. I don't know what we're going to do.

Mary and Rachel catch up to Anne and Jill. The pouring rain isn’t a consideration.

RACHEL

Let me get the car.

JILL

No, I'll come with you. I have to get out of here.

The women quickly proceed down the street to the car. Rachel and Mary get in the front seat with Jill and Anne in the back. Jill sits motionless, staring out the window as the others try to adjust themselves in their wet clothes.

RACHEL

Jill, I'll do whatever you want me to do.

Jill remains silent.

ANNE

Take her home.

Rachel turns around to face the backseat and looks for confirmation from Jill.

RACHEL

Is that what you want, Jill?

Jill silently puts her head in her hands and begins to cry. Anne puts her arm around Jill and pulls her to her shoulder.

ANNE

Take her home.

Rachel nods, starts up the car and pulls away from the curb.

JILL'S HOUSE - 20 MINUTES LATER

Rachel pulls up in front of Jill's house and puts the car in park.

RACHEL

Are you sure you're going to be okay?

Jill says nothing.

ANNE

Do you want us to come inside?

Jill silently shakes her head.

MARY

Do you want to stay with one of us?

Jill continues to silently decline.

RACHEL
Do you want me to set fire to everything he owns?

Mary smacks Rachel in the shoulder for the inappropriate comment.

JILL
(Softly)
What I want is for this entire evening to be a bad dream.

The women share concerned looks.

MARY
Know we love you and we'll be right here if you need us.

ANNE
That's right. Don't worry about what time it is. Just promise us you'll pick up the phone and call if you need anything.

Jill nods gently as she opens the car door and steps out. The women stay in the car and watch her go into her house.

RACHEL
I don't like this.

ANNE
What do you propose we do, Rachel?

RACHEL
I gave my suggestion, and I got smacked for it.

Rachel silently fumes.

MARY
Let's just all check on her frequently.

Rachel grips her steering wheel tightly.

RACHEL
Christ, what I'd do for a cigarette!

ANNE
Don't, Rachel. You've been doing so well.

MARY
Actually, I don't even smoke and I was thinking the same thing.

A car comes around the corner and pulls into Jill's driveway. John gets out of his car and runs into the house.

MARY
Now what do we do?

ANNE
Nothing. This is between them.

RACHEL
Nothing?!

ANNE
Nothing.

MARY
Should we stay here?

ANNE
No. Let's go home. Everyone, go home and wait. They need to figure this out by themselves.

RACHEL
You expect me to go home and do nothing?!

Anne leans her body into the front passenger compartment.

ANNE
Rachel, this is none of our business. All we can do is be here for Jill when, or even IF, she needs us.

MARY
She's right.

Rachel reluctantly concedes to Anne.

NEIGHBORHOOD STREET - CONTINUOUS

Anne and Mary get out of the car. Anne turns back to the driver's side and taps on Rachel's window.

ANNE
(Through the glass)
It's none of our business.

Rachel patronizingly nods and drives down the street to her house.

MARY

Anne, do you mind if I hang out at your house for a bit? The thought of seeing that woman makes me want to stab myself in a vital organ.

Anne motions for Mary to follow her.

ANNE

I'll pour.

JILL'S HOUSE- CONTINUOUS

Megan is asleep inside a blanket fort with all three children when slamming doors and loud voices wake her up. She gently navigates around the sleeping kids, gets out, and goes to the hallway. She listens for a few moments then realizes the conversation is very serious. Trapped upstairs, she pulls out her phone.

ANNE'S KITCHEN - CONTINUOUS

Anne is finishing up pouring two glasses of whiskey for herself and Mary.

ANNE

I'm skipping straight to the serious stuff.

MARY

Please.

Anne's phone rings.

ANNE

Oh shit! I totally forgot! Megan is over there.

Anne answers her phone using the speaker.

ANNE

Megan?

JILL'S UPSTAIRS - CONTINUOUS

MEGAN

(Whispering)

Mom! Mr. and Mrs. Michaels are downstairs fighting and I'm stuck upstairs. What do I do?

ANNE

Can you hear what they're saying?

MEGAN

(Whispering)

Not really. Mom, I don't want to be here. What do I do?

ANNE

Okay, okay. Is there any way for you to get out without them knowing you're there?

Megan frantically looks around.

MEGAN

(Whispering)

No, they're in the living room, right between me and the front door.

RACHEL'S HOME OFFICE - SIMULTANEOUSLY

Kevin works at his computer as Rachel enters the doorway.

RACHEL

Hi.

Kevin looks up from his computer screen.

KEVIN

Hi.

Rachel points to a Pete Rose autographed baseball bat prominently displayed on the wall.

RACHEL

Can I borrow that?

KEVIN

What for?

Rachel takes the bat from the wall.

RACHEL

To keep from smoking.

Rachel leaves the room. Kevin returns to his computer screen.

KEVIN
(To himself)
Can't imagine how that's going to help.

ANNE'S KITCHEN - CONTINUOUS

Anne grows frustrated trying to help Megan out of Jill's house.

ANNE
Can you slip out a window?

JILL'S UPSTAIRS - CONTINUOUS

MEGAN
(Whispering)
What if the house alarm is still on?

ANNE
Look, Megan, if you're not even going to try any of the ideas I give you...

MEGAN
(Whispering)
Why don't you try giving me a less stupid idea!

MARY
Megan, this is Mrs. Hueston. How about if you make a bunch of noise so they remember you're up there.

Voices from downstairs become louder and more impassioned.

MEGAN
(Whispering)
They're getting louder. Mrs. Michaels is crying. Mom, these are YOUR friends! Get me out of here!

ANNE
Okay Megan, unfortunately, I don't think there's any way out. Go back and lie down with the kids. You'll just have to wait this out.

MEGAN
(Whispering)
Wait this out?! Can't you come over here and ring the doorbell or something?

Anne looks at Mary for input on Megan's suggestion.

Mary vigorously shakes her head.

ANNE
I'm sorry, Megan. You're in this by yourself.

The arguing abruptly stops.

MEGAN
(Whispering)
Wait. They've stopped.

ANNE
They stopped? Are they making up?

A loud commotion gets Megan's attention.

MEGAN
(Whispering)
Shhh. I hear something.

ANNE
(Frantically)
What? What do you hear? What's going on?

MEGAN
(Whispering)
It's like... like... glass breaking.

ANNE
Glass breaking?

MEGAN
(Whispering)
There it is again.

Anne covers the phone's microphone.

ANNE
(To Mary)
This can't be good.

MEGAN
(Whispering)
They opened the front door. They're going outside.

Mary grabs Anne by the hand and they rush out of the front door. Anne shouts back at her phone.

ANNE

Go now, Megan!

JILL'S DRIVEWAY - CONTINUOUS

Mary, Anne, Jill, John, and Megan all come out of their respective homes and converge on the driveway. Rachel has the baseball bat resting on her shoulder as she stands at the front of John's vehicle. Every window has been smashed in.

RACHEL

I saw a cat sitting on your car, John. I didn't want it to scratch your hood, so I scared it off. I know how precious this car is to you.

Rachel takes a final swing and destroys the car's grill.

MARY'S BATHROOM - NEXT MORNING

Mary steps out of her shower with a towel wrapped around her. She begins to get herself ready for her day when she looks on the counter and sees her phone. She stops what she's doing, picks up the phone, and thinks for a moment. She locks her bathroom door and engages her camera.

MARY'S BEDROOM - LATER

Mary is dressed and ready for the day. She checks her phone and is disappointed to see no messages. She dials Craig's office number.

CRAIG'S OFFICE - CONTINUOUS

CRAIG

Hello?

MARY

Well?

CRAIG

Well, what?

MARY

I expected to hear something back from you after the picture I sent.

CRAIG

Huh?

MARY

I sent you a naughty picture after I got out of the shower.

Panic begins to set in.

MARY

Tell me you got it!

CRAIG

I left my phone with my mom. She doesn't have one and she's taking the kids...

Mary doesn't bother listening to the rest of his explanation. She throws the phone to the floor and runs out of her bedroom.

MARY'S KITCHEN - CONTINUOUS

Patricia is feeding the boys breakfast. Craig's phone sits on the coffee table in the family room. The message indicator rhythmically sounds every thirty seconds.

PATRICIA
(Bothered)

What keeps making that noise?

ETHAN

It's dad's phone.

PATRICIA

Can you make it stop, Ethan?

Ethan gets up from the kitchen table, walks into the family room, and picks up the phone. Simultaneously, Mary sees him from the balcony and panics. She leaps from the second story to the ground floor while reaching out to snatch the phone.

She successfully breaks her fall with the couch but not without causing an injury to her arm. Patricia and Charlie look up at the sound of Mary hitting the couch and quickly head to the family room.

CHARLIE

Mom! That was freaking awesome!

PATRICIA
Mary, what in God's name is wrong with you?!

Mary cradles her wrist as she struggles to keep the phone in her hand. She looks at the screen to see her message has not been retrieved. She musters up her most polite and carefree tone.

MARY
Patricia, would you be a dear and call Anne for me.

Patricia shows no sympathy as she turns to get the house phone. Mary continues to rock back and forth in pain while mouthing profanities.

MARY'S KITCHEN - MOMENTS LATER

Mary sits on a chair in her kitchen while Anne gently examines her injury.

ANNE
Charlie tried to explain, but I didn't quite understand. How did this happen?

MARY
Where are Patricia and the boys?

Anne looks over her shoulder.

ANNE
Outside.

MARY
I'm such an idiot. After seeing Jill's perfect marriage disintegrate in front of us last night, I decided it wouldn't be such a bad idea to do something different in my own. You know, to keep Craig's interest. I got out of the shower and figured I'd send him an unexpected photo text. Little did I know he left his phone here for his mother to use.

ANNE
Oh God.

MARY
Wait, it gets so much worse. I called Craig and he said the phone was here, so I ran out of my bedroom to grab it when I saw Ethan pick it up.

ANNE

No!

MARY

Yes! So, watching the scene unfold from upstairs, I had to decide: do I swan dive fifteen feet, risk paralysis, and try to grab the phone OR do I stand there and helplessly watch my son's head explode?

ANNE

Did you get it?

MARY

Yes, thank God.

ANNE

Well, I don't think you broke your arm.

MARY

Oh good.

ANNE

I think you fractured your wrist.

MARY

(Deflated)

Great.

ANNE

Either way, you definitely need an x-ray.

MARY

This is what happens when I try to do something spontaneous and sexy.

ANNE

You're probably going to be in a cast for four to six weeks.

MARY

(Sarcastically)

Well, at least I have my mother-in-law here to help me.

ANNE

Come on, I'll take you to the hospital.

MARY'S BEDROOM - LATER THAT EVENING

Mary sits on her bed in her new wrist cast. Craig stands while looking at his phone and admiring the picture.

CRAIG
Wow, the cost of the hospital visit will probably end up being cheaper than Ethan's therapy.

MARY
You would have saved money with me moving out.

CRAIG
Don't get me wrong, I love the thought, but what the heck made you do this? You've never done anything like this before.

MARY
Exactly.

Mary stands to face Craig.

MARY
Jill is beautiful and thin and much nicer to John than I am to you. And yet, he still went out and found someone else.

CRAIG
Well, I think you're just as beautiful as Jill, but you could be a little nicer to me.

MARY
You didn't mention I was as thin as her.

Craig stalls in thought as he thinks of a response that won't aggravate the situation.

CRAIG
That's because I think Jill is TOO thin.

MARY
(Impressed)
Oh, you are so getting laid tonight.

Mary kisses Craig.

CRAIG
When are you women going to understand that a man cheating on his wife says everything about him, not her? A guy like John is going to find any reason not to appreciate what he has.

MARY
And what about you?

CRAIG
What about me?

MARY
Do you appreciate what you have?

CRAIG
I really appreciate this picture you sent.

MARY
Seriously, Craig, do I have to worry about walking into a restaurant one day and finding you with another woman?

CRAIG
No, you don't have to worry about that. I'm too cheap to take my mistress to a restaurant. I'd just run her through a drive-thru before we do it in the back of the minivan.

Mary lifts her broken wrist and hits Craig in the shoulder. She's reminded of the break as the pain shoots through her arm. She cradles her cast as Craig hugs her.

CRAIG
I always have, and I always will, appreciate you.

RACHEL'S POOL - ONE WEEK LATER

Rachel walks out of her house with two cocktails in her hand. Mary sits near the pool, relaxing. Rachel hands one of the cocktails to Mary.

RACHEL
Here.

MARY
I don't know if I should drink while taking pain medication.

RACHEL
You're fine. It's not like there's a warning on the label.

MARY
Actually, there is... in bold capital letters.

RACHEL
(Dismissive)
They print that on multi-vitamins. You're fine.

Mary apprehensively accepts the drink. Rachel taps the glass with her own and sits down.

RACHEL
How's the wrist?

MARY
It'll heal. My ego, on the other hand...

RACHEL
Hey, at least you can send your husband naked pictures. If I did that, Kevin would be the one jumping head first over the balcony.

Mary laughs, then a quiet moment passes.

MARY
Have you talked to her?

RACHEL
No, you?

MARY
Anne said she told Megan that John's moved to a hotel, but the kids think he's on a business trip.

RACHEL
He's such a reprehensible bucket of chum. If she forgives him, she's as stupid as he is repugnant.

Mary raises a brow at Rachel's unsympathetic language.

MARY
How do you think this will end?

RACHEL

If there's any justice in this world, it'll end with his hyperactive custard launcher in the hands of a taxidermist.

MARY

I can't imagine Jill leaving John.

RACHEL

She's a fool if she stays.

Kevin opens the house door and shouts to the women seated with their backs to him.

KEVIN

I'm leaving to play golf!

Rachel neglects to turn around as she yells back to him.

RACHEL

Fine!

Kevin closes the door and goes back into the house.

RACHEL

(Quietly)

Enjoy your trip to Broke "Back- Nine" Mountain.

A moment passes as Mary builds up the courage to broach the next subject.

MARY

Rachel, you realize your harsh criticism of Jill can just as easily be applied to you.

Rachel shakes her head.

RACHEL

Jill's different.

Mary furrows her brow.

MARY

What? What do you mean by THAT?

RACHEL

(Becoming irritated)

I don't want to talk about this.

Mary becomes increasingly protective of Jill.

MARY

No, tell me you understand the similarities here. You're outraged by John's behavior, and you're ready to condemn Jill for looking the other way, but you've been doing the exact same thing for years.

RACHEL

You know, you're welcome to go home and spend the rest of the afternoon with your mother-in-law.

Mary doesn't back down.

MARY

How is Jill different?

As Mary persists, Rachel becomes more annoyed.

RACHEL

Look, Mary, I know Psychologist #2 is listed on your resume, but you understand you're not actually an expert, right?

MARY

Stop avoiding the question.

RACHEL

Stop ASKING the question!

MARY

How is Jill different?

Rachel uncomfortably searches her thoughts then blurts out the answer.

RACHEL

Jill deserves better!

Mary shifts her tone.

MARY

And you don't?

Rachel physically struggles with the memories of her guilt-ridden past and lashes out.

RACHEL

No, Mary, I don't!

Concern washes over Mary's face.

MARY
Why would you say that?

Rachel shakes her head, regretting her comment.

MARY
(Gently)
You deserve everything Jill does.

Rachel becomes physically pained hearing the compliment and turns away.

RACHEL
You don't know what you're talking about, Mary.

Mary studies Rachel's evasive body language.

MARY
I know YOU, Rachel Easton. And yes, you're guilty of biting insults and offensive behavior, but you've done NOTHING that would make me think you deserve anything less than anyone else.

Rachel takes a moment to get a handle on her emotions, then faces Mary.

RACHEL
I appreciate your astutely inaccurate analysis, Mary, but trust me, if you dropped your pants and started forming words with your butthole, you'd sound more intelligent.

Rachel stands and abruptly walks into her house. Mary's face fills with confusion as she silently watches her friend exit.

JILL'S HOUSE - THE FOLLOWING DAY

Wil opens the front door to Mary, Anne, and Rachel standing on the front porch.

MARY
Hi, Wil. Is your mom here?

WIL
Yeah. She's upstairs.

Wil opens the door wide and shouts upstairs.

WIL

Mom!

JILL'S LIVING ROOM - CONTINUOUS

The women enter, glancing around for any hints on the status of the situation.

WIL

I'll go get her.

Wil turns to head upstairs but Rachel stops him.

RACHEL

Wil, would you and your sisters like to go swimming over at my house?

WIL

Yeah!

RACHEL

Ask Miss Megan if she'll take you over there.

WIL

Okay!

Wil runs upstairs.

MARY

Rachel, I know you have strong opinions, but please, try to keep from looking like you have an agenda here.

RACHEL

(Insulted)

I don't have an agenda.

Jill makes her way down the stairs. Her normally manicured appearance is now disheveled and neglected. Her eyes are puffy and tired from several sleepless nights. She looks as fragile as she is.

JILL

Hey. What are y'all doing here?

Anne and Mary share sincere hugs with Jill while Rachel keeps her usual distance from human contact.

JILL

Oh, my goodness. What happened to your wrist?

RACHEL
An amateur porn accident.

Jill looks to Mary for clarification.

MARY
Ignore her. I fell.

ANNE
We haven't seen you in a few days. We just wanted to make sure you're okay.

JILL
(Unconvincingly)
Yeah, I'm okay.

ANNE
(Concerned)
Are you sure?

RACHEL
Because you look like a hot southern mess.

Mary rolls her eyes at Rachel's bluntness.

JILL
I've been busy lately, that's all.

RACHEL
Doing what?

Jill shrugs her shoulders.

JILL
Normal things... cleaning the house, laundry, tending to the kids.

Megan comes down with the kids in their swimsuits.

JILL
Where y'all going?

MEGAN
Wil said Miss Rachel invited us to swim at her pool.

Jill looks at Rachel, who nods her approval.

JILL

Okay, just remember your manners over there.

Megan and the kids walk out of the front door.

JILL

Do y'all want something to drink?

The women share looks of concern as they follow Jill into the kitchen. There is an awkward silence as they watch Jill grope around the kitchen, trying to prepare coffee. Anne quietly positions two dice between countertop appliances.

Rachel's patience wears thin, watching Jill fumble about.

ANNE

(Gently)

Jill, we don't need anything to drink.

Rachel blurts out her feelings.

RACHEL

We need to know you're not going to fall for any of John's bullshit.

Jill becomes irritated at Rachel's comment.

JILL

Excuse me?

Mary tries to calm the growing tension.

MARY

We're just concerned, that's all.

Rachel's frustration grows.

ANNE

Is there anything we can do for you?

JILL

I just need time to process everything.

RACHEL

He's a festering cock scab! Process complete.

Mary tries to cue Rachel to calm down by placing her hand on her shoulder.

MARY

Jill, we can only imagine how difficult things are for you right now, and we want you to know we will support any decision you make, no matter what.

JILL

Thank you.

RACHEL

Unless you decide to forgive that limp butt noodle!

MARY

(To Rachel)

Is this you not having an agenda?

Jill becomes defensive.

JILL

Of all people, Rachel, I thought you'd be the one to understand my position.

Anne sees the hostility growing between Jill and Rachel.

ANNE

Okay, let's just focus on being the supportive friends here.

Rachel interrupts Anne's placid approach.

RACHEL

Jill, I do understand. I understand he's a manipulative fart stain who'll never look out for anyone but himself!

Jill becomes agitated.

JILL

So, y'all think I should leave him?!

All answer simultaneously.

MARY/ANNE

No.

RACHEL

Yes!

Mary hurriedly tries to redirect the conversation.

MARY
No, what we think doesn't matter. This is your life, your decision.

RACHEL
You deserve better than that cheating twat monkey.

ANNE
(Quietly to Rachel)
Maybe less derogatory monikers will create the illusion of impartiality.

RACHEL
Fuck that lying cum weasel!

Anne abandons hope for civility and throws up her hands.

JILL
So, what am I supposed to do, Rachel?! Throw away thirteen years of marriage?! Arrange weekend visitation for the kids?! Spend every night alone?!

ANNE
We shouldn't have brought Rachel, I mean, come over here.

JILL
Everything about my life has been turned upside down and destroyed! I'm paralyzed with betrayal, and I don't know what to do!

RACHEL
(Curtly)
Dump him.

Jill addresses Rachel.

JILL
Look, as far as I'm concerned, you don't get an opinion on this. You were bought and paid for years ago.

Mary takes Rachel by the arm.

MARY
This was a mistake, we should go.

Rachel ignores Mary's attempt to leave and continues to confront Jill.

RACHEL
I just figured you had more self-respect! He's humiliated you, and you're seriously considering staying!

JILL
It's not that simple, Rachel! It's not just me! I have kids to think about! You've stayed for years without even having THAT as an excuse!

MARY
Okay, stop! None of this is helping!

Jill folds her arms as she turns her back on the women. Rachel pulls away from Mary and walks up behind Jill to calmly address her.

RACHEL
You know what, you're right. I have stayed, but Kevin hasn't embarrassed me in front of the world. He's had the decency to screw me from behind.

Jill turns back around to face Rachel.

JILL
No, Rachel. He's screwing someone else from behind.

Terror blankets the faces of Anne and Mary as they anticipate a cage match style rumble to break out. Rachel absorbs the insult for a moment, then steps toward Jill and speaks with an unexpectedly calm tone.

RACHEL
Hasn't my life taught you anything?

Rachel storms out.

RACHEL'S HOUSE - MOMENTS LATER

Rachel enters her front door, slams it shut and goes straight for a drawer in her china cabinet. She opens the drawer and pulls out a box of cigarettes and a lighter. She unwraps the box, pulls a cigarette out, and slaps it in between her lips. She struggles with her lighter then quickly gives up. She crushes the unlit cigarette from her mouth along with those remaining in the box, then hurls the crumbled box across the room. Her hands come to rest on her hips as she does her best to regain control.

Her attention is drawn to the children playing outside in her backyard. She moves to the window and watches them frolic in the pool.

JILL'S KITCHEN - CONTINUOUS

Mary, Anne, and Jill continue.

JILL
I can't believe she's being like this!

ANNE
She's just worried about you.

JILL
She should be less concerned with my cheating husband and more with her own!

MARY
You're right, Jill, I can't figure her out. Most prison psychiatrists couldn't figure her out, but I know all she wants to do is protect you.

JILL
Or she's getting some degree of satisfaction watching me in this awful situation.

Mary is shocked by Jill's accusation.

MARY
You can't really believe that?

Jill slumps into a chair at the kitchen table. She buries her head in her folded arms on the table and begins to cry. Anne bends down next to Jill's chair to comfort her.

JILL
(Through sobs)
I don't know what to believe anymore. I've lost faith in everything.

Mary sits down next to Jill and puts her hand on her shoulder. Jill lifts her head from the table.

JILL
I don't know what to do.

Jill calms and turns her tear-filled eyes to Mary.

JILL
Maybe this was partly my fault. Maybe I didn't make him a priority.

MARY

Your family has always been your priority, Jill.

JILL

Everyone makes mistakes, right?

MARY

Yes, everyone makes mistakes.

JILL

There's infidelity in lots of couples. Just because it happens doesn't automatically mean a marriage is over.

MARY

You're right. It doesn't.

JILL

We could go to counseling through the church. I could tell people we're volunteering.

MARY

You don't need to tell people a damn thing. This is nobody's business but yours.

Anne pulls up a chair next to Jill and sits.

ANNE

Jill, this decision is one hundred percent yours. You shouldn't factor in how Rachel feels or what anyone might think. But understand, if you decide to stay with John, you have to be prepared to let this go forever. You can't let it silently eat away at you. If you want to forgive him, truly forgive him and don't think about it again.

JILL

What if I can't?

ANNE

Then... you can't.

Mary and Anne remain silent as Jill takes a moment to think.

JILL

I don't want to be divorced.

MARY

Then don't get divorced.

JILL
I don't know if I can stay married.

ANNE
I'm sorry, Jill. There isn't another option.

JILL'S CAR - ONE WEEK LATER, AFTERNOON

Jill sits in her car for a few moments in a hotel parking lot. She wipes away tears as she reads a stamped, handwritten letter. She breathes deeply in an effort to compose herself. Resolutely, she slides the keys out of the ignition, gathers her purse, tucks the letter inside it, and gets out of the car.

CINCINNATIAN HOTEL LOBBY - MOMENTS LATER

Jill is visibly nervous as she waits for an elevator. After a few moments, the elevator door opens. With a start, Jill recognizes the person in the elevator and her anxiety quickly flares to anger.

RACHEL'S HOME OFFICE - LATER THAT EVENING

Rachel is reading articles on her computer titled, "How To Be A Non-Smoker." The browser's search engine is not yielding anything helpful. Her phone rings.

RACHEL
Hey.

NURSE STATION

ANNE
Rachel, is Jill with you?

RACHEL
No. Why would she be?

ANNE
Megan said Jill's been gone since this afternoon and she doesn't know where she is.

RACHEL
I don't know either, Anne. I haven't talked to her since last week. If I had to guess, she's probably in John's hotel room apologizing for HIS infidelity.

Anne, concerned with privacy, lowers her voice and cups her hand over the mouthpiece.

ANNE

She's definitely not doing that. John was just brought into the emergency room.

Rachel sits up in her chair as Anne has piqued her interest.

RACHEL

The emergency room? For what?

ANNE

A gunshot.

RACHEL

What?!

ANNE

Someone shot him, and Jill's not answering her phone.

Rachel smirks and shakes her head.

RACHEL

Okay, very funny. I'm not falling for this, Anne.

ANNE

Rachel, listen to me. I wish this was a joke, but it's not. This is very real.

Rachel's disbelief shifts to concern.

RACHEL

Is he going to be okay?

ANNE

I don't know. He came in unresponsive with a bullet in his chest. The police want to talk to his wife. You have to find Jill.

RACHEL

All right. I'm going to get Mary. I'll call you when I know something.

The call ends and Rachel heads for the door.

MARY'S FRONT PORCH - MOMENTS LATER

Rachel repeatedly rings the doorbell. Patricia answers the door with an irritated tone.

PATRICIA
Good God, Rachel, why all the urgency?! Has your liquor cabinet sprung a leak?

RACHEL
As much fun as listening to all your crap is, I'm going to have to take a rain check. Where's Mary?

PATRICIA
(Insulted)
If you think I'm going to stand here and let you talk to me that way...

Rachel has no patience for Patricia and pushes her way through the door.

MARY'S KITCHEN - CONTINUOUS

Rachel finds Mary preparing dinner, and the boys watching videos at the kitchen table. Patricia follows.

MARY
Hey, Rachel. What are you doing here?

RACHEL
I need you.

MARY
We're just about to eat.

RACHEL
(Earnestly)
Jill's missing.

Mary trusts the tone of Rachel's voice. She drops her dinner preparations and starts for the door. Patricia stops her.

PATRICIA
Wait! You're not seriously thinking of leaving?

MARY
Patricia, please feed the boys. I don't know when I'll be back.

PATRICIA
Mary, I can't believe you're abandoning your family to go play with your friends again.

MARY
(Boldly)
I'm not abandoning them. You're here.

Mary kisses her preoccupied boys on the head.

MARY
Be good for your grandma, boys.

Mary follows Rachel out of the front door.

NEIGHBORHOOD STREET - CONTINUOUS

Rachel brings Mary up to speed as they hurry to Jill's house.

MARY
What do you mean she's missing?

RACHEL
That's not the worst part. Someone shot John.

MARY
What?!

RACHEL
Anne just called me. He's there at the hospital.

MARY
Who shot him?

RACHEL
He's unconscious, they don't know.

MARY
You don't think Jill could have...

Rachel holds up her hand to interrupt.

RACHEL
Let's just find her.

Mary and Rachel walk up Jill's driveway.

JILL'S LIVING ROOM - CONTINUOUS

Mary and Rachel burst through the door. Megan is pacing the living room floor and texting while the children play in the family room.

MARY

Megan!

Megan is startled by their entry.

MEGAN

What?!

Rachel races upstairs.

MARY

When was the last time you heard from Mrs. Michaels?

MEGAN

About four hours ago. She came home from the grocery store, went upstairs for a bit, then came back down and asked me to stay longer while she went out.

MARY

Out where?

MEGAN

I don't know.

JILL'S BEDROOM - CONTINUOUS

Rachel enters the immaculately kept bedroom and looks around for any clues to Jill's whereabouts. Clothing, strewn around the bathroom, catches Rachel's attention. She steps closer to the bathroom and sees that the discarded clothing is covered in blood.

RACHEL

(To herself)

What did you do, Jill?

She quickly returns downstairs.

JILL'S LIVING ROOM - CONTINUOUS

Mary continues to question Megan.

MARY
Did she give you any indication of where she might be going?

MEGAN
She had a letter in her hand.

MARY
Do you know who it was from?

MEGAN
No.

Rachel enters the living room.

RACHEL
Megan, take the kids over to your house for the night.

Rachel leads Mary to the door.

MEGAN
Okay. Is everything all right?

Rachel opens the door for Mary.

RACHEL
Keep the kids away from this house until I tell you otherwise.

Rachel and Mary exit.

NEIGHBORHOOD STREET - CONTINUOUS

Mary and Rachel hurry down the street to Rachel's car.

MARY
Where are we going?

RACHEL
I don't know! Where would she go to find solace? Her church? A yoga class? Pottery Barn?

Rachel and Mary reach Rachel's car.

RACHEL'S CAR - CONTINUOUS

MARY
You don't think she did anything stupid, do you?

RACHEL
I wish you asked me that three minutes ago.

MARY
(Concerned)
What happened in the last three minutes?

Rachel hesitates before continuing.

RACHEL
The less you know, the better off you are.

Hours pass as they drive aimlessly around the greater Cincinnati area looking for Jill. Finally, Rachel's phone rings with an unfamiliar number.

RACHEL
Hello? Yes, it is. Who's this?

Rachel's face fills with relief.

RACHEL
Okay, thanks. I'll be right there.

Rachel ends her call.

MARY
Who was that?

RACHEL
You're not going to believe where she is. Call Anne and let her know we found her.

BACK ALLEY BAR - MOMENTS LATER

Rachel and Mary walk into the restaurant and up to the hostess stand. Lisa, the hostess familiar with Rachel, is waiting for them.

LISA
I'm sorry to call you, Mrs. Easton, I know she's a friend of yours and...

Rachel interrupts.

RACHEL

It's fine, Lisa. Where is she?

LISA

She's in the bathroom. She came in a few hours ago and went straight to the bar. She seemed really upset.

Rachel and Mary give each other a concerned glance.

BACK ALLEY BAR BATHROOM - CONTINUOUS

Rachel and Mary open the door slowly to the bathroom.

MARY

Should I be concerned the staff has your phone number?

Rachel ignores Mary's comment.

RACHEL

Jill?

MARY

Jill? Honey, are you in here?

They hear a commotion from a stall and approach it cautiously.

RACHEL

Jill?!

They look into each stall and find them all empty. They reach the final stall and slowly push the door open. The open door reveals Jill, curled up next to the side of the toilet bowl. She is barely coherent.

MARY

For this evening's performance, the role of Rachel Easton will be played by Jill Michaels.

RACHEL

Let's get her up.

Rachel and Mary help the very inebriated Jill to her feet and escort her out of the bathroom.

BACK ALLEY BAR - CONTINUOUS

LISA

Is she going to be okay?

RACHEL

She'll be fine. Thank you for calling me. Does she owe you anything?

LISA

Let me ask Caleb.

RACHEL

Do me a favor and tell him to hang onto it. I'll come in tomorrow and take care of it.

LISA

Sure, Mrs. Easton.

BACK ALLEY BAR PARKING LOT - CONTINUOUS

Rachel and Mary put Jill in the front seat and fasten her seat belt.

RACHEL

Mary, you get behind me and help her if she needs it.

MARY

Okay.

Mary and Rachel load themselves into the car. Rachel leans over, lifts Jill's chin, and tries to communicate.

RACHEL

Hey! Jill! Are you going to be okay? Do you think you'll need to throw up?

Jill fights the weight of her eyelids.

JILL

(Mumbling)

A proper southern woman never throws up.

Rachel lets Jill's chin drop back to her chest.

RACHEL

Uh-huh. A proper southern woman doesn't take a nap on a public bathroom floor, either. If you feel like you have to, tell me so I can lower the window, okay?

Jill drifts in and out of consciousness.

RACHEL

Jill! Did you hear me?!

JILL

Yeah.

Rachel starts the car and cautiously heads home.

MARY

(Concerned)

This is so unlike her. She's never done anything like this before.

RACHEL

(Somberly)

She's never felt disposable before.

Mary falls silent as she detects empathy in Rachel's tone. Several quiet minutes pass as Rachel continues the drive home. After a few miles, Jill starts to sit up in her seat.

RACHEL

Jill, ya okay? Are you going to be sick?

Jill closes her eyes and breathes deeply.

RACHEL

Do you need me to lower the wi...

Rachel's sentence is interrupted by Jill violently throwing up all over the dashboard and front seat. Mary silently cringes in the backseat.

Rachel doesn't say a word. She pulls into the closest gas station and gets out. A few moments pass with Mary horrified in the back seat, and Jill barely able to hold her head up. Rachel re-enters her car with a pack of cigarettes. She unwraps the pack, pulls one out, lights it, and inhales a lengthy and therapeutic drag.

JILL'S DRIVEWAY - 10 MINUTES LATER

Rachel pulls into the driveway and parks the car. Mary comes around the car and opens the door to get Jill out. She gags at the sight of the mess in the front seat as Rachel comes to her side.

MARY

How are we ever going to clean this?

RACHEL

I have no intention of cleaning this. Tomorrow I'll take the car to a cornfield and torch it.

They extract Jill from the car.

JILL'S BEDROOM - MOMENTS LATER

Mary and Rachel help Jill upstairs and into her room.

MARY

We can't put her to bed like this. We have to clean her up.

They sit Jill down on the bed and take off her vomit-covered outer layer and shoes. With a wrinkled nose, Mary gathers up the soiled clothes.

MARY

I'm taking these down to the laundry room.

Jill stirs in a panic as Rachel tries to help her into bed.

JILL

The kids!

RACHEL

They're fine. Megan has them at her house.

Jill lets out a sigh of relief before falling onto her bed.

JILL

I lost the baby.

Rachel sympathetically lowers her head and sits on the bed next to Jill.

RACHEL

I'm sorry.

Jill brings her hands to her face as she begins to cry.

JILL

She was there.

Rachel lifts her head.

RACHEL

WHO was WHERE?

Tears and mucus begin to flood Jill's face.

JILL

I can't believe this is happening.

Rachel watches Jill wipe her eyes and runny nose onto her forearm.

RACHEL

You're not going to be satisfied until you get your body fluids all over everything tonight, are you?

Rachel grabs a few tissues from a box on the bedside table and tries to hand them to Jill.

RACHEL

Here.

Jill pushes the offer away.

JILL

I don't care. I don't care about anything anymore. He ruined everything.

Jill rolls over and buries her head in the surrounding pillows.

JILL

(Muffled)

I always hated that gun.

Rachel stands and becomes very concerned.

RACHEL

What?!

JILL

(Muffled)

I left him there. I don't care what happens. Nothing matters anymore.

Rachel pulls the pillow off Jill's face.

RACHEL

Jill, what happened tonight?

Jill begins to fade into sleep.

JILL

Tell the kids I'm sorry.

Jill passes out. Rachel replaces the pillow next to Jill, steps away from the bed, and goes downstairs.

JILL'S LIVING ROOM - CONTINUOUS

Rachel meets Mary at the bottom of the stairs.

RACHEL

She told me she lost the baby.

Mary exhales heavily.

MARY

(Dejectedly)

No.

RACHEL

Yeah.

MARY

Did she say anything else?

Rachel thinks for several moments before answering.

RACHEL

Yeah.

Mary thoughtfully hesitates.

MARY

Do I want to know?

The doorbell rings.

MARY

Now what?

JILL'S ENTRY HALL - CONTINUOUS

Rachel and Mary hurry to the front door, and Rachel opens it. DETECTIVES CLARKE and BELL are standing on the front porch.

RACHEL
Can I help you?

DETECTIVE BELL
Yes, ma'am. I'm Detective Bell and this is Detective Clarke. Are you Mrs. Michaels?

RACHEL
No.

DETECTIVE CLARKE
Who are you?

RACHEL
Rachel Easton.

DETECTIVE CLARKE
Is this the Michaels' residence?

RACHEL
Yes.

DETECTIVE BELL
Is Mrs. Michaels here?

RACHEL
Yes.

DETECTIVE BELL
Can we speak with her, please?

RACHEL
You can try, but you risk getting covered in projectile vomit. She's completely passed out drunk.

DETECTIVE CLARKE
Are you a friend of hers?

RACHEL
Yes. I've been here with her all night.

Mary's eyes widen as she hears the lie come out of Rachel's mouth.

DETECTIVE CLARKE
(To Mary)
And are you a friend as well?

Mary steps closer to Rachel in the entry hall.

MARY
Yes.

DETECTIVE CLARKE
What's your name?

MARY
(Flustered)
Mary. Mary Hueston.

DETECTIVE CLARKE
You've been with Mrs. Michaels all evening too?

Rachel interrupts before Mary can answer.

RACHEL
No, she just came over not too long ago. Mrs. Michaels and I were discussing what an enormous asshole she's married to, and the evening got away from us.

DETECTIVE BELL
I assume you're referring to John Michaels?

RACHEL
You're familiar with him then.

The detectives do not react to Rachel's sarcasm.

DETECTIVE CLARKE
Are you aware Mr. Michaels was shot this evening?

RACHEL
No, I wasn't aware of that. Is he alive?

DETECTIVE BELL
For now.

RACHEL
Damn.

DETECTIVE CLARKE
Do you have any idea who may want to hurt Mr. Michaels?

RACHEL
I'd like to turn his ball sack inside out.

DETECTIVE CLARKE
Is that a confession?

RACHEL
Have you asked his whore girlfriend?

DETECTIVE BELL
He has a girlfriend? Do you know her name?

Detective Bell pulls out a pad to take notes. Rachel pretends to offer assistance by spelling out the girlfriend's name.

RACHEL
C-U-M-D-U-M-P-S-T-E-R

Detective Bell is not amused by Rachel's attempt at humor.

DETECTIVE BELL
Mrs. Easton, I would appreciate less sarcasm and more cooperation.

RACHEL
I don't know her name. The only time I saw her, I had Mr. Michaels' testicles in my fist. I was more interested in choking off his sperm count and less on formal introductions.

DETECTIVE BELL
Any idea where we can find her?

RACHEL
Forehead deep in a crotch forest, I would suspect.

The detectives can see they won't get anywhere with Rachel.

DETECTIVE CLARKE
Okay, well, please let Mrs. Michaels know we need to speak with her at her earliest convenience.

Detective Clarke pulls out a business card and hands it to Rachel.

RACHEL

I will let her AND her attorney know.

Rachel shuts the door on the detectives. Mary stands flabbergasted by Rachel's blatant falsehood.

MARY

I can't believe you just lied to the police!

Rachel hushes Mary.

RACHEL

You've seen Jill unable to handle the grandstand admission crowd at Churchill Downs. You think she could last five minutes in the general population of an Ohio Correctional Facility?

MARY

Yeah, but now WE could go to prison!

RACHEL

Not WE, ME. I said you just came over.

MARY

Rachel, if Jill did have anything to do with shooting John, you can't cover it up.

RACHEL

Trust me, they're not always interested in the truth. Now, you go home and get some sleep. Your mother-in-law is probably on the verge of petitioning for custody of the boys.

Mary rolls her shoulders in a futile effort to release the tension that has developed in the past few hours.

MARY

Is Jill going to be all right?

RACHEL

She should be. She threw up everything she's eaten since grade school.

MARY

What are you going to do?

RACHEL
I'll stay here and keep an eye on her. I have to get up early in the morning and commit insurance fraud anyway.

MARY'S HOUSE - MOMENTS LATER

Mary quietly enters her front door and is immediately greeted by Patricia. Mary is startled by her presence in the darkness.

MARY
Wow. You scared me, Patricia. What are you doing up so late?

Patricia is irritated and blunt.

PATRICIA
What's going on, Mary?

MARY
(Nervously)
What do you mean?

PATRICIA
Don't insult me by playing dumb. You fly out of here with that degenerate, you're gone for hours, and when you finally come back, the police follow.

Exhausted, Mary abandons kindness and maturity.

MARY
I would appreciate it if you didn't refer to Rachel as "that degenerate." She's my friend and she needed my help.

PATRICIA
I know you're a selfish woman, Mary, but you have exceeded ALL of my expectations tonight.

MARY
Selfish? What I was doing for the past several hours was not for me.

PATRICIA
Meanwhile, your family was at home alone.

MARY
(Exasperated)
You weren't alone, you had each other. And besides, these women are much more a part of my family than you are.

Patricia is beyond offended.

PATRICIA
I begged Craig not to marry you.

MARY
(Indignant)
Well, he did, and isn't it about time you accepted it? I am a great wife, a devoted mother, and a loyal friend. I can't imagine how you justify your treatment of me.

Patricia folds her arms as her tone becomes haughty.

PATRICIA
You're just not the kind of woman I would have picked for my son.

MARY
What kind of woman would you have picked? Someone like Jill Michaels? Well, let me tell you where I've been all night. I've been holding Jill's head out of her own vomit since she tried to drink away the knowledge of her husband cheating with a twenty-year-old.

A wave of disgust washes over Patricia's face.

MARY
Oh, and one more thing, the reason the police were there tonight is because they think she shot him.

PATRICIA
(Appalled)
I can't believe the company you keep! I can see the only answer for you women is at the bottom of a liquor bottle.

Mary steps back and laughs as she realizes the discussion is pointless.

MARY
Yes, Patricia, liquor is the only way we know how to deal with the assholes in our lives. Have you noticed? I've gone through three liters since you arrived.

Patricia stands speechless in a pout.

MARY
Now, if you'll excuse me, I have to go upstairs and fuck your son. I'll need him in a good mood when you whine about this conversation tomorrow.

Mary storms past Patricia and proceeds upstairs.

JILL'S BACKYARD - NEXT MORNING

Rachel sits at the patio table chain smoking. Jill opens the back door and surprises Rachel. Jill is very hungover, disheveled, and cradling her head.

RACHEL
Good morning. Your children spent the night with Megan.

Jill sits down next to Rachel. She places her head in her hands as she rests both elbows on the table.

RACHEL
You may want to throw them a vegetable when they come home. I'm pretty sure refined sugar is the only food group in Anne's pantry.

Jill's speech is muffled by her palms.

JILL
I am the worst mother ever.

RACHEL
Why? Because you got drunk? Sorry, you're going to have to do something much worse to win that title.

Jill lifts her head from her hands.

JILL
My life is completely falling apart. I'm doing things I never thought were possible.

RACHEL
Do you remember much about last night?

Jill ignores Rachel's question and notices her cigarette.

JILL

Are you smoking again?

RACHEL

A little bit.

Rachel crushes her cigarette into a cereal bowl overflowing with butts and ash.

JILL

I was so terrible to you the other day. From the bottom of my heart, I am so sorry.

RACHEL

I deserved it. Who am I to give advice? This is between you and John.

JILL

I don't think there is a "me and John" anymore.

Rachel faces Jill and takes a very serious tone.

RACHEL

Jill, what happened yesterday?

Jill struggles to keep from crying.

JILL

I lost the baby.

RACHEL

I know. You told me.

Jill nervously brings her fingers to her lips.

JILL

(Concerned)

What else did I tell you?

Not wanting to put words in Jill's mouth, Rachel begins her own line of questioning.

RACHEL

Did you see John yesterday?

Jill nods.

JILL

Yes. He sent me a letter apologizing and begging me to forgive him, along with some other... stuff. I had to tell him about the baby, so I figured I'd just go to his hotel.

RACHEL

Then what?

JILL

Then everything went bad. As I got on the elevator, I saw HER leaving.

RACHEL

Her, who?

Jill gives a "you know who" look to Rachel.

JILL

HER.

RACHEL

And?

Jill shakes her head as she continues with her vague recollection.

JILL

And then lots of words turned into lots of emotion that turned into...

The doorbell rings and interrupts Jill's thought.

JILL

Are you expecting someone?

Jill gets up and Rachel follows her.

RACHEL

Jill, wait. There's something I have to tell you!

JILL'S ENTRY HALL - CONTINUOUS

Jill looks out her front window and sees several police cars.

JILL

It's the police.

Rachel blocks Jill from answering the door.

RACHEL

Jill, say nothing.

JILL

What do you mean?

RACHEL

Trust me. I have experience with this. You need to get an attorney before you answer any questions.

The doorbell rings an impatient second time.

RACHEL

Something happened last night.

The doorbell rings a third time. Rachel angrily opens the door.

RACHEL

You can direct all questions to Mrs. Michaels' attorney!

Rachel tries to shut the door, but Jill stops her.

JILL

Rachel, please.

Jill opens the door wide. Several officers accompany Detectives Clarke and Bell into the house and fan out both up and downstairs.

DETECTIVE BELL

Mrs. Michaels?

JILL

Yes.

DETECTIVE BELL

We have a warrant to search your residence.

Detective Bell holds out the warrant for Jill's inspection.

JILL

A search warrant? What for?

RACHEL

(Forcefully)

Jill, don't say a word.

Detective Bell steps closer to Rachel and speaks softly to her.

DETECTIVE BELL
You said your name was Rachel Easton?

Rachel refuses to answer Detective Bell.

DETECTIVE BELL
Formerly, Rachel Fitzpatrick from Chicago, Illinois?

Rachel stands silently locked in an intimidation stare down with Detective Bell. An officer comes downstairs with Jill's bloody clothes in an evidence bag and holds it up to show the detectives. Detective Bell reaches for his handcuffs.

DETECTIVE BELL
Jill Margaret Michaels, you are under arrest for the attempted murder of John Michaels.

Detective Bell takes Jill's wrists and cuffs them behind her back. Jill appeals to Rachel as she cooperates with the officer.

JILL
(Terrified)
Rachel...

Rachel quietly advises Jill.

RACHEL
Don't say anything.

DETECTIVE BELL
You have the right to remain silent. If you choose to waive that right, anything you say can and will be used against you. You have the right to have an attorney present during questioning. If you cannot afford an attorney, one will be appointed to you by the court.

Jill lowers her head.

DETECTIVE BELL
Do you understand these rights I have just read to you?

Jill shamefully nods.

DETECTIVE BELL
I can't hear you, Mrs. Michaels.

JILL
(Quietly)
Yes.

Jill holds back her tears as she implores Rachel.

JILL

Take care of the kids.

RACHEL

I will. I'll get you out as soon as I can.

DETECTIVE BELL

It's Saturday, Mrs. Easton. Bail won't be set until her arraignment on Monday.

Detective Bell escorts Jill out her front door.

DETECTIVE CLARKE

The hotel desk clerk identified Mrs. Michaels and said he remembered her both arriving and leaving, alone. Do you want to revise your statement about being with Mrs. Michaels all night?

RACHEL

I'll let my attorney do that.

Detective Clarke nods.

DETECTIVE CLARKE

I'm advising you not to go too far, Mrs. Easton. After we talk to Mrs. Michaels, we may be issuing another arrest warrant. Oh, and in Ohio, the penalty for obstructing justice in an attempted murder case carries the same penalty as the attempted murder itself.

Rachel stands motionless.

DETECTIVE CLARKE

But... you already know how this works.

Detective Clarke walks out to join his partner. Rachel is left in the house with the crime scene investigators as they tear Jill's house apart, looking for more evidence. Rachel's phone rings.

RACHEL

Hello?

ANNE'S LIVING ROOM - CONTINUOUS

Anne is still in her work scrubs, looking out her window, and talking on her phone.

ANNE
Rachel?! What's going on?!

Rachel looks around at the police listening to her every word.

RACHEL
I really can't talk now, Anne.

ANNE
I just got home. Was that Jill in handcuffs?

RACHEL
I'm coming over there.

Rachel heads for the door.

ANNE'S LIVING ROOM - MOMENTS LATER

Anne opens the door for Rachel.

ANNE
What's going on?

RACHEL
Where are the kids?

ANNE
Out back.

RACHEL
Jill's been arrested.

ANNE
What?!

RACHEL
That's not all.

Rachel takes a deep breath.

RACHEL
I think she did it.

ANNE

No way!

Rachel nervously shakes her head.

RACHEL

She said some things last night, Anne...

Anne's eyes widen with concern.

ANNE

Like what?

Rachel stares at Anne in a way that says everything without saying anything.

ANNE

(Skeptically)

You're wrong.

RACHEL

I hope I am. She won't be arraigned until Monday, so she's got at least forty-eight hours of incarceration in front of her.

ANNE

She'll never make it.

RACHEL

She may have company. Last night I lied and said I had been with Jill all night. The police talked to someone who said they saw her coming out of John's hotel room.

ANNE

Oh my God.

RACHEL

Yeah, and I was threatened with an obstruction of justice charge.

ANNE

You're kidding.

RACHEL

I wish. Any chance John won't remember anything when he wakes up?

ANNE

There's a chance he never wakes up.

RACHEL
I don't know what to hope for.

ANNE
What are you going to do?

RACHEL
First, get an attorney.

ANNE
(Surprised)
I would have thought you already had one.

RACHEL
I did, but she stopped taking my calls.

Rachel nervously rubs her forehead. Both of them hear a message notification sound.

RACHEL
What is that?

ANNE
Oh! It's John's cell phone. He had it on him when they brought him in. I took it to give to Jill.

Anne removes the phone from her pocket.

ANNE
It's been going off every now and then. I don't know how to make it stop.

RACHEL
You realize by taking that you tampered with evidence.

ANNE
Should I give it to the police?

RACHEL
God, no! Give it to me.

Rachel grabs the phone and begins to push buttons. She accesses the phone and reads from the screen.

RACHEL
There's a text message from someone.

ANNE

Who?

RACHEL

I don't know, it's just a number. It was sent yesterday. It says, "Meet you in the bar tomorrow, noon."

ANNE

Is that his girlfriend?

RACHEL

Jill said she saw her at the hotel yesterday. If this is her, she may know something.

Rachel pauses for a moment.

ANNE

What are you thinking?

RACHEL

I'm thinking I should go down there.

ANNE

That's a horrible idea.

RACHEL

No, listen, if she doesn't show up, maybe it's because SHE had something to do with it.

Anne is not enthusiastic about Rachel's plan.

ANNE

Let's just tell the police.

RACHEL

They aren't very fond of me right now.

Anne rolls her eyes at Rachel.

RACHEL

I'll just go down there, watch for her, and then tell the police anything I find out.

ANNE

Maybe it's best if I go with you.

RACHEL

No, you have three extra kids out back that probably need an explanation about where their parents are.

Rachel turns to leave.

ANNE

What should I tell them?

Rachel addresses Anne as she continues walking out of the door.

RACHEL

Tell them they're out shopping for Christmas presents.

HAMILTON COUNTY JAIL - LATER

An officer escorts Jill down the corridor of the county jail facility. They stop at a cell, and the officer inserts the key into the lock. Jill tentatively steps inside the cell and looks at her fellow inmates: prostitutes, drug addicts, and derelicts. Jill tries to retreat when the officer forces her back inside. The inmates look Jill up and down as the officer steps away from the door. Jill shudders as she hears the deafening sound of the lock securing behind her.

CINCINNATIAN HOTEL LOUNGE - LATER THAT DAY

Rachel enters the lounge and positions herself discreetly at the corner of the bar. After a few minutes, Rachel spots TERESA, John's young mistress, as she enters the lounge. Teresa motions to the BARTENDER and sits at a table. Rachel recognizes Teresa and continues her surveillance. The bartender notice's as Rachel observes Teresa.

BARTENDER

Can I get you anything, ma'am?

RACHEL

Do you know that woman sitting over there?

Rachel points out Teresa.

BARTENDER

Teresa? She's a regular. What do you want to know?

RACHEL

(Sinisterly)

Is she capable of murder?

The bartender is taken aback by Rachel's question.

BARTENDER

Uh, not sure about THAT, but her nickname around here is "Lara Croft."

RACHEL

What does that mean?

The bartender leans over the bar and speaks quietly.

BARTENDER

You know, Lara Croft, Tomb Raider. She hunts down successful married men, discovers their riches, and steals everything.

Rachel is outraged.

RACHEL

So, she's a home-wrecking slut.

BARTENDER

Basically.

Rachel leaves the bar and approaches Teresa's table. Teresa acknowledges her.

TERESA

Can I help you?

Teresa has a vague recollection of Rachel but can't place her.

TERESA

Have we met?

Rachel pulls out a chair and sits down at Teresa's table.

RACHEL

Once. I'm a friend of John's wife.

TERESA

Oh, yeah, now I remember. You were part of that ugly scene at the Riverview.

RACHEL

So, what's going on between you two? Are you still seeing him?

TERESA

How is this any of your business?

RACHEL

My friend, Benjamin, wants to know.

Rachel pulls a one-hundred-dollar bill out of her pocket and slides it across the table. Teresa smiles, scoops up the bill, folds it in half twice, then tucks it into her cleavage.

TERESA

Yes, I'm still seeing him.

RACHEL

It doesn't bother you that he's married with three kids?

TERESA

Look, don't play the guilt card with me. I didn't steal him from his family, he came willingly. Several times, I might add. You suburban wives get all caught up in your play dates and PTA meetings, then you wonder why your husbands go looking for attention elsewhere.

RACHEL

And what's your hourly rate for attention these days?

TERESA

Oh, very funny, a whore joke. Let's see who's laughing in my bed later.

Rachel and Teresa remain locked in a death stare as the bartender approaches the table and sets down Teresa's drink.

RACHEL

I hope you plan on paying for that drink yourself. John won't be joining you.

Rachel stands.

TERESA

Did that wife of his freak out on him?

RACHEL

Yeah. Yeah, she did. Then she shot him in the chest.

Teresa reacts with genuine surprise.

TERESA

What?! Is he okay?!

RACHEL

We'll see. And just so you know, she's the most rational woman in the suburbs. So, I suggest you be more careful the next time you decide to screw a man for the chance to move in on a life you didn't help build.

Rachel turns to leave as Teresa stands and shouts after her.

TERESA

You tell that psycho wife of his that while she's rotting in a jail cell for the next thirty years, I'll be redecorating her house, sleeping in her bed, and screwing her husband better than she ever did!

Rachel stops and slowly turns back around to face Teresa.

TERESA

(Indignantly)

And her kids will be calling ME mom.

Rachel clenches her fist.

GROCERY STORE - ONE HOUR LATER

Mary speaks on her phone while pushing her shopping cart through the aisles.

MARY

When will she be released? Oh my God, Anne, this is unreal. I'll finish up here then come by and help with the kids. Do you need anything? Okay, see you soon.

As Mary ends the conversation, she runs into KELLY WATTS, the local gossip and a former bunco member.

KELLY

Hello, Mary.

Kelly notices Mary's cast.

KELLY

Oh, my goodness, what happened to your arm?

Mary would rather talk to anyone else.

MARY

Hi, Kelly. I fell and broke my wrist.

KELLY

(Insincerely)

That's just awful. Things aren't going well in the old bunco group, are they?

MARY

What do you mean?

KELLY

I mean Jill and John Michaels. I heard she was arrested for shooting him after he cheated on her.

Mary looks at her phone, still warm from her conversation.

MARY

How did you find out?

KELLY

Cindy Kramer's husband is with Cincinnati PD. I have to admit, when we first heard someone was taken into custody on your block, we figured it had to be Rachel Easton. Did Jill really shoot him?

Mary takes a deep breath and debates how to answer.

MARY

It's a tough time for Jill right now.

KELLY

I can just imagine. You know, her husband always did seem too good to be true. Heck, her whole life always seemed too good to be true. Looks like there was more sugar coating going on there than she would have us believe.

Mary bristles at Kelly's comment and tone.

MARY

I don't think...

Kelly talks over Mary's comment to start gossiping.

KELLY

As soon as I heard, I just knew this wasn't the first time.

MARY

I'm sure you didn't.

KELLY

I mean, it wouldn't surprise me if he had phone numbers of women all over the area.

MARY

Where are you getting this?

KELLY

C'mon, Mary. It's not that hard to figure out. John's a good-looking guy, he's got a good job, and he spends lots of time away from home.

Mary is both stunned and infuriated by Kelly's remarks.

MARY

(Calmly)

You are such a bitch.

KELLY

(Insulted)

Excuse me?

MARY

You heard me. You don't know a damn thing about Jill's situation, but that doesn't stop you from spreading any rumor that happens to develop in your head.

KELLY

What are you talking about?

MARY

It took you less than thirty seconds to tell me what you've heard and what you think. The truth is, two people are having a tough time, and the last thing they need is peripheral gossip making things worse.

KELLY

I'm sorry if you think I'm making things worse.

MARY

You are. So, if it's possible, keep your rumors and theories to yourself.

Kelly, insulted, starts to push her cart away from Mary.

MARY

Oh, and Kelly...

Kelly looks over her shoulder.

MARY

...Jill would never say or do anything to hurt anyone. So, if you're going to make up lies about someone, make them up about me. I talk shit about you all the time.

BACK ALLEY BAR - LATER

Rachel enters and is relieved to see her friend Caleb tending bar. She pulls out a stool and sits down. Caleb notices an abrasion across the back of her knuckles.

CALEB

What happened?

Rachel tries to conceal her wound by placing her left hand over her right. Caleb takes Rachel's hand, grabs a napkin, and gently wipes blood off the back of her knuckles. Rachel becomes uncomfortable but allows Caleb to finish tending to her injury.

RACHEL

Thanks.

Caleb looks into Rachel's hair and pulls out a small white mass.

CALEB

Is this a tooth?

Rachel grabs the tooth out of Caleb's hand and pitches it into the trash can behind him. An audible "clink" echoes. Caleb smiles at Rachel.

CALEB

You're in here early.

RACHEL

I wish it was for pleasure and not business. A friend of mine was in here last night and she left without paying.

CALEB

Left? Weren't you carrying her?

RACHEL

Yeah, well, if you saw the inside of my car, you'd thank me for getting her out of your bathroom.

Caleb goes to his register and pulls out Jill's bill.

CALEB

Jill, right?

RACHEL

That's her. Did you hear her talking about anything last night?

Caleb hands the receipt to Rachel.

CALEB

Not really. She mostly just cried. I tried to cheer her up, but nothing I said seemed to make her feel any better.

RACHEL

Did she mention anyone in particular?

CALEB

She did say something about a guy named John, but it was more mumbling than talking. I couldn't really understand her.

Rachel thinks about his comments for a moment then looks at the receipt.

RACHEL

Wow, seventy-six bucks. At least she paved the way to her blackout with the good stuff.

CALEB

Sorry. She was indiscriminately ordering drinks based on the style of the bottle.

Rachel reaches into her pocket and pulls out the one-hundred-dollar bill, folded in half twice. Caleb turns to the register to process the sale.

RACHEL

Yeah, she doesn't have much experience with this. She doesn't know the good stuff smells exactly the same as the cheap stuff when regurgitated into air conditioning vents.

Caleb cringes as he places her change in front of her. Rachel pushes the pile of money back at him.

RACHEL

Keep it. I assume you were good to her last night.

CALEB
(Flirtatiously)
You know me, I'm always good.

Caleb winks at Rachel. She awkwardly smiles as Caleb scoops up the gratuity and drops it into the community tip jar.

CALEB
Can I get you anything?

RACHEL
I have to meet with an attorney later, so I should probably be on my best behavior.

Caleb prepares her an iced tea.

CALEB
Attorney? That WAS a rough night.

RACHEL
You have no idea.

Caleb puts Rachel's tea in front of her.

CALEB
Oh, Jill left her purse here.

Caleb pulls Jill's purse out from behind the bar. Rachel places it on the stool next to her.

RACHEL
Thanks for hanging onto it.

CALEB
My pleasure.

Caleb becomes a bit coy.

CALEB
Can I ask you something?

RACHEL
Sure.

CALEB
What do you do when you're not drinking here?

Rachel shifts her eyes as she thinks for a moment.

RACHEL

Drinking at home.

CALEB

Would you ever want to... get a drink with me?

Rachel stares wide-eyed and shocked.

RACHEL

You're kidding, right?

Caleb smiles and shakes his head.

CALEB

No.

Rachel looks Caleb up and down.

RACHEL

How old are you?

CALEB

Why? Does that matter?

RACHEL

Not really, but indulge me.

CALEB

I turn thirty-seven on the twenty-third.

Rachel can't contain a smirk.

RACHEL

That would make me, Mrs. Robinson.

Rachel begins to drink her tea.

CALEB

Who's Mrs. Robinson?

Rachel gasps and begins to choke on her tea.

RACHEL

(Through coughs)

From "The Graduate?"

Caleb shows no sign of recognition. Rachel continues to clarify between hacks.

RACHEL

Simon and Garfunkel...?

Caleb shakes his head.

RACHEL

Never mind. You proved my point.

Rachel's attention is pulled to her phone ringing. Caleb turns to tend the other side of the bar.

RACHEL

Hello?

ANNE'S KITCHEN - CONTINUOUS

ANNE

Rachel, anything happen with the girlfriend?

RACHEL

Her future meals will require a blender.

Anne shakes her head at Rachel's confusing comment.

ANNE

My co-worker Tanya just called. He's conscious. The police are on their way to get his statement.

RACHEL

Great. I better go pick out something to wear for my mug shot.

ANNE

Rachel, a check's not going to make the situation go away this time.

RACHEL

I know.

ANNE

This is prison we're talking about. You have to be honest with the police.

RACHEL

I know.

Rachel feels the sting of defeat as she ends the call. After a moment, Rachel looks down to gather her things. She sees Jill's purse and opens it. A letter addressed to Jill is inside. Rachel holds it up to show Caleb.

RACHEL

Caleb! Did you put this in here?

Caleb returns and looks over the letter.

CALEB

Nope.

Rachel opens the letter, reads a few sentences, then joyously grabs Caleb's face and kisses him. She lets him go and jumps off the stool toward the exit.

Caleb stands motionless.

After a few seconds, Rachel returns, hurdles the bar, and engages him in a very passionate kiss. Several moments pass before they release and remain in a half embrace.

RACHEL

I'm sort of married.

CALEB

You are? Well, let me know when that changes.

Rachel reluctantly gets off the bar, grabs Jill's purse and letter, and runs out of the restaurant.

HOSPITAL CORRIDOR - LATER

Rachel is running full steam down the long hospital corridor. Tanya comes out of John's hospital room, closes the door behind her, and stops Rachel in her tracks.

TANYA

Where do you think you're going?

Rachel is out of breath and panting heavily.

RACHEL

Please... please... let me in there.

TANYA

This patient is not allowed any visitors.

Rachel continues to catch her breath.

RACHEL
But... I have... to talk... to the police.

Rachel holds up the letter.

TANYA
Then call 9-1-1. You aren't going in there.

Rachel holds up her hands as if to surrender to Tanya.

RACHEL
Okay... okay.

Rachel pretends to walk away, then turns and starts banging on John's door.

TANYA
You did NOT just do that...

Detective Bell opens the door and interrupts Tanya's scolding. He steps into the corridor with Rachel and Tanya. Rachel hands him Jill's letter.

RACHEL
Here! Read it! He threatens to kill himself if she doesn't take him back. That means HE may have pulled the trigger!

Detective Bell takes the letter.

DETECTIVE BELL
He did.

Rachel pinches her brow with confusion.

RACHEL
Wait, what? He did?

DETECTIVE BELL
That's what he told us.

Rachel shifts her eyes back and forth as she struggles to hide her confusion.

RACHEL
Well then... if he says he shot himself, you have nothing to keep her on.

Tanya walks away and leaves them alone. Detective Clarke comes out of John's room to join the gathering in the hallway. Detective Bell passes the letter to Detective Clarke.

DETECTIVE BELL
Mrs. Easton brought us the letter Mr. Michaels spoke of.

DETECTIVE CLARKE
How did you get a hold of it?

RACHEL
She left her purse at a bar last night. I went by just now and picked it up. The letter was inside.

DETECTIVE BELL
Last night? You told us you both were at the house last night. If you're admitting to misleading us, I can arrest you, Mrs. Easton.

Rachel trades looks between both detectives.

RACHEL
Did I say, last night? I meant two nights ago. Last night we were definitely at her house... all night. Drinking and puking... she did most of the puking... and the drinking for that matter. Which is what caused the puking...

Detective Bell stares down Rachel.

DETECTIVE BELL
Stop talking, Mrs. Easton.

Rachel obediently curls her lips shut. Detective Bell continues his intimidating stare-down until Detective Clarke breaks the tension.

DETECTIVE CLARKE
Mrs. Michaels is being processed for release now. She'll be out within the hour.

Detective Clarke signals Detective Bell to leave.

DETECTIVE CLARKE
Mrs. Easton, I expect you'll be more cooperative if we ever have a reason to meet again.

Rachel compliantly nods. Detective Clarke seems satisfied and follows Detective Bell down the hall.

HAMILTON COUNTY JAIL - LATER

A deputy escorts Jill to the main booking area and processes her release. After signing some paperwork, she is led into the lobby where Rachel is waiting for her.

RACHEL
If someone told me I'd be picking up a friend from jail,
I'd have put money on it being Mary.

Jill half-heartedly smiles. They walk out to the parking lot. Jill focuses on the ground beneath her as she struggles to ask the question she most wants answered.

JILL
Is John all right?

RACHEL
He'll live.

The women walk a few strides in silence.

RACHEL
As much as I hate him, I have to give him credit for
covering for you.

Jill lifts her head.

JILL
(Confused)
What?

RACHEL
He told the police he shot himself.

Jill takes another moment.

JILL
He did. I mean, he threatened he would.

Rachel grabs Jill's arm to stop her.

RACHEL
Wait. WHAT? He DID shoot himself? You didn't do it?

JILL
(Offended)
No, I didn't do it!

Jill recoils and lowers her voice.

JILL

He begged me not to leave him and said if I did, he would...

Jill holds back tears, unable to detail John's threat.

JILL

I can't let him manipulate me anymore.

Jill starts to walk again. Rachel takes a moment to put all the pieces together. She hesitates long enough to require a hurried jog to catch up.

RACHEL

Jill, why didn't you tell the police that when they arrested you?

Jill stops and faces Rachel.

JILL

YOU told me not to talk to them! You said you had EXPERIENCE with this!

RACHEL

I told you not to talk to them because I thought you did it.

Jill is dumbfounded.

JILL

Why would you think I did it?!

Rachel looks around to ensure privacy.

RACHEL

(Quietly)

There was blood all over your clothes in the bathroom.

Jill sighs with embarrassment.

JILL

Those were the clothes I was wearing when I miscarried. With everything happening, getting them to the laundry was the least of my concerns.

Jill's explanation sets a slow epiphany in motion. As Rachel realizes she inaccurately interpreted the evidence, she sheepishly walks away. Jill hurries after her.

JILL
(Appalled)
Dear Lord, Rachel. After years of knowing me, you really thought I could've shot John?

Rachel lights a cigarette as she picks up her pace.

RACHEL
Look, Jill, your normally photoshoot-ready bathroom was littered with bloodstained clothes. You left the kids with Megan and disappeared for hours. You weren't answering your phone. When Mary and I DID find you, you were obliterated at the base of a bar room toilet. You were acting completely out of character! So, YES, color me PESSIMISTIC, I thought you could've shot John!

The two women come to a stop and face each other. Jill's outrage takes a backseat to humiliation.

JILL
(Shamefully)
I was next to a toilet?

Rachel takes a long drag from her cigarette and blows the smoke into the air.

RACHEL
No, Jill, you weren't next to it. You had the porcelain equivalent to carnal knowledge of it.

Jill shakes her head as it sinks into her hands. Rachel attempts to console Jill.

RACHEL
So, you got drunk and threw up... it happens.

Jill looks up as revelations continue.

JILL
I threw up?

Rachel throws her cigarette down and opens the door of an unfamiliar vehicle.

JILL
(Confused)
What's this?

Rachel feigns ignorance.

RACHEL

What do you mean?

JILL

I mean this isn't your car. What happened to yours?

Rachel nervously laughs.

RACHEL

Well, it didn't inexplicably combust and roll into a pond
if that's what you're asking.

JILL'S LIVING ROOM - LATER

The women are enjoying coffee together. Jill is sitting on her couch with both twins asleep on either side of her. Mary and Anne are sitting across from Jill on the opposite couch. Rachel is in an oversized chair, fighting to stay awake with Wil curled up next to her.

MARY

You'll all be happy to hear that due to the criminal
element in the neighborhood, my mother-in-law is
packing up and leaving tomorrow.

RACHEL

Thanks for taking one for the team, Jill.

The women share a gentle chuckle.

ANNE

Have you talked to John?

JILL

I'm going to let my attorney do that.

MARY

So, it's divorce then?

JILL

I could never stay after everything that's happened.

ANNE

For what it's worth, I think you're doing the right thing.

MARY

So do I.

JILL

Thanks.

Rachel raises her cup to her mouth, making the abrasion on the back of her hand visible.

MARY

What's that on your hand?

Rachel sets down her coffee and inspects her injury.

RACHEL

That? That's the most gratifying check I'll ever write.

END OF ROUND 2

ROUND 3

How to Score Points

20 MONTHS LATER

CATHOLIC CHURCH - LATE WINTER, DAY

A group is sitting together in a crowded sanctuary: Anne, Bill and Megan; Mary and Craig; Jill; and Kevin, with his daughters PAIGE EASTON and JENNIFER EASTON. They are solemnly waiting for the service to begin.

Several moments pass before Kevin checks his watch, then anxiously looks over his shoulder and scans the room. After not finding what he's looking for, he motions to the PRIEST to start the service. The priest cues the funeral procession to begin.

CAR PARKED IN CATHOLIC CHURCH PARKING LOT - MOMENTS LATER

Rachel sits behind the wheel of her car and stares blankly out of the front windshield. She ashes her cigarette off the edge of her open window.

A side door to the church opens. Mary emerges and walks up to the car. Rachel doesn't flinch as Mary tries to lift the locked door handle. Mary waits a moment, bends down to look in the car, and knocks on the window. Rachel reluctantly triggers the unlock button. Mary opens the door and sits down in the passenger seat sideways. Rachel evades eye contact while Mary tries to get her attention.

MARY
I thought you were going to quit.

Rachel takes an extra-deep inhale from her cigarette, then obnoxiously blows smoke throughout the entire car.

RACHEL
I thought you were going to lose weight.

MARY
Okay. I'm going to let that slide, under the circumstances.

RACHEL
Look, Mary, I really don't feel like a therapy session.

MARY
Okay.

Mary shifts her body to sit forward in the seat and joins Rachel in staring out of the front window. After a few silent moments, Mary can't help but try to engage Rachel again.

MARY
The service has started.

Rachel rolls her eyes at Mary's inability to stay quiet.

MARY
Think you should, maybe, go inside?

Rachel continues to peacefully smoke her cigarette.

MARY
This is your mother's funeral, Rachel.

After a few more awkward moments of watching Rachel stare out the window, Mary tries to engage her in conversation again.

MARY
I think it would be better if you talked about it.

Rachel slaps her cigarette between her lips, leans across Mary, and opens the door. Mary takes the cue, surrenders, and gets out of the car.

MARY
I'm here if you want to talk.

Rachel ignores Mary's comment, stretches across the passenger seat, and pulls the door shut. Mary is left to address the sealed car door.

MARY
(Facetiously)
Of course, with your history of mental stability, I'm sure you're rock solid.

Defeated, Mary returns to the service.

CATHOLIC CHURCH GATHERING ROOM - LATER

Guests are milling around the crowded room while they indulge in the ceremonial post-service coffee and food. Jill, Anne, and Mary are gathered in a corner. Kevin approaches the women.

KEVIN
Have any of you seen my wife?

MARY
Yes, Kevin. She's outside in her car.

KEVIN
(Irritated)
In her car? People are asking for her.

MARY
I think this may be more difficult for her than she expected.

KEVIN
(Unsympathetic)
Difficult or not, she has responsibilities here. When you see her, remind her of that.

Kevin leaves to tend to other guests.

ANNE
I know he's gay, but he has lived with her for fourteen years.

JILL
Maybe we should try to coax her inside.

MARY
Jill, I think we'd have an easier time trying to get a cranky raccoon into a bathing suit.

A preoccupied man bumps into Jill and spills a tonic water all over her. ROBERT FITZPATRICK is a tall, athletic, and charismatic man in his 40s.

ROBERT
(Embarrassed)
I am so sorry.

Robert keeps his head down as he quickly pulls the handkerchief from his suit pocket and begins to blot up the liquid he has spilled. He dries off Jill's sleeves and purse.

ROBERT
I can't believe I did that. I'm so glad I turned down the red wine I was offered.

Jill tries to minimize the man's embarrassment.

JILL

It's fine.

Robert continues to insist on wiping up every last drop.

ROBERT

Funerals always make me nervous.

Robert looks up for the first time and makes eye contact with Jill. He is instantly attracted to her.

JILL

I don't know anyone who enjoys these gatherings.

ROBERT

I'm Robert.

Robert extends his hand to Jill. She is struck by his charm and good looks. She smiles and shakes his hand.

JILL

I'm Jill.

The two share a flirtatious stare as they release hands, oblivious to the others. With raised eyebrows and sharing a smile, Anne and Mary take the opportunity to slip away from the conversation.

ROBERT

I'm very sorry for your loss.

JILL

Oh, thank you. I didn't really know her. I'm here to support a member of her family.

ROBERT

Oh, really? Which member?

Rachel quietly comes around the corner and up behind Robert. Her arms are folded, and she has a disgusted look on her face.

RACHEL

You realize you're out of your jurisdiction, Lieutenant Brasshole.

Robert recognizes the familiar voice and neglects to turn around.

ROBERT

You must not have heard, I made captain.

RACHEL
My apologies.

Rachel sarcastically corrects herself.

RACHEL
CAPTAIN Brasshole.

Robert smiles as he turns to face Rachel.

ROBERT
Always looking for a fight, Ellie.

RACHEL
And you're always running from one, Bobby.

A moment passes between the three before Jill realizes their relationship.

JILL
Is this... your brother?

Rachel and Robert stand locked in the kind of penetrating stare only siblings can share. Jill continues to flirt with Robert.

JILL
Rachel hasn't told us much about you. Are you in town long? Is your wife waiting for you?

Rachel doesn't let Robert answer.

RACHEL
Jill, why don't you go find Mary and Anne and ask them to kindly extinguish the fire in your crotch.

Jill bashfully excuses herself from the conversation, leaving Rachel and Robert alone.

RACHEL
What are you doing here?

ROBERT
Our mother died.

RACHEL
Yeah, and she's been dying for the past three years. Where were you then?

ROBERT

Hey, you were the one trying to prove something. You never wanted my help.

RACHEL

You turned out to be quite useless when I needed help.

Robert becomes irritated at the re-introduction of a tired topic.

ROBERT

Jesus, Ellie, it's been over twenty years. Let it go.

Rachel struggles to contain her agitation at Robert's comments.

ROBERT

Look, what happened to you was unfortunate, but if you had exercised even the smallest amount of self-control, it might not have turned out like it did.

Rachel shakes her head in disgust.

ROBERT

I don't know what you expected me to do. I wasn't going to jeopardize my career for your screw-up.

RACHEL

You never disappoint me, Bobby. You always seem to take thinking about yourself to a whole new level.

Rachel turns to walk away. Robert forcibly grabs her arm and turns her toward him.

ROBERT

That's not fair, Ellie.

RACHEL

(Quietly incensed)

Don't you dare talk to me about what's fair.

Robert acknowledges Rachel's anger and releases her.

RACHEL

(Condescendingly)

Congratulations on making captain. I'm so relieved my reckless behavior didn't leave a lasting scar on your spotless record.

Rachel turns to leave but Robert stops her again.

ROBERT

(Sincerely)

I'm truly sorry, Ellie. If I could do it over, I'd do things differently.

Rachel is unmoved by his seemingly heartfelt apology.

RACHEL

Wouldn't we all?

Rachel walks away and rejoins Jill, Mary, and Anne in the corner.

ANNE

Was that your brother?

RACHEL

(Disgusted)

Yes.

Rachel directs her next comments at Jill.

RACHEL

And I would appreciate it if you didn't fawn all over him like a sex-starved schoolgirl.

JILL

(Embarrassed)

I'm sorry. It's been over a year since my divorce.

RACHEL

Well, buy a dildo for Christ's sake!

Jill is mortified at Rachel's suggestion.

MARY

Come on, Rachel, what's the harm?

Rachel addresses the entire group with an authoritative tone.

RACHEL

Listen to me. None of you are allowed to talk to him! And if I find out you are, I'll knock you unconscious, shave off your pubic hair, and super glue it to your upper lip.

The women all curl their upper lips into their mouths.

RACHEL

Not that anyone would notice on you, Mary.

JIM ALLENBACH, a grey-haired, round-bellied man in his 70s, approaches Rachel.

JIM

Hello, Ellie.

Rachel's anger is lifted by the sight of his familiar face.

RACHEL

Mr. Allenbach, how are you?

JIM

You're not a child anymore, Ellie. You can call me Jim.

RACHEL

That wouldn't feel right.

Rachel and Jim share a cordial embrace.

RACHEL

These are my friends: Mary, Jill, and Anne.

They all share handshakes and greetings.

RACHEL

This is Mr. Allenbach. He's been around for as long as I can remember.

JIM

Nice to meet you ladies. Ellie, I was worried about you after you were released, but I can see you made a nice life for yourself down here.

Mary catches his reference to her "release." Rachel quickly takes Mr. Allenbach by the arm and pulls him away.

RACHEL

Let's not bore them with our memories. Why don't we catch up over here?

Rachel walks away with Mr. Allenbach as the women are left to close ranks and talk amongst themselves.

JILL

It's hard to imagine Rachel was once a child.

ANNE
I always figured she was conjured by members of a questionable religion.

Mary quickly addresses Jim's comment.

MARY
Did you catch that?

JILL
(Oblivious)
Catch what?

MARY
"After you were released." She's been to jail.

JILL
What?!

ANNE
I heard him. Smart money has always been on her doing time.

JILL
What are you two talking about?

MARY
Didn't you hear that old guy? He said, “After you were released."

Jill shrugs off Mary's insinuation.

JILL
That could mean a number of things.

MARY
Name one.

Jill takes a minute to think but comes up empty.

JILL
(Insistent)
She hasn't been to jail. She just likes to talk tough.

MARY
You're right, Jill. Rachel never exhibits the kind of behavior that would get her sent to jail.

Mary dramatically puts her finger to her face as if she's thinking.

MARY

Oh wait, wasn't it just last Christmas she got drunk and dismembered an animatronic Santa because, in her words, "He was looking at me!"

JILL

(Dismissive)

Santa Claus can be a disturbing figure.

Mary shakes her head in disbelief.

MARY

Yeah, if you're a toddler.

Mary looks to Anne to plead her case.

GATHERING ROOM CORNER - CONTINUOUS

Rachel and Jim Allenbach continue to talk privately in the corner.

JIM

I'm very sorry about your mom.

RACHEL

I appreciate that.

JIM

She was a difficult woman.

Rachel quietly laughs in agreement.

JIM

I never once saw her issue or accept an apology in the fifty years I knew her.

Rachel shakes her head.

RACHEL

No, she didn't.

Jim misreads Rachel's stoic nature as fragility.

JIM
(Sympathetically)
You know, the forgiveness you're looking for is from yourself.

Rachel forces a seemingly grateful smile.

JIM
The past is the past, Ellie. Just close the lid on it.

Rachel puts her hand on Jim's shoulder.

RACHEL
You're right. Thank you, Mr. Allenbach.

She leaves him and slowly walks to the side of the open casket. She hovers over the body of her dead mother for a few moments. The priest approaches.

PRIEST
Rachel, we're ready to take your mother to the gravesite. Just let me know whenever you're ready.

Rachel reaches over and knocks the hinge of the casket lid free. The lid slams down and startles everyone in the room. She turns and instructs the priest.

RACHEL
(Enthusiastically)
Let's do this!

Robert watches as Rachel dramatically storms past him and out of the room.

EASTON LIVING ROOM - LATER

Rachel is sitting in her living room, surrounded by her stepdaughters Paige and Jennifer. Paige is in her late 20s and not shy about her dislike for Rachel. Jennifer is in her mid-20s, sweet, and quick to compensate for Paige's mistreatment of Rachel. Kevin comes out of the kitchen, walks into the living room, and hands Rachel a drink.

KEVIN
That was... an interesting funeral.

Rachel takes the drink as Kevin heads back to the kitchen.

RACHEL
When you visit a gorilla pen, you can't be surprised when shit gets thrown at you.

PAIGE

At least now I know what the accepted code of conduct is when I attend your funeral.

RACHEL

You're assuming I'm going to die before you.

PAIGE

That's true, I shouldn't. You'll probably evade death like a horror film villain. We'll arm ourselves with every pitchfork and torch in the village, but it'll never be enough to end your reign of terror.

Paige gets up and walks into the kitchen. Jennifer moves closer to Rachel and places her left hand on top of Rachel's knee.

JENNIFER

Ignore her. She's cranky because she just found out she's not going to be the center of attention for a while.

Rachel takes a moment to soak in Jennifer's sincerity.

RACHEL

How did you two fall out of the same vagina?

Jennifer smiles. Rachel looks down to acknowledge Jennifer's gesture when a large engagement ring gets her attention.

RACHEL

What's that?

Jennifer smiles.

JENNIFER

Matt finally asked me.

Rachel raises Jennifer's hand to admire the ring.

RACHEL

When?

JENNIFER

Tuesday night.

RACHEL

Does your dad know?

JENNIFER

Yes. Matt stopped by to ask his permission. Your mom had just passed away, so dad didn't want to make any announcement. If Matt had known, he would have waited.

Rachel releases Jennifer's hand and a smile spreads across her face.

RACHEL

I'm glad he didn't.

The two share a quiet moment.

JENNIFER

Rachel, I know it wasn't easy for you. I can't imagine what it was like walking into this family when you did. Mom's death was hard on all of us, but especially for Paige. She was going to make it difficult for anyone who stepped into this house. You tried. You respected our boundaries and didn't try to force a relationship on us. I just want to say thank you and tell you how much I'm looking forward to sharing my wedding day with you.

Rachel's silent gratitude is interrupted by Paige re-entering the room.

PAIGE

Rachel, dad's making dinner. Do you want some actual food, or is the nutritional value of simple syrup enough to sustain you?

MARY'S LIVING ROOM - TWO DAYS LATER, EVENING

Jill helps Mary set out food and prepare for bunco, while Rachel sits on the couch, nursing a cocktail. Rachel is in the middle of reliving the encounter with her stepdaughters.

RACHEL

...and then, she throws an alcoholic insult at me. Like that isn't the easiest place to go! Get some new material, you over-privileged, unimaginative gutter shrew! I drink because your daddy has sex with men!

Jill and Mary look at each other like they know they're in for a rough night. Jill tries to lighten the mood.

JILL

So, a wedding! That'll be exciting for y'all.

RACHEL

Oh no, don't think you're getting out of it. I expect all three of you there, WITH your spouses, racking up Kevin's bar bill.

MARY

That means you're going to need a date, Jill.

JILL

Oh, please don't make me.

RACHEL

You were named the most gorgeous woman in South Carolina. Why is this so difficult for you?

JILL

When you finally get the courage to register with one of those online dating sites, and the first responses you get are from men with the screen names, "FiveHourFootLong" and "TheMoanMaker," you quickly lose hope for a meaningful relationship.

MARY

You're kidding?! Men really think that kind of username is going to get the attention of a serious woman?

RACHEL

Serious? No. Desperate? Yes.

Rachel leans over to Jill.

RACHEL

Don't delete the contact information for "FiveHourFootLong."

Anne, still in her nurse scrubs, enters Mary's house and makes her way into the living room.

ANNE

Grab your parkas, ladies. Hell is officially freezing over.

MARY

Megan's off academic probation?

Anne scoffs.

ANNE

No.

Anne takes a deep breath.

ANNE

I just signed up to run the Cincinnati marathon.

MARY

(Happily surprised)

You're kidding?!

JILL

(Excited)

You've been talking about doing that for years!

RACHEL

(Disgusted)

Why?!

Anne becomes consumed with regret and sits on the couch next to Rachel. She helps herself to the drink in Rachel's hand.

ANNE

I don't know. I've always thought about it. Every time I see one of those marathon ovals on the back of a car, I think, I'd love to have one of those. And then today, the hospital announced it's sponsoring a team, and everyone was talking about it and I just got caught up and before I knew it, I committed.

Rachel takes her glass back as she stands up to get a refill at the liquor cabinet.

JILL

How far is that?

ANNE

Twenty-six point two miles.

JILL

Twenty-six miles? That's like from here to downtown.

ANNE

(Worried)

And back.

MARY

How long will that take?

ANNE

I have no idea. Five? Six hours?

RACHEL

Five or six hours? That is the dumbest waste of time I've ever heard of.

Jill sits down next to Anne.

JILL

Don't listen to her. We're incredibly excited for you. We'll help you get ready for it, and we'll go down the day of the marathon and cheer you on.

ANNE

You will?

MARY

Of course, we will. As will Rachel.

Rachel continues to concern herself more with getting the right ratio of whiskey to water.

RACHEL

(Patronizingly)

Yes, Anne. We will enable your reckless decision to destroy your joints and stress your body, all for the unparalleled glory that only a car magnet can bring.

Anne smiles and shrugs her shoulders.

ANNE

Thanks.

MARY

What did Bill say?

Rachel returns to the couch.

ANNE

I haven't told him yet. I came straight over here from work. I'm afraid to hear what he's going to say.

JILL

He'll support you. Why wouldn't he?

ANNE

It's a huge time commitment. I'll need to get up early in the morning to do my runs before my shift. That means no late nights. I'll have to bike and swim to cross train, buy new shoes and better running clothes, and then I'll have to do a ten to twenty mile-long run every weekend.

RACHEL

(Sarcastically)

Sounds AWEsome.

MARY

He'll be fine. It's not like you're making him do any of those things with you.

ANNE

I hope so.

MARY

Grab a drink. You've got all night to figure out how to tell him.

The doorbell rings. Mary leaves the women in the living room to answer the door.

MARY'S FRONT PORCH - CONTINUOUS

DIANE KHOURI, a young woman in her late 20s, stands on the front porch with her hands in her pockets and her head lowered.

Mary opens the door and has no recollection of her visitor.

MARY

Hello?

Diane lifts her head into the light and makes eye contact with Mary.

DIANE

Hi. I'm sorry to bother you. I'm hoping you can help me. I'm looking for Mary Pugh, forty-four years old, originally from Indianapolis, Indiana.

A sudden blast of recognition paralyzes Mary.

MARY'S LIVING ROOM - CONTINUOUS

Mary frantically re-enters her living room.

MARY

Get out!

Surprised, the women turn their attention to Mary.

ANNE

What?! We just got here.

Mary is increasingly agitated as she speaks more quietly and checks over her shoulder.

MARY

I know, but I need you to leave.

Rachel holds up her glass.

RACHEL

I just poured this.

Mary helps Rachel off the couch.

MARY

Take it with you. I just need you all to go.

RACHEL

Who the hell rang your doorbell?

Mary continues to herd the women out of her house.

MARY

Never mind. Use the back door.

JILL

Why the back door?

MARY

I'll explain later, please, just go.

Mary successfully corrals the women out of the back door, locks it, and takes a deep breath before turning around to face her guest.

NEIGHBORHOOD STREET - NEXT MORNING

Jill, Anne, and Mary are standing at the bus stop with their children: Emma, Grace, Wil, Jack, Ethan, and Charlie. An unspoken tension hangs in the air.

WIL

Can you drive?

JACK

Yeah, I can drive.

WIL

Then why do you still ride the bus?

ANNE

He can't drive alone yet, Wil. He only has his temps.

WIL

What are temps?

JACK

Temps let me drive with my parents or teacher in the car. I'll get my license in a couple months.

ANNE

Not if you don't learn to look behind you when you're in reverse.

JACK

(Defensively)

I look behind me!

ANNE

Tell that to the dent in the mailbox.

The bus approaches, stops, and opens its doors.

JILL

Be good. I'll see y'all when you get home.

MARY

Charlie, remember to ask Mrs. Delgado for extra help in math.

Mary addresses Jill and Anne.

MARY

He's only in the sixth grade and I'm already useless.

The kids load onto the bus and pull away.

MARY

I should get going. I have a lot to do today.

Jill attempts to keep Mary in the conversation.

JILL

Wait. Would you like to come over for a cup of coffee?

MARY

No, thanks.

JILL

I can make you a smoothie. I got some fresh blueberries from the farmers market.

MARY

No, thank you.

JILL

How about...

Mary becomes more annoyed and interrupts Jill.

MARY

NO. Thank you.

ANNE

Look, Mary, Jill is just trying to be pleasant and not appear to be invading your privacy. Rachel, on the other hand...

Anne points over Mary's shoulder. Mary turns around to see Rachel standing behind her with a cigarette in her mouth and determination in her attitude.

RACHEL

So, who was it? An old boyfriend? Craig's bookie? Your agent with an offer for an adult diaper commercial?

Mary struggles for several moments while trading looks between each woman. She fails to come up with a believable explanation and succumbs to their pressure. She takes a deep breath, lowers her head, and shamefully speaks.

MARY

It was my daughter.

Jill and Anne share confused looks.

ANNE

I'm sorry, what did you say?

RACHEL

She said, DAUGHTER!

Mary becomes both irritated and embarrassed.

MARY

Could you be any more of an asshole, Rachel?

ANNE

Since when do you have a daughter?

Mary begins to fight back tears.

MARY

Since I was sixteen.

Mary loses her battle and tears begin to stream down her face. She buries her face into her hands. Jill and Anne rush to comfort her.

JILL

Come on, let's go inside.

JILL'S ENTRY - CONTINUOUS

The women file into the house. Anne leads Mary to the living room while Jill hurries to the bathroom to get a box of tissues. Rachel pauses at the door to extinguish her cigarette on the front porch. As Jill returns, she witnesses the careless discard of Rachel's cigarette.

JILL

You better be planning to do something with that disgusting butt.

RACHEL

Hey! Let's hear her story before we start calling her names.

Rachel smirks as she storms past Jill and enters the house.

JILL'S LIVING ROOM - CONTINUOUS

Anne consoles Mary on the couch.

JILL

Here you go, Mary.

Jill hands Mary the tissue box while Rachel and Jill sit down.

MARY

Thank you.

Mary fumbles with getting tissue from the box. Anne tries to help by taking the box and setting it down on the coffee table.

ANNE

I'm sorry for pressuring you to tell us.

JILL

We had no idea it was this personal. We don't need to know the details.

RACHEL

I need to know!

Mary blows her nose and takes a moment to dry her eyes.

MARY

I was fifteen. I didn't know anything. I mean, I knew how things worked, but no one ever went into detail about the way things snowball when your hormones are raging. I was at a party, and I met a boy. We started messing around and one thing led to another. Four weeks later, when I didn't get my visit from Aunt Flow, I realized I was pregnant.

RACHEL

(Confused)

Aunt Flo? Was she some sort of teenage health and safety officer?

ANNE

No, Rachel, her period!

RACHEL

Oh, why didn't she just say her period then? This story is hard enough to follow without the addition of needless characters.

ANNE
Haven't you ever heard your period referred to as a visit from Aunt Flow?

RACHEL
Never. I've heard riding the cotton pony, on the rag, surfing the crimson wave, spreading your red wings, code red, birthing a blood diamond, checking into the Red Roof Inn, shark week...

MARY
(Frustrated)
Back to me!

ANNE
I'm sorry, honey, continue.

MARY
I didn't know what to do. I was so scared, and I kept hoping it would just go away.

RACHEL
(Sarcastically)
Flawless strategy.

MARY
I know! By the time I had the courage to tell my mom, giving her up for adoption was my only option.

ANNE
Does Craig know?

MARY
Yes. He's always known, but the boys don't.

JILL
So, you have a daughter and she wants a relationship with you. That's wonderful.

MARY
No, she doesn't. She made it very clear she has loving parents and doesn't need a woman who doesn't know her coming in and acting like a mother.

ANNE
Then why bother finding you?

Mary takes a moment before finding the courage to continue.

MARY

Her son is sick.

Mary begins to cry.

MARY

He needs a bone marrow transplant and he's running out of time.

The seriousness of the situation washes over the room.

RACHEL

So now what?

MARY

What do you mean, "now what?" Now, the boys and I get tested.

ANNE

Are you going to tell them why?

MARY

We're going to tell them they need to give blood and that's all. The situation is complicated enough.

ANNE

I can ask to administer if you think that would be easier for them.

MARY

Thanks.

JILL

And I'll get tested too.

MARY

You will?

JILL

Of course, I will.

ANNE

I'm already in the database.

MARY

Thank you both so much.

A quiet falls over the room as all heads turn toward Rachel.

RACHEL
What kind of selfish monster do you people think I am?

The women keep all comments to themselves.

MARY
Thank you. Thank you all so much.

Mary receives reassuring hugs and concern from Jill and Anne while Rachel gets up to finish her cigarette.

UPSCALE RESTAURANT BAR - TWO WEEKS LATER, NIGHT

Jill is sitting alone at the bar with a drink in front of her. She scans the area and checks her watch. A familiar man walks by.

JILL
Robert?

Robert Fitzpatrick turns around and is pleasantly surprised to see Jill.

ROBERT
Jill! How are you?

Robert and Jill share that awkward moment in between a hug or a handshake. They arrive at a handshake.

JILL
I'm fine. How have you been?

ROBERT
Good. I'm actually meeting someone here to talk about a career change.

JILL
A department down here?

ROBERT
Something like that. Are you meeting Ellie?

JILL
No...

Jill rolls her eyes.

JILL
...I'm foolishly giving internet dating one more try.

BRUCE GILLIAM, a well-dressed, middle-aged man, shouts to Robert from across the bar.

BRUCE

Fitz!

ROBERT

Gilliam!

Bruce makes his way over to Jill and Robert. The men shake hands.

ROBERT

Bruce, this is Jill.

Bruce hesitates as he extends his hand.

BRUCE

Have we met before?

Jill recognizes Bruce as an agent from the Kentucky division of the FBI. Not wanting to be recognized, she abruptly turns her face away.

JILL

I don't believe so.

BRUCE

I'm sorry, it's just that you look really familiar.

Jill continues to direct her attention away from Bruce.

ROBERT

Stand down Gilliam, she said she doesn't know you.

Bruce does a head-to-toe visual assessment of Jill.

BRUCE

I'm sure I know you. It'll come to me.

Robert sees that Jill is very uncomfortable.

ROBERT

Go get a table. I'll be there in a minute.

Bruce leaves.

ROBERT

I'm sorry about that. His job makes him suspicious of everyone.

JILL

It's fine.

ROBERT

I should get going.

JILL

(Warmly)

It was nice seeing you.

ROBERT

Yes, it was. I'm in town for the next couple of days. Any chance of taking you to dinner?

Jill hesitates, being torn between her desire to accept the invitation and Rachel's threat.

ROBERT

I'm sorry. You're sitting here waiting for a date, I shouldn't be asking you out.

JILL

No, no, it's just that...

Jill stumbles in thoughts and words as Robert waits anxiously for her response.

JILL

I'd love to.

ROBERT

Great.

Feeling the pressure to get back to his job interview, Robert pulls out his business card and hands it to Jill.

ROBERT

Here's my card. If your date doesn't turn out to be your dream man, text me your number.

Jill takes his card.

ROBERT

I hope I hear from you.

Robert leaves and Jill is left alone with her drink and a smile.

An obnoxious, arrogant MAN approaches Jill.

MAN

Are you Jill?

Jill thinks for a moment.

JILL

I'm sorry, no.

MAN

(Flirtatiously)

Do you want to be Jill?

Jill uncomfortably smiles, then pulls out her phone and adds Robert's contact information.

RUNNING STORE - ONE WEEK LATER

Anne and Jill are browsing the store. Anne is overwhelmed by this brand-new world.

ANNE

Thank you so much for coming with me. I'm so intimidated by these places.

JILL

My pleasure. I actually need to talk to you about something.

Anne gives Jill her full attention.

ANNE

Oh yeah? What about?

JILL

You know the kind of luck I've been having with the dating scene...

ANNE

Yeah.

JILL

Well, the other night I ran into Robert.

ANNE

Robert?

JILL
Rachel's brother.

ANNE
Really?

JILL
And, he asked me to dinner.

ANNE
Are you asking me if I think you should go?

JILL
I went already.

ANNE
You did? How was it?

JILL
I had a really nice time.

ANNE
That's wonderful! Are you going out again?

JILL
I want to.

ANNE
What's stopping you?

JILL
Rachel's threat to my lady curls, that's what.

Anne chuckles.

ANNE
Oh, please! Is she afraid he'll tell us what a nut job she is? Like we don't already know? Besides, she never needs to find out. It's not like you two can get serious. He lives in Chicago.

JILL
He's moving to Cincinnati.

Anne's interest is piqued.

ANNE
Is he? Do you see a future with him?

JILL

Maybe. I mean, it was just one date, but I really enjoyed myself.

ANNE

You realize he and Rachel come from the same gene pool. Are you sure you want to go swimming in that sea of crazy?

JILL

They're nothing alike. He's kind and gentle and thoughtful.

ANNE

Maybe he's adopted.

Jill's affection for Robert becomes more apparent as she continues.

JILL

We just sat and talked for hours about everything and nothing.

ANNE

Wow, Jill. It sounds like you really like him.

JILL

I know. What should I do?

ANNE

Sleep with him.

Jill is shocked at Anne's suggestion.

JILL

What?!

ANNE

Sleep with him.

JILL

I can't sleep with him! What kind of a person would I be if I jumped into bed with the first interesting man I dated?

ANNE

I'm not going to touch that comment. You said yourself, he's different. I just think, it's been a long time and he sounds like a guy you should take a chance on.

JILL

It's the "long time" that scares the heck out of me.

KATIE, a young running enthusiast, approaches the women.

KATIE

Hello, ladies. Is there anything I can help you with?

ANNE

Yes, everything. I just signed up to run the marathon
and I'm consumed with regret.

Katie nods sympathetically.

KATIE

I've been getting that a lot lately. Let's start with shoes.

RACHEL'S ENTRY HALL - TWO WEEKS LATER, EARLY AFTERNOON

Kevin hurries to answer a knock at the front door. Robert Fitzpatrick stands on the porch with a medium-sized cardboard box in his arms.

KEVIN

Hello, Robert.

ROBERT

Hi, Kevin.

Kevin opens the door wide for Robert and welcomes him inside.

KEVIN

I was just on my way out, let me get Rachel.

ROBERT

Thanks.

Kevin leaves Robert to stand alone in the entry hall with nothing to do except admire the surroundings. After a few awkward moments, Kevin emerges, escorting Rachel down the hallway.

KEVIN

Here she is.

Rachel communicates only a silent glare.

ROBERT

Hi, Ellie.

Kevin feels the tension between the two.

KEVIN

I'll leave and let you two talk. It'll give me an opportunity to squeeze in a few holes.

Rachel folds her arms and rolls her eyes.

ROBERT

Nice seeing you, Kevin.

KEVIN

You too, Robert. Make sure you clear your calendar for the first weekend in May. My daughter is getting married.

Rachel redirects her disgust at Kevin as he walks out of the front door.

RACHEL

The guest list hasn't been finalized, so I wouldn't go making any hotel arrangements if I were you.

Robert looks around the house.

ROBERT

Nice house.

RACHEL

(Curtly)

I know. I pay a huge price for it.

Robert smiles, then draws attention to the box.

ROBERT

Mind if I put this down?

RACHEL

What is it?

ROBERT

It's mom's stuff. You never returned the hospital's messages, so they called me.

RACHEL

You came down just for that?

Robert sets the box down on the floor.

ROBERT

No, not just for that.

Rachel remains cold and disgusted.

ROBERT

I've been offered a position in the Bureau's northern Kentucky field office.

RACHEL

Nice guys. They were very gentle with my body cavity search. I only had to use a safe word twice.

ROBERT

I wanted you to hear it from me.

Rachel remains stoic.

RACHEL

Okay, I've heard it from you.

Robert digs deep to make a peace offering.

ROBERT

Call me a jackass, but I thought with mom gone and me moving down here, we might be able to put everything behind us.

RACHEL

You're a jackass.

Robert sighs heavily.

ROBERT

You're just like mom. Never willing to let anything go.

Rachel becomes furious. She reaches down, grabs the box, shoves it back into Robert's arms, and starts to tear into it.

RACHEL

When did you EVER experience mom not letting go?! Let's see...

Rachel pulls out framed pictures of Robert from years past.

RACHEL

Here she is not letting go of your senior picture!

Rachel throws the framed picture onto the hard floor of the entry hall. The frame breaks and glass shatters. She digs another picture out.

RACHEL

Here you are graduating from college!

Again, she throws the picture down and reaches in for another.

RACHEL

Here YOU are graduating from the academy!

She strikes the frame with her fist, cutting her hand. Still, she continues to rummage through the box. She randomly throws pictures out, adding her blood to the layer of broken frames and glass.

RACHEL

Here you are getting your Sergeant's shield! And, where am I?

She continues to dramatically empty the box's contents onto the floor before pulling out a yellowed newspaper clipping.

RACHEL

Ah, yes! Here I am!

She holds up an aged newspaper article and shoves it in Robert's face.

RACHEL

You know where she kept this?! Right over her bed! So every time I'd give in to her Irish Catholic guilt and visit, there was no possible way I could avoid being reminded.

She throws the newspaper on the ground.

RACHEL

Don't you EVER talk to me like we had the same upbringing! You were the pride of the Fitzpatricks! You made captain before you were forty! I was the embarrassment! The one whose name was whispered so no one would know I was part of the family!

Robert tosses the now-empty box onto the floor.

ROBERT

You're right. Mom was merciless. But she's dead, and it was twenty-two years ago. Don't you think you should move on?

Rachel is dumbfounded by Robert's levity.

RACHEL

Do me a favor and close your eyes. Go on! Close them!

Robert apprehensively closes his eyes.

RACHEL

Where does your mind go? What you're going to do on your day off? What you're going to eat next? Your inability to satisfy a woman?

Robert opens his eyes with an insulted expression.

RACHEL

Mine goes to the blood-covered face of a nine-year-old boy, lying dead on the ground. Now, you tell me how long it would be before you could ignore that image and MOVE ON?!

Rachel shakes her head, tired of the conversation.

RACHEL

Thanks for the stroll down Misery Lane, you can leave now.

Robert turns to leave but stops.

ROBERT

Ellie, you were screwed. It was so hard watching what they did to you. I should have come to your defense. I'm sorry.

Robert walks out and closes the door behind him. Rachel struggles with her boiling emotions. She kicks over the box left on the floor and storms out of the room.

NEIGHBORHOOD STREET - THREE HOURS LATER

Anne turns onto her street and finishes her run as Jill pulls her trash cans down her driveway.

JILL

Hey, Anne! How far did you go?

Anne does a cool-down walk over to Jill's driveway.

ANNE

Fifteen miles. I may have made a huge mistake signing up for this thing. I don't know if I'll be able to find the energy to go another eleven.

JILL

You'll be okay. You still have two months.

ANNE

Oh God! Is that all?!

Mary comes rushing out of her house and joins the women.

MARY

They found a match!

ANNE

Who is it?

MARY

I don't know. Diane said a donor matched preliminary markers. Whatever that means.

ANNE

It means more testing needs to be done before they can determine if the donor is a viable match.

JILL

That's encouraging.

MARY

Yeah, this is the first potential donor they've found.

ANNE

Does Rachel know?

MARY

No, she's not answering her phone.

JILL

Well, she's home. Her car is in her driveway.

RACHEL'S FRONT PORCH - CONTINUOUS

Mary, Jill, and Anne approach Rachel's front door.

Peering through the front window, Mary can see the aftermath of broken glass, splintered frames, pictures, newspaper clippings, and blood on the entry floor.

MARY

Oh my God!

Mary checks the doorknob, finds it unlocked, and slowly opens the front door.

RACHEL'S ENTRY HALL - CONTINUOUS

MARY

Rachel!

The women proceed cautiously across the dangerous floor.

JILL

What is all this?

ANNE

Maybe we should call the police.

MARY

And tell them what? We'd like to report a mess.

Anne points out the blood spots on the ground.

ANNE

That looks like blood.

The women continue to venture farther into the house.

RACHEL'S LIVING ROOM - CONTINUOUS

The women discover a disturbing scene of overflowing ashtrays, empty liquor bottles, and a vibrating cellphone dancing across the coffee table. Rachel is passed out cold on the couch with some sort of makeshift bandage around her hand.

MARY

It looks like the centerfold of Kamikaze Health magazine.

Anne goes to the couch and makes sure Rachel is still breathing.

JILL

Is she alive?

ANNE

Yeah, just passed out.

JILL

It's not even four o'clock yet.

Anne inspects Rachel's injury.

MARY

What happened?

Anne holds up Rachel's hand.

ANNE

It looks like she cut the back of her hand during whatever rock-star-fit she threw, and then tried to stop the bleeding by duct taping a beer koozie to her knuckles.

Rachel's phone vibrates across the table.

MARY

That's probably the mental institution letting her know her room is ready.

Mary picks up the phone and becomes horrified as she recognizes the incoming number.

MARY

No. No. No. No. No. NO! NO! NO!

JILL

Who is it?

Mary answers the phone.

MARY

(Apprehensively)

Hello?

Mary grimaces.

MARY

Yes.

Anne and Jill trade looks of confusion.

MARY

Yes, all right.

ANNE

Should you be answering that?

Mary waves off Anne and covers her exposed ear to hear better.

MARY

Yes, I will. Okay. Thank you. Goodbye.

Mary ends the call and tosses the phone onto Rachel's unconscious body.

MARY

Well, it's official. God hates me. Guess who the potential donor is!

JILL

(Clueless)

Who?

MARY

Who do you think?!

Mary dramatically points to Rachel.

MARY

The high priestess of self-destruction herself!

Jill and Anne unintentionally synchronize their heads as they turn to look at Rachel.

MARY

She needs to be at the hospital tomorrow morning for an interview and more blood work.

Mary surveys Rachel's condition. Her desperation grows.

MARY

What am I going to do? This is the only thing I can contribute to a daughter and grandson I'll never know. I can't believe it's in the hands of someone Charlie Sheen would find toxic.

JILL

It'll be okay, Mary. It's still early. She can recover by tomorrow morning.

Mary looks around and finds a glass half-filled with liquid. She picks it up and throws it in Rachel's face.

Rachel remains motionless.

JILL

Maybe they have an opening in the afternoon.

Mary's frustration begins to turn to anger.

MARY

She did this on purpose! I can't depend on her for anything!

JILL

What are you talking about? You answered her phone. She has no idea what's going on.

MARY

We're always excusing her bad behavior! She just manufactures misery so she can treat people like shit!

Anne tries to be the voice of reason.

ANNE

All right, Mary, this is just a stressful situation with some unexpected circumstances. Don't start saying things you don't mean.

Faced with the prospect of failing her daughter's only request, Mary abandons reason and begins to panic.

MARY

I do mean it! She is the most selfishly miserable person on Earth! Her only contributions to humanity are bitterness, sarcasm, and insults!

JILL

Now, just a minute. I think you're being way too hard on her. She has her good traits.

MARY

Name one!

Jill thinks for a moment.

JILL

She got me out of jail.

MARY

It was her advice that PUT you in jail!

JILL

She paid for my kitchen remodel.

MARY

After she set it on fire trying to light a cigarette with your toaster oven!

JILL

Our range did have burners that were quite difficult to ignite.

ANNE

Jill, stop helping.

MARY

She thinks she's the only one hurt by life! We've all felt unloved and unappreciated. Look at you, your husband was screwing someone else for months behind your back!

Jill's eyes widen at the mention of her painful history.

JILL

(Exasperated)

Why?

MARY

I'm just saying, you didn't wallow in self-loathing. You didn't spread your misery like an STD. You got a divorce, and you are trying to find happiness. Anne, you've got two teenagers, the greatest source of disrespect and frustration in the world, and you don't feel like everyone around you should share in your suffering. I'm struggling with the guilt from giving up a child.

Mary turns her accusations at a comatose Rachel.

MARY

We all have pain in our lives. We're all able to go on without taking it out on the world. What makes you think your pain is any greater than ours?!

ANNE

Enough, Mary. I know you're frustrated, but screaming at her while she's unconscious is pointless.

Mary takes a deep breath to calm down.

ANNE

Now, I think the best thing we can do is clean up this mess, let her sleep it off, and hope she's not obnoxiously hungover tomorrow.

Jill follows Anne back into the entry. Mary slowly inspects the scene of alcohol and nicotine overindulgence. She moves to the couch and quietly addresses Rachel's motionless body.

MARY

Why couldn't it have been Jill, or Anne, or anyone but you? You're so busy destroying yourself, you don't have time for anything else. I will never understand why you are the way you are. You do everything to show how strong and tough you are, but honestly, you're the weakest person I have ever known.

Mary's voice cracks as she fights back tears.

MARY

I hate that I have to count on you for this.

ANNE (FROM THE OTHER ROOM)

Mary!

Mary shakes her head in disgust before leaving Rachel and going into the entry hall.

RACHEL'S ENTRY HALL - CONTINUOUS

Jill and Anne are standing in the center of the mess, holding the newspaper clipping and a picture. Jill has tears forming in her eyes.

MARY

What? Did you find her parole paperwork?

ANNE

Not quite.

Anne hands Mary the yellowed newspaper clipping.

MARY

What's this?

ANNE

Read it.

Mary takes a deep, irritated breath and starts to read the headline aloud.

MARY

"Two Dead in Provoked Murder-Suicide."

Mary hands the newspaper back to Anne.

MARY

So what?

Anne pushes the newspaper back to Mary.

ANNE

Keep reading.

Mary rolls her eyes with annoyance as she moves the paper farther from her face to focus on the smaller print.

MARY

"The Chicago Police Department responded to a domestic violence call in the 1300 block of 65 St. in Englewood last Wednesday. Upon arrival, police found an active hostage situation. Officers were instructed to stand down and await negotiation teams. Reports indicate the initial officer on the scene ignored the order, entered the residence, and attempted to disarm the suspect. The situation ended when James Roth, Sr. shot and killed James Roth, Jr. before turning the gun on himself. Witnesses provided conflicting reports of the degree of danger Mr. Roth exhibited at the time the officer entered the apartment. Department officials said in a prepared statement that Officer Rachel Fitzpatrick claims her actions were motivated solely by the imminent threat the suspect posed to the hostage."

Mary looks up from the newspaper.

ANNE

Finish it.

MARY

"Neighbors who knew the suspect reported he was incapable of killing his 9-year-old son and voiced concern that it was Officer Fitzpatrick's entry into the residence that provoked the tragedy. Officer Fitzpatrick has been suspended without pay, pending an investigation."

Jill hands Mary a photo of Robert and Rachel embracing, dressed in Chicago police uniforms.

JILL

I found this.

Mary's demeanor humbles.

MARY

Oh my God.

Jill fights back tears.

JILL

I had no idea.

ANNE

None of us did.

MARY

Where did this stuff come from?

ANNE

I don't know.

Mary, still holding the picture and newspaper, sits down on the stairs.

MARY

This pretty much explains everything. Ever.

Jill starts moving toward Rachel.

JILL

I need to give her a giant hug.

Anne grabs her arm to stop her and brings her back.

ANNE

Don't you dare! She's gone to great lengths to keep this from us. You can't do something as out of character as HUG her. Conscious or not, she'll immediately know something's up.

MARY

So, what do you propose we do?

ANNE

Nothing.

JILL

Nothing?

ANNE

Let's clean this up, get her to bed, and forget we know any of this.

JILL

I don't know if I can forget this.

ANNE

You have to. And don't go asking Robert any questions about it either.

MARY

Robert?

ANNE

Jill's dating Rachel's brother.

MARY

(Flabbergasted)

What?! Are you trying to do everything you can to send her over the edge? She made it very clear she wanted us to have nothing to do with him. Probably because she was afraid we'd find out about this. Her frontal lobe is going to decorate the wall when she finds out.

ANNE

She's not going to find out. Not about this or Jill and Robert.

Anne grabs a broom out of the hall closet and hands it to Mary.

JILL

I'll go get a trash can.

ANNE
(Resolutely)
No. We'll put everything in that box and take it with us so there's no trace it was ever here.

MARY
She's going to remember going ninja assassin in here. She's going to wonder what happened to the carnage.

ANNE
Let her wonder. This won't be the first time we cover up her bad behavior and I doubt if it will be our last. You want to keep her frontal lobe intact? Keep your mouth shut.

The women start to clean up in silent agreement.

RACHEL'S BEDROOM - EIGHT HOURS LATER, NIGHT

Rachel wakes up in her bed, groggy and confused. She slowly gets out of bed and proceeds downstairs. As she enters the living room, she sees Kevin reading a book on the couch.

RACHEL
What time is it?

Kevin checks his watch without taking his attention away from his reading.

KEVIN
Quarter to midnight.

Rachel struggles to put the pieces of her afternoon together.

RACHEL
Have I been in bed all night?

KEVIN
You were there when I got home.

Rachel raises her hand to her head and notices a proper bandage dressing around her knuckles. She goes to inspect the spotless entry hall.

KEVIN
Mary called. She said you have an appointment with her in the morning. She'll pick you up at ten.

RACHEL (FROM THE OTHER ROOM)
Did you clean up in here?!

KEVIN
Clean up what?

Kevin's attention is finally pulled away from his reading as he hears Rachel's thundering footsteps racing back upstairs.

RACHEL'S MASTER BEDROOM CLOSET - CONTINUOUS

Rachel is frantically digging through the bowels of her closet. She shifts boxes and containers in an effort to locate the box Robert delivered.

She moves a heavily taped, square box to the front of the closet. After a few minutes, she ends her search baffled.

She raises her hand to her throbbing head and tumbles back into bed.

DOCTOR'S OFFICE - NEXT DAY, MORNING

Rachel and Mary sit waiting for the doctor. Rachel is hungover and impatient. Her disheveled appearance is complemented with dark sunglasses. Mary tries to hide her increasing anxiety level.

MARY
I can't thank you enough for doing this.

Rachel ignores Mary's gratitude. She fumbles with a cigarette box for a few moments before successfully getting one in her mouth.

RACHEL
Do you have a light?

MARY
Rachel, this is a hospital.

DR. GARCIA, a young, attractive woman in her early 30s, enters the room with a chart under her arm. Rachel pulls her sunglasses down the bridge of her nose to verify her age and appearance. Rachel dramatically rolls her eyes and pushes her sunglasses back up her face.

DR. GARCIA
I'm sorry to keep you waiting. I'm Dr. Garcia.

RACHEL

Do you have a light?

DR. GARCIA

This is a hospital.

RACHEL

Why does everyone keep saying that?

DR. GARCIA

You must be Mrs. Easton.

RACHEL

And you must be looking forward to getting your first period.

Mary loses her patience. She grabs the cigarette out of Rachel's mouth and rips the sunglasses off her face.

DR. GARCIA

And you're the patient's maternal grandmother?

MARY

Yes, but it's more complicated than that.

Dr. Garcia and Mary shake hands.

DR. GARCIA

Anything I need to know about?

MARY

Not really.

Dr. Garcia sits down, opens Rachel's chart, and begins to look over the results.

DR. GARCIA

Mrs. Easton, you have been identified as a preliminary match for a bone marrow recipient. Although hopeful, this in no way finalizes the process. There are several more tests we need to conduct as well as measure extenuating factors to determine your suitability as a donor.

MARY

(Concerned)

What extenuating factors?

DR. GARCIA

Should Mrs. Easton turn out to be a suitable donor, she would need to go under general anesthesia. Although a routine and relatively safe procedure, it does come with its risks. We would need to minimize those risks by addressing certain health-related behaviors.

Rachel continues her malcontented demeanor.

RACHEL

Before you continue, I have the mother of all hangovers. You don't have a little something that could take the edge off, do you?

Dr. Garcia patronizingly smiles.

DR. GARCIA

Mrs. Easton, this is a very serious and complicated procedure. I can't, in good conscience, consider you a candidate if it puts you in danger. And, after looking over all the information we have from your initial screening, I can say with a high degree of certainty that I've known hobos with better general health than you.

RACHEL

I don't believe you.

Dr. Garcia takes a very serious tone as she leans forward in her chair and reads over Rachel's chart.

DR. GARCIA

According to your own admission, your diet consists mainly of nicotine, alcohol, and caffeine. Your initial screening shows you have high blood pressure, high cholesterol, and elevated enzyme levels in your liver. You're borderline diabetic. And you're more than a few years older than the ideal candidate.

RACHEL

None of that proves you know a hobo.

DR. GARCIA

(Unamused)

And most importantly, you're not convincing me you have any real desire to be an active participant in the treatment of this patient.

Mary anxiously shifts in her chair while trading looks between Dr. Garcia and Rachel.

MARY
Can we have a moment alone please, doctor?

DR. GARCIA
(Aggravated)
Sure.

Normally the picture of professionalism, Dr. Garcia stands up in a frustrated pout.

RACHEL
Yeah, why don't you go get a juice box or something?

Dr. Garcia and Rachel glare at one another as Dr. Garcia leaves the room.

RACHEL
It's none of my business, Mary, but don't you think you should have hired a doctor familiar with the concept of pubic hair.

Mary squeezes her eyes shut and struggles to find the right words to impress upon Rachel how very important this is.

MARY
Listen to me. I've never asked you for a single thing in our entire friendship. I've put up with your insults, your tirades, your phone calls in the middle of the night looking for the phone that you are speaking through. I'm not saying you owe me, but God damn it, you owe me! You want me to beg, I'll beg. You want me to grovel, I'll grovel. Just please, please do this for me.

Rachel feels the desperation in Mary's plea and drops her charade of indifference. She becomes as sincere as she's capable of.

RACHEL
Mary, there's nothing I want more than to help this boy.

MARY
Really?

RACHEL
Yes, really.

MARY

Thank you! Thank you so much. I'll never ask you for another thing as long as I live!

Mary moves to put her arms around Rachel. She instantly reverts back to her sardonic self and throws up her arm to stop her.

RACHEL

You can thank me by lowering that skull-piercing voice of yours.

Mary retracts. A wave of relief blankets her entire body, as she sits back in her seat.

RACHEL

And that phone call thing only happened once.

A knock precedes Dr. Garcia's re-entry into the room.

RACHEL

Okay, Doctor Polly Pocket, let's pretend I end up being a match. What do I need to do?

Dr. Garcia takes a seat behind her desk.

DR. GARCIA

As I said, we still have several tests to run and that will take several weeks. What you need to do now is get healthy enough should the transplant proceed. You need to - immediately - stop smoking, stop drinking, increase your activity level, and focus on a well-balanced diet.

Rachel says nothing as she glares at Mary.

DR. GARCIA

You're going to have to resist every one of your natural impulses, but if successful, you'll play the vital role in saving this child's life.

BACK ALLEY RESTAURANT - LATER THAT EVENING

Rachel, Mary, Anne, and Jill are seated at a table. Caleb finishes delivering fresh non-alcoholic beverages to everyone. Rachel sits aloof and disengaged.

CALEB

Nice to see you ladies in here again.

Caleb smiles at Rachel as he walks away. Mary lifts her glass.

MARY

To Rachel! You've always been a thorn in my ass, but today, you're my needle in the haystack!

Anne and Jill enthusiastically raise their glasses while Rachel reluctantly lifts hers. They toast and drink.

ANNE

This is amazing. The odds are literally astronomical.

MARY

The doctor said Rachel needs to start preparing herself for the transplant. We've got to get her eating better and doing some regular exercise.

JILL

(To Rachel)

I have tons of recipes to make just about anything healthy. Name it, and I'll make it for you.

Rachel continues to sit silent.

MARY

What kind of exercise would be good for her?

Anne becomes wide-eyed and excited.

ANNE

I know...

Rachel prepares herself for a ridiculous suggestion.

ANNE

...she can work out with me while I train for the marathon.

Rachel dramatically rolls her eyes and pushes herself away from the table.

MARY

That's a great idea!

ANNE

It'll keep us both accountable.

MARY

It'll put her in a routine.

JILL
It'll get her out into the fresh air.

Rachel can't take the planning of her life any longer and walks away from the table.

RACHEL
Don't mind me, I'm just going to go step into oncoming traffic.

Rachel heads for the back door. Caleb notices her leaving and follows her.

BACK ALLEY RESTAURANT - CONTINUOUS

Once outside, Rachel takes a deep breath, exhales, and looks to the sky.

RACHEL
(Quietly)
Don't screw this up.

Caleb comes out of the back door and startles her.

CALEB
Oh, sorry, am I interrupting something?

Rachel smiles.

RACHEL
Just my daily mantra.

CALEB
I'll leave you alone.

Caleb turns to leave, but Rachel reaches out for him.

RACHEL
No.

Caleb stops and turns back around. Uncomfortable with Caleb's attention, Rachel folds her arms.

RACHEL
(Casually)
I mean, it's your bar. You can go wherever you want.

Caleb moves closer to her.

CALEB
You didn't look very happy in there.

Rachel shakes her head.

RACHEL
They're trying to be helpful.

CALEB
I was surprised when you walked in. You haven't been here in over a year.

Rachel lowers her head in humiliation.

RACHEL
Yes, well, it turns out they don't make greeting cards that say, "Sorry I molested you."

Caleb smiles then gently takes Rachel's hand from her defensive posture.

CALEB
No need to be sorry.

Rachel savors the unfamiliar feeling of her hand in someone else's.

CALEB
Do you want to talk about it?

Rachel suppresses her desires and gently pulls back her hand.

RACHEL
It's a boring story.

Caleb smiles and nods.

CALEB
Okay.

Caleb thoughtfully changes the subject.

CALEB
Oh, hey, I found out who Mrs. Robinson is.

RACHEL
What?

CALEB

Last time you were here, when you thought your friend had killed her husband, you said if we ever went out, you'd be Mrs. Robinson.

RACHEL

Not that it's critical to the story, but I thought she just shot him, not necessarily killed him.

Caleb smiles.

CALEB

My mistake. Did you know the woman who played Mrs. Robinson was only six years older than the actor she was seducing? That's not far off from you and me.

Rachel stares at Caleb with disbelief.

RACHEL

Why would you want to have anything to do with me?

Caleb thinks for a moment then speaks through a smile.

CALEB

Why wouldn't I?

Caleb takes Rachel and kisses her passionately. Rachel simultaneously engages in the kiss and softly pushes him away.

RACHEL

Caleb...

Caleb shows disappointment with Rachel's rejection.

CALEB

You're still married.

Rachel expresses her regret with a deep sigh.

RACHEL

Yeah.

Rachel's head drops under the weight of her ingrained Catholic guilt. Caleb takes a deep breath as he struggles to decipher Rachel's conflicting signals.

CALEB

Do you have your phone?

Rachel takes her phone out of her pocket and hands it to him.

CALEB

What's your passcode?

Rachel apprehensively stammers.

RACHEL

Uh... zero, seven, two, three.

Caleb brings his attention up from the phone.

CALEB

That's my birthday.

Rachel's eyes nervously shift as she tries to act surprised.

RACHEL

Is it?

Caleb contains a smile as he returns his attention to her phone. Rachel struggles to mask her anxiousness as she watches Caleb begin to push buttons.

RACHEL

(Under her breath)

Why wasn't I raised Methodist?

Caleb looks up from the phone.

CALEB

What did you say?

Rachel nervously smiles.

RACHEL

Nothing.

Caleb hands the phone back to Rachel. She reads his contact information as The Graduate's seduced character, "Benjamin Braddock."

CALEB

Just in case you find yourself in a situation wanting it.

Caleb puts his hands on Rachel's face and draws her in for one last kiss. He breaks their embrace and walks back into the restaurant. Rachel closes her eyes and longingly leans toward the space Caleb was occupying. She extends too far, stumbles forward and falls up against the closed door.

RUNNING STORE - THREE WEEKS LATER

Anne and Rachel enter a crowded running store. Several athletic people are browsing around and testing products. Rachel is very uncomfortable.

RACHEL
I had a vision of Hell once. It looked just like this.

ANNE
Don't embarrass me.

The women are approached by Katie, the enthusiastic sales associate.

KATIE
Hi. I'm Katie. Is there anything I can help you with today?

ANNE
Yes, Katie. You helped me find a pair of running shoes a few weeks ago, and I was hoping you could do the same for my friend.

Anne points to Rachel.

KATIE
Sure.

Katie cheerfully turns to Rachel.

KATIE
Have you ever been fit before?

RACHEL
(Annoyed)
Why? Is there some baseline conditioning that's required to engage in this sadistic sport?

Katie stands speechless and confused. Anne clarifies.

ANNE
Not physically fit, Rachel. Fit for running shoes.

Katie humbly nods in agreement.

RACHEL
Oh. No.

KATIE

Well, the right pair of shoes can make your run much more enjoyable.

RACHEL

Unless they effortlessly propel me forward, I guarantee my run won't be enjoyable.

Katie struggles to remain pleasant.

KATIE

Hey, now, don't underestimate the power of a good run. A brisk five-miler and a hot shower can make everything right in the world.

RACHEL

Really? I would say a winning lottery ticket and a ten-inch dick would make everything right in the world. Let's ask around and see what others think... the women, I mean.

Rachel points out a very effeminate man.

RACHEL

And that guy.

Katie gives up.

KATIE

Let me go get some options for you.

Rachel smirks as Katie leaves.

ANNE

You're an awful human being.

RACHEL

Three weeks without alcohol or cigarettes and now you're making me exercise. You're lucky I'm not randomly punching people in the throat.

ANNE

Yes, we should all thank you.

RUNNING PATH AROUND A SMALL LAKE - LATER

Rachel and Anne are running together along an asphalt-covered path. Anne is patiently running at a speed much slower than her normal pace. Despite Anne's attempts to remain supportive, Rachel begins to fall behind.

ANNE

You okay?

Rachel pants heavily.

RACHEL

(To herself)

I couldn't... hate you... more... if I tried.

Anne looks at her watch and calculates how much time she has.

ANNE

Rachel, I have to get twenty miles in. Do you mind if I run ahead and allow you to run at your own pace?

RACHEL

Are... you... joking?!

ANNE

I'll meet you back at the house!

Anne quickens her pace and the gap widens between them. She continues on the path and passes several Canadian geese nesting on the banks of the lake. Feeling threatened, the geese move closer to the path and take an aggressive position.

Rachel approaches the birds, expecting them to move, but instead they hiss, spread their wings, and charge her. Presented with the options of fight or flight, Rachel's instinct is the former. She starts cursing threats and wildly swinging her fists at the birds. The commotion gets the attention of Anne, as well as a park ranger patrolling the area.

ANNE

(To herself)

Of course.

Anne quickly runs back toward the interspecies rumble. The park ranger turns on his lights and siren.

RESTAURANT - THE FOLLOWING EVENING

Jill and Robert are seated across from each other, talking over a pre-meal glass of wine. It's obvious that they are enjoying each other's company very much.

JILL
Did you always want to be in law enforcement?

ROBERT
Oh yeah. Our dad was a cop. Didn't Ellie ever tell you that?

JILL
No, she didn't.

Robert's fondness for his father comes through his voice.

ROBERT
He was the best. Everyone loved him. He was like this giant, ginger teddy bear who protected the whole neighborhood. People rarely tried to mess with him, and if they did, he'd use his humor to resolve the conflict.

JILL
I wish I could have met him.

ROBERT
He would have liked you. He liked people who smiled easily.

Jill bashfully smiles.

JILL
What about your mom?

Robert's tone changes.

ROBERT
My mother? She didn't like anyone. She was the exact opposite of my dad. She was distant, unforgiving, and downright mean. She hated being married to a street cop and never let him forget it. She always wanted nicer things, and to move out of the neighborhood.

JILL
Sounds like she was a difficult person to get along with.

ROBERT
That's being kind. I never understood why my dad married my mother. Then I married a woman who turned out to be just like her.

JILL
Is it too early to ask why it ended?

Robert's comfort with Jill disarms his filter.

ROBERT
We tried to start a family, and that didn't go well. We both seemed to want different things and have different priorities. Everything went from bad to worse. Our conversations became more biting and accusatory. We both looked for reasons to stay away from home. I didn't want to live like that, so I talked her into going to counseling. One night, I came home early so we could drive to our session together. She wasn't home so I checked the voice mail. There were two messages. The first was her telling me she had to work late and wouldn't be able to make it. The second was thirty minutes of her having sex with a co-worker.

JILL
What?

ROBERT
She must have accidentally redialed our number, and the voice mail captured every auditory detail.

JILL
Robert, I am so sorry.

Robert shrugs his shoulders.

ROBERT
Don't feel too bad for me. It was what I needed to justify ending it.

JILL
Justify?

ROBERT
When you're raised in a strict Irish Catholic family, mild humiliation isn't enough to accept divorce. It has to reach a certain level of... egregiousness.

JILL

That definitely qualifies.

ROBERT

It worked out. I threw myself into work, got a few promotions, and now I'm sitting here with you.

Robert takes Jill's hand from across the table. Jill quickly gives in as he gently draws her closer. They kiss.

ANNE'S LIVING ROOM - SIMULTANEOUSLY

Mary walks right in the front door and looks around for Anne. The usual junk food and desserts are substituted with healthy snacks, vegetables, and fruit.

MARY

It's just me!

Anne walks in from the kitchen carrying bottles of water and cans of juice.

ANNE

Want one?

MARY

Anything with caffeine?

ANNE

Rachel's not supposed to have caffeine.

MARY

Fine. Give me this one.

Mary grabs a can of sparkling water. Anne sets the rest on the table.

ANNE

(Conspiratorially)

Okay, so before Rachel gets here, Jill's not coming. She's out with Robert.

MARY

What?! Again?

ANNE

I know.

MARY

We're pushing our luck. Rachel is vice-deprived and ready to snap. If she finds out...

Anne sits down on the couch.

ANNE

She won't find out.

MARY

What if she asks me?

ANNE

You were a professional actress, Mary. ACT like you don't know.

A knock at the door precedes Rachel letting herself in and walking into the living room.

RACHEL

Here!

Rachel tosses an envelope to each woman.

ANNE

What's this?

Rachel sits down.

RACHEL

They're invitations to Jennifer's wedding.

Rachel notices the healthy buffet.

RACHEL

What the hell is this?

ANNE

It's food.

RACHEL

That's your word, not mine.

Rachel looks around the room.

RACHEL

Where's Jill?

MARY

On a date.

Mary takes a seat and transforms into the working actress she once was.

RACHEL

She's been doing that a lot lately. Is this all the same guy? It's "FiveHourFootLong," isn't it?

Mary speaks in her tried-and-true soap opera tone.

MARY

Jill doesn't share the details of her love life with me.

Rachel's suspicions are piqued by Mary's seemingly scripted answer. She shifts her skeptical glare to Anne, who throws up her hands.

ANNE

She hasn't told me a thing.

Mary changes the subject.

MARY

How did your run go the other day?

ANNE

(To Rachel)

Do you want to tell her or should I?

MARY

What happened?

RACHEL

Nothing!

ANNE

Nothing?! Most people come away from a three-mile run with a sense of accomplishment. Rachel came away with a court date.

RACHEL

That goose was an asshole!

MARY

What?

ANNE
How long have you lived in Cincinnati?! All geese are assholes!

MARY
Oh my God, what did you do?

RACHEL
Nothing! I was minding my own business running, for you I might add, and a flock of those honking douchebags attacked me!

Mary's smile turns into a giggle, then into a belly laugh.

RACHEL
(Irritated)
Eat a dick, Mary.

Rachel gets up and goes into the kitchen. Mary shouts out after her.

MARY
I'm sorry! Come back! I want to hear how it ended!

ANNE
It ended with a ranger witnessing the melee and giving Rachel a ticket for harassing protected wildlife.

Rachel comes back into the room, eating straight from a jar of peanut butter.

RACHEL
If anyone was harassed, it was me!

Mary desperately tries to control her laughter.

MARY
So, who won?

ANNE
There were no winners.

Anne opens up the envelope.

ANNE
The wedding is May third?

RACHEL
Yeah, so?

ANNE
So, that's the day of the marathon.

MARY
What time does it start?

ANNE
Six-thirty, but I can't guarantee I'll be finished in time for a five o'clock wedding.

MARY
That's over ten hours. You really think it's going to take you that long?

ANNE
I make no promises.

RACHEL
I had nothing to do with picking the date. I've had nothing to do with any planning whatsoever. Paige has been very clear with her expectations of me.

MARY
And what are those?

RACHEL
Shut up and remember I'm not part of their family.

Mary and Anne are flabbergasted.

ANNE
She did not say that!

RACHEL
You're right. Her exact words were, "Don't think for a second you're going to have any meaningful role in this wedding."

MARY
Why would she be like that?

RACHEL
Because, Mary, tact and civility are foreign concepts to her. Much like a nose hair trimmer is to you.

MARY
You are the reigning authority on tact and civility.

ANNE

Jack has a baseball tournament that day too. Maybe I should just back out of the race.

RACHEL

Oh, no! You're not forcing me to do all this exercise crap and then backing out. You've seen a hundred of Jack's baseball games. Send Bill. Have him record the highlights. You're doing it!

COUNTRY ROAD - TEN DAYS LATER

Anne and Rachel are taking a brisk bike ride along a two-lane winding road. Anne is pulling away from Rachel as they begin climbing a steep hill. Anne begins to hear car horns behind her. The farther she travels up the hill, the louder and more frequent the horns become. She takes a quick look over her shoulder to see Rachel far behind, struggling to pedal up the hill. A line of cars is forced to wait as Rachel battles the grade and unsteadily drifts into the traffic lane. Anne unclips from her pedals, stops her bike, and watches the scene unfold. Rachel continues to struggle as she waves the cars to pass.

RACHEL

Go around me!

The cars continue their merciless honking. A DRIVER yells out the window.

DRIVER

Get off the road, slowpoke!

Rachel's fury is unleashed as she unclips from her pedals and drops her bike in the middle of the road. She takes off her helmet and hurls it at the windshield of the driver's car.

ANNE

Of course.

The driver watches in horror as Rachel takes off her bike shoe and uses the metal cleat to scratch the letters "B-I-T-C-H" into her hood.

RECREATIONAL LAKE - FOUR DAYS LATER

Rachel and Anne are in wetsuits, swim caps, and goggles, standing on the shore. Rachel's lack of enthusiasm is on full display with her crossed arms and clenched jaw. Mary floats in a kayak a hundred yards from shore.

ANNE

All right. We're going to swim out to Mary in the kayak. Don't worry about staying afloat because the wetsuit won't let you sink.

RACHEL

I'm not worried about sinking. I'm worried about the mythological-sized river creatures lurking underwater.

ANNE

There are no river creatures. You'll be fine. Just focus on your breathing and try to make it all the way out to Mary without stopping.

Anne leads Rachel into the water.

ANNE

You ready? Let's go.

They wade out to waist-deep water before both of them put their faces in the water and begin swimming. Anne pulls away from Rachel and swims out to Mary. Anne hugs the side of the kayak as they watch Rachel's progress.

MARY

She's doing well.

ANNE

Yeah, maybe we finally found an activity she'll do a second time.

Suddenly, Rachel stops swimming and starts frantically flailing about.

ANNE

Or not.

Rachel begins furiously yelling and smacking at her back.

RACHEL

Get it off me! It's on me!

Rachel swims as fast as she can toward shore, stopping occasionally to scream and thrash in the water. Anne glides effortlessly through the water, and Mary quickly paddles back to the shore.

Rachel climbs out of the water and continues to take swipes at her back.

RACHEL

It's still on me! I feel it! Get it off!

Anne rushes out of the water to aid Rachel.

ANNE

What is it?!

RACHEL

I don't know! I can feel it! Get it off!

Anne does a quick check of Rachel's body.

ANNE

There's nothing on you!

RACHEL

Yes, there is! It's back there! Get it off!

Anne looks on Rachel's back and grabs the long wetsuit zipper cord.

ANNE

You mean this!?

Mary beaches the kayak and jumps out.

RACHEL

What the hell is that?!

ANNE

It's your zipper! It came loose from the Velcro fastener!

Rachel stands silent and humiliated as her panic calms. Mary and Anne can't keep their smiles from turning into full-out laughter.

RACHEL

Screw you both.

Laughter continues as Rachel's phone sounds. Rachel reaches into the kayak and grabs her phone out of a backpack.

RACHEL

What?!

Rachel's face indicates the call is serious. Mary and Anne fall silent.

RACHEL

Yes.

Rachel fails to blink as she focuses on Mary.

RACHEL

I understand. Thank you.

Rachel ends the call.

MARY

(Apprehensively)

Who was that?

HOSPITAL ROOM - ONE WEEK LATER

Rachel sits up in a bed, primed for a trip to the operating room. Anne enters the room.

ANNE

How ya doing?

RACHEL

I don't know what's thinner, this gown or the toilet paper.

ANNE

Your catheter will eliminate the need for toilet paper.

RACHEL

(Sarcastically)

Oh goody.

ANNE

Did you tell your family you're here?

RACHEL

Why? So Paige can tell me to drop dead to my face? I'll be home before they miss me.

ANNE

You're going to be pretty sore. You may need some help getting around.

RACHEL

I'll manage.

Anne reluctantly nods.

ANNE

I won't be in the room during the procedure, but I know someone who will. She'll keep me updated on your condition.

Mary and Jill knock lightly and enter the room.

MARY

Hello.

Rachel rolls her eyes.

ANNE

(To Rachel)

I think they want to say something to you.

Rachel grabs Anne's arm.

RACHEL

(To Anne)

God, no, please. They're going to make this all sentimental and weird.

Anne gently pulls her arm away from Rachel.

ANNE

(To Rachel)

Let them.

Anne pats Mary on the shoulder as she exits.

MARY

How are you feeling?

RACHEL

(Aloof)

Fine.

Mary struggles to find the right words.

MARY

Rachel, I just want to tell you...

Rachel quickly interrupts.

RACHEL

Please don't.

MARY

Just let me say this.

RACHEL

(Irritated)

I really wish you wouldn't.

Mary's frustration bubbles over.

MARY

Just shut up for half a minute and let me talk!

Rachel sighs heavily and looks away from Mary.

MARY

Jesus, you're an asshole. And not just an average asshole, you're the most aggravating, obnoxious, abusive asshole ever...

Rachel raises her eyebrows as she looks back at Mary.

MARY

...and yet you're doing this incredibly selfless, generous thing.

Mary's voice begins to crack as her emotions well up.

MARY

I will never be able to express how grateful I am for everything you've done. I know it wasn't easy, and I love you for doing it.

Mary quickly turns and exits before Rachel can comment.

Jill approaches Rachel's bedside.

JILL

I'll be praying for you.

RACHEL

I don't believe in that, Jill.

JILL

I know you don't, but I do.

Jill smiles, takes Rachel's hand, and slips something into her palm.

A NURSE enters the room.

NURSE

Time for your catheter.

Jill lets go of Rachel's hand and turns toward the door. As Rachel watches Jill leave, she opens her fist and finds two dice. She squeezes them tightly in her hand.

The nurse holds up the catheter for Rachel's inspection.

NURSE

(Enthusiastically)

Are you ready?

RACHEL

It's been a while since I've spread my legs. You may need to have maintenance send up an auger.

HOSPITAL CORRIDOR - HOURS LATER

Mary nervously paces outside a waiting room. Jill exits a nearby elevator carrying two cups of coffee.

JILL

Here you go. Crazy Frank was down there claiming to be King of Condiment Island. I hope you don't mind, it's black.

Jill hands one cup to Mary.

MARY

Thank you.

JILL

Do we know anything?

MARY

Not yet.

Mary's attention is drawn to an anxious, middle-aged couple walking down the corridor. Mary hands her coffee back to Jill.

MARY

Jill, would you mind taking this into the waiting room. I'll be there in a minute.

Jill takes the coffee and heads toward the waiting room. Mary approaches NEIL and LAURA ENGLISH.

MARY

Excuse me. Are you Diane's parents?

LAURA

Yes.

Mary hangs her head for a moment before garnering the courage to continue.

MARY

I just wanted to tell you what a wonderful job you did raising Diane. She's a remarkable woman who loves you both dearly.

NEIL

Thank you.

LAURA

I'm sorry. Have we met?

MARY

(Reluctantly)

I'm Mary Pugh.

Neil and Laura realize Mary's identity. Laura silently steps toward Mary and, with a lifetime of gratitude, hugs her tightly. Their embrace is interrupted by Anne rushing up to Mary.

MARY

Is he okay?

Jill hears the commotion and rejoins everyone in the corridor.

ANNE

He's fine. They were able to complete the procedure.

Relief sweeps over everyone.

ANNE

But, Mary, Rachel suffered a cardiac event.

MARY

What do you mean a "cardiac event?"

HOSPITAL ROOM - HOURS LATER

Rachel is slowly waking up. Kevin and Jennifer are at her bedside.

KEVIN

Funny finding you here.

Rachel struggles to emerge from her anesthetized haze.

RACHEL

Huh?

Kevin is more irritated than sympathetic.

KEVIN

You can imagine my surprise when I got a call from the hospital telling me there was a problem with my wife, and I had no idea what they were talking about.

RACHEL

What WERE they talking about?

Dr. Garcia enters the room.

DR. GARCIA

I'm sorry. I didn't mean to interrupt.

KEVIN

It's fine. We were just leaving.

Kevin stands and leaves the room. Jennifer reaches out for Rachel's hand.

JENNIFER

You did an amazing thing. I'm so glad you're okay.

Jennifer stands up and follows her father out of the room.

DR. GARCIA

Nice family.

RACHEL

They're not mine.

DR. GARCIA

The procedure was successful. We've transplanted your bone marrow into the recipient and so far, things are looking good. We'll know more in the coming weeks. We had a little problem with you though. Your heart became quite erratic toward the end of the harvest. We were forced to use the paddles to shock it back into rhythm.

Rachel repositions herself in the bed.

RACHEL
Is that why I feel like I've been thrown from a speeding car?

DR. GARCIA
Nothing we did today will make you feel good. I'm ordering an EKG and we're keeping you overnight for observation. My guess is the radical change to your diet and lifestyle had more to do with it than anything. You could have just as easily had an episode walking down the street. We just want to be sure. Get some rest. I'll see you tomorrow.

Dr. Garcia turns and leaves the room as Anne enters.

ANNE
How ya feeling?

RACHEL
(Irritated)
Why did you call Kevin?

ANNE
I didn't call him, the hospital did. You listed him as the next of kin on your paperwork.

Rachel throws her head back onto her pillow in disgust.

DOWNTOWN CINCINNATI RIVER WALK - THE FOLLOWING EVENING

Jill and Robert leisurely walk hand in hand, enjoying the evening and each other's company.

JILL
So, what can you tell me about your new job?

ROBERT
I could tell you everything, but then I'd have to kill you.

JILL
Don't be specific.

ROBERT
Okay. No matter how sophisticated the crime, criminals always get caught by doing something really stupid.

JILL

Like what?

ROBERT

Like not realizing their cell phones are creating a digital roadmap to their crimes.

JILL

People do that?

ROBERT

Most actually. People sign up for these free apps that track locations, interests, and internet searches. It doesn't take long to put the pieces together.

Jill laughs.

ROBERT

Who needs the FBI when everyone volunteers for personal surveillance?

Jill lets go of Robert's hand and puts her arms around him.

JILL

I need the FBI.

Robert leans over and kisses Jill.

ROBERT

I leave for training tomorrow. I'll be gone until May.

Jill can sense the suggestive nature of Robert's voice.

JILL

May is only a couple weeks away.

Robert masks his disappointment with a smile, but Jill senses his frustration.

JILL

What?

ROBERT

Nothing.

Jill steps back.

JILL

Look, I'd be lying if I said I haven't thought about it, but things are complicated.

ROBERT

What's complicated?

JILL

My children, for one.

ROBERT

I love children. I've been looking forward to meeting yours since you told me you had them.

JILL

Rachel, for two.

Robert sighs heavily.

ROBERT

That will always be complicated.

JILL

Okay. How are we supposed to be together and keep her from vandalizing my... undercarriage?

Robert chuckles at Jill's characterization.

ROBERT

I don't know, but I promise I'll do everything in my power to protect your undercarriage.

Jill loses her battle to keep from smiling.

JILL

I just need a little more time to figure out how this is all going to work, okay?

ROBERT

Okay.

They kiss and continue their walk.

JILL'S LIVING ROOM - ONE WEEK LATER

A buffet of customary food and drink decorates the table. Mary, Anne, and Rachel are positioned in comfortable chairs while Jill delivers beverages to her guests.

RACHEL
There you are! I've missed you so much!

Rachel takes the alcoholic drink, cradles it in her palms, and speaks to it like an old friend.

RACHEL
You wouldn't believe what I've been through. They made me eat good and exercise and mean animals attacked me...

MARY
So, you have no desire to stick with clean living?

RACHEL
God, no. Why would you even ask?

MARY
Well, you did have a heart attack.

RACHEL
I did NOT have a heart attack. Anne, tell her it wasn't a heart attack.

ANNE
It wasn't a heart attack. It was as close as you can get to having a heart attack without actually having a heart attack, but no, it wasn't a heart attack.

MARY
So, it was like cardiac foreplay.

ANNE
Exactly.

RACHEL
My own vital organs refuse to go all the way with me.

Jill sits down.

JILL
We're just so glad you're all right. You have no idea how scared we were.

ANNE
What did Kevin say?

RACHEL

That egomaniac was more concerned about his image with the hospital receptionist than my well-being.

MARY

I saw Jennifer was there.

RACHEL

Yeah, given the sentiment of her family, her decency always amazes me.

JILL

(Hesitantly)

Did you tell Robert?

The mood suddenly takes a serious shift.

RACHEL

Why would I?

JILL

He's your brother. It's not out of the ordinary for people to share health scares with their family.

Mary sees the tension building.

MARY

Are you trying to give her another heart attack?

RACHEL

It was not a heart attack!

JILL

I just don't understand what he could have done that was so unforgivable.

Anne cringes and shakes her head.

ANNE

If you want to poke bears, Jill, I'll take you to the zoo.

Rachel remains uncharacteristically calm.

RACHEL

No, Anne, I'll answer her.

Rachel leans closer to Jill.

RACHEL

When someone puts their wants above another person's needs, that's unforgivable. Robert made it very clear where I fall on his list of priorities years ago. I will never share ANY aspect of my life with him again.

Jill nods with understanding as she retracts. Mary and Anne are shocked at Rachel's rational response.

MARY

Wow. Having a near-death experience really changed you.

RACHEL

I did not have a near-death experience, you blathering idiot! And if you say I did one more time, I'm going to rip out your tongue and shove it up your colon!

ANNE

There she is.

ANNE'S LIVING ROOM - MARATHON/WEDDING DAY, BEFORE DAWN

Anne nervously stands with her arms in the air as Mary safety pins the marathon bib on her shirt. Jill enters from the kitchen with a prepared bagel, banana, and water bottle.

JILL

Here you go.

Jill hands Anne her breakfast.

ANNE

I don't think I can eat.

Anne lowers her arms and takes the meal.

JILL

Is Rachel coming?

MARY

Jennifer asked her to stay and help her get ready.

JILL

That was nice of her.

Mary finishes.

MARY

There! You're ready to go.

Anne bends at the waist, drops her food onto a nearby table, runs to the bathroom, and slams the door.

MARY

That's the third time this morning.

JILL

Do you think it's just nerves?

MARY

Yeah, I used to get the same way before every audition.

JILL

Since we have a minute...

The toilet flushes.

MARY

Or more.

JILL

Can I get your opinion on something?

MARY

Always.

JILL

Do you think I should end things with Robert?

MARY

What?! Why? Has something happened I don't know about?

JILL

No. Things couldn't be better. It's just that, with Rachel's animosity toward him, we can never truly get serious.

MARY

Are you sure that's why you're considering breaking up?

JILL

Of course. Why else would I end a relationship with the most amazing man I've ever met?

MARY

Listen to yourself.

The toilet flushes again.

MARY

Is it really because of Rachel? Or is it because you know what the inevitable next step is?

Jill hushes Mary.

MARY

Jill, you've got to drop this puritanical attitude toward sex. You've been dating a few months, he's all you ever talk about, and I've never seen you happier. Not to sound like an athletic ad, but just do it.

JILL

That's so easy for you to say. I've never been with anyone besides John. There was always a very consistent sequence of events I could expect.

The toilet flushes again.

MARY

God, I feel sorry for you. Okay, fear of him introducing some bizarre Kama Sutra position aside, do you want to sleep with him?

JILL

What's karma hookah?

MARY

Kama Sutra. Never mind. Forget I brought that up. Do you want to?

Jill takes a deep breath.

JILL

Yes, but...

MARY

No buts. All you have to do is let it happen. Things will progress naturally. Stop thinking so much, you'll be fine.

JILL

You sure?

MARY

I'm sure. It's like riding a bike, just jump on and enjoy the ride.

Anne emerges from the bathroom pale and sweaty.

MARY

Demon exorcised?

ANNE

I don't know what's wrong with me.

MARY

You're expected to run over twenty-six miles today. The thought makes my intestines liquefy, and I'm just standing on the curb with a cowbell.

Anne takes a deep breath and gathers her things. The three walk out of the front door.

ANNE'S LIVING ROOM - EIGHT HOURS LATER

The front door bursts open. Mary and Jill carry Anne into the house. Anne is sunburnt, crusty with dried sweat, and exhausted. They take her into the living room and sit her down on the couch. The weight of Anne's finisher medal hanging around her neck pulls her face down into the cushions.

MARY

You did it! How do you feel?

Anne speaks with her face buried between cushions.

ANNE

(Muffled)

Like I've pissed off every muscle in my body.

JILL

Are you going to be able to make it to the wedding?

Anne slowly sits up.

ANNE

I honestly don't know. I have aches where I've never felt aches before. I swear, pain is radiating out of my spine into what feels like a tail.

Mary's phone rings.

MARY

What is it, Ethan?

Loud arguing can be heard as Mary pulls the phone away from her ear.

MARY

All right! Tell him to stop! I'll be home in a minute!

Mary hangs up.

MARY

I'm sorry, Anne. I've got to get home and save the dog.

Mary bends down and hugs Anne.

MARY

Congratulations. We are so proud of you.

Anne can only gratefully lean into Mary's embrace.

ANNE

Thank you so much for all of your help today. I wouldn't have been able to do it without you.

Mary turns to leave.

MARY

That's not true. You would have rocked that run with or without us. I'll see you in a few hours.

ANNE

I'll make sure Jack goes over as soon as he gets home.

Mary's phone rings again as she walks out of the front door.

MARY

I'm looking right at you, Charlie! Stop putting chip clips on his ears! He's going to bite you!

Jill checks her watch.

JILL

I should get going myself.

ANNE

Can I ask you to do one more thing before you go?

JILL

Of course.

ANNE

Can you help me get to the bathroom?

JILL

Sure.

Jill positions herself in front of Anne and helps her up. Anne can't help but grimace as she straightens her legs and stands.

ANNE

Oh God. That was so hard.

Jill helps Anne into the bathroom and positions her near the toilet.

JILL

Can you manage it from here?

ANNE

I think so.

Jill closes the door and stands outside. She overhears Anne's moans and groans as she checks the messages on her phone. Robert has sent several texts asking about her projected arrival time. Jill becomes more anxious with every passing moment. Finally, she turns and speaks to the closed door.

JILL

Anne! If you don't need me anymore, I'm going to go get ready for the wedding, okay?

After a few moments of silence, Jill hears soft sobs coming from inside the bathroom.

JILL

Anne, are you okay?

ANNE (THROUGH THE CLOSED DOOR)

No.

JILL

Oh honey, what's wrong?!

ANNE

I can't stand.

JILL
What can't you stand?

ANNE
I can't stand! I'm stuck on the toilet and I can't straighten my legs!

JILL
Okay. Do you want me to come in and help you?

ANNE
I don't think I have a choice.

Jill opens the bathroom door.

ANNE'S BATHROOM - CONTINUOUS

Jill tries to help Anne feel less embarrassed as she bends down and helps her to her feet.

JILL
Need help with your shorts?

ANNE
(Mortified)
Yes.

Jill does her best to preserve Anne's dignity. She keeps her head turned away as she bends down, grabs Anne's shorts, and lifts them to her waist.

ANNE
I don't know what I'd do without you.

Jill checks her watch.

JILL
Will Bill be home soon to help you get ready?

Anne silently shakes her head as the pain and her predicament force tears down her face.

ANNE
We didn't know when Jack's tournament would end. We planned to meet at the church. I had no idea I would be this helpless.

Jill checks her watch again.

ANNE

Just go. I don't want you to miss anything.

Jill surveys the situation, takes a deep breath, and pulls out her phone.

ANNE

What are you doing?

JILL

I'm just letting Robert know I'll meet him at the wedding.

ANNE

I'm sorry for ruining your plans.

JILL

You didn't ruin any plans. Now, come on, let's go upstairs and get you cleaned up.

ANNE

(Pathetically)

Not stairs.

Jill supports Anne as the two exit the bathroom and slowly make their way upstairs.

ANNE'S BEDROOM - ONE HOUR LATER

Bill hastily enters his bedroom while calling out for Anne. He is brought to a silent standstill when he hears the shower running and two female voices in his bathroom.

ANNE (THROUGH THE DOOR)

I can't believe it took you forty-five minutes to get me into the shower. Thank you for being so gentle.

Bill quietly moves closer to hear more clearly.

JILL (THROUGH THE DOOR)

I know you're full of regret, but you did it. You can stop wondering if you're capable of it.

Anne speaks through painful moans.

ANNE

Promise me you won't tell anyone I was this bad.

JILL

I just hope the hot water will help you feel better. I was surprised at how hard it was to get you out of your clothes.

Bill's eyes widen.

ANNE

I think this officially takes our friendship to a new level.

JILL

I put the shower head on massage. If it's too hard, I can make it softer.

Anne's moans intensify as her sore muscles are massaged by the shower head.

ANNE

No, it's perfect. Thank you for talking me into this.

JILL

I don't know if you want Bill to know you were this dirty. He may never look at you the same way again.

Bill silently loses his mind.

ANNE

(Lost in pleasure)

Bill who?

Jill walks out of the bathroom carrying Anne's dirty running clothes and runs into Bill.

JILL

Bill! You're home.

Bill tries to mask his flustered demeanor.

BILL

Jill! Hi! I just walked in. How are you? What are you doing up here?

Jill doesn't understand Bill's unhinged behavior.

JILL

I'm taking your wife's running clothes down to the laundry.

BILL

Running clothes?

Bill continues to act oddly.

JILL

She ran the marathon today.

BILL

Oh yeah, the marathon! How'd she do?

JILL

She finished! She's in a lot of pain though. I stuck around to help her get upstairs and into the shower.

BILL

Oh, thanks.

JILL

Now that you're home, I'll let her tell you all about it.

Bill awkwardly laughs.

JILL

I'll drop these off on my way out. See you at the wedding.

Bill wipes the sweat off his forehead as he watches Jill walk out. He rushes to the bathroom. Anne is motionless, enjoying the water stream of her shower.

Bill opens the shower door and startles Anne.

BILL

Was Jill in here helping you take a shower?!

ANNE

What?

BILL

Just tell me if that really happened!

ANNE

Yes, that happened, but I assure you there was nothing sexy about it.

Bill holds up his hand to stop her from continuing.

BILL
Don't say another word. I'll fill in the blanks, myself.

Bill shuts the shower door.

CHURCH VESTIBULE - DUSK

Mary and Craig socialize with Jill as guests arrive at the church.

MARY
You should have come and got me. Craig could have hosed down the boys.

CRAIG
So, you undressed Anne, then helped her take a shower...

Mary decides to torture her husband a little more with a seductive extension of his fantasy.

MARY
Didn't you say you tried a sponge bath before the shower, but you used too much soap and the sponge kept slipping all over her body?

Craig's interest in the story is brought to an abrupt end by the evil smirk that spreads across Mary's face.

CRAIG
Why do you have to ruin everything?

Jill bashfully corrects Craig's impression.

JILL
I'm sorry, Craig, but I only helped her INTO the shower. She was able to manage everything from there.

Robert enters the vestibule and approaches the trio.

MARY
Bobby, right? You're Rachel's brother.

ROBERT
Actually, it's Robert.

MARY
My apologies, Robert. I'm Mary Hueston and this is my husband, Craig.

The guys shake hands.

MARY
And this is Jill. I think you two spoke at your mom's funeral.

Jill goes along with the charade.

JILL
Hello.

Robert also plays along.

ROBERT
Nice to see you again.

MARY
How did you snag an invitation to this?

ROBERT
Kevin invited me.

Mary nods.

MARY
Well, if you're looking to avoid your sister, I know she'll be in the family gathering area until she's escorted down for the ceremony. Which gives you...

Mary looks down at her watch.

MARY
...thirty minutes.

Jill immediately exits with Robert following behind.

CRAIG
What was that all about?

MARY
Jill and Robert have been dating against strict instructions from Rachel not to. Jill has finally accepted the fact that it's time to take the relationship physical and was probably going to this afternoon until her impromptu episode of Three's Company got in the way. So, since they won't be able to go anywhere near each other once this party starts, they're taking advantage of the next thirty minutes.

CRAIG
Why does Rachel care if Jill goes out with her brother?

MARY
That's personal, Craig. I can't tell you that.

CRAIG
What the hell do you call everything you just told me?

MARY
(Dismissive)
That's just bunco stuff.

CHURCH FAMILY GATHERING ROOM - CONTINUOUS

Rachel, Kevin, Paige, and Jennifer are taking pictures and mingling with the rest of the wedding party. Kevin steps away from the women.

JENNIFER
Paige, did you get mom's sixpence?

PAIGE
No, I thought you got it.

RACHEL
What are you asking about?

PAIGE
Nothing that concerns you.

JENNIFER
It's an English tradition to put a sixpence coin in your shoe on your wedding day. My mother saved hers for us to use. I can't believe I'm going to get married without it.

RACHEL
Where do you think it is?

JENNIFER

I know exactly where it is. It's with mom's things in a taped-up square box in your bedroom closet.

RACHEL

I'll go get it.

JENNIFER

Oh, thank you, Rachel.

PAIGE

No, she won't. I'm the maid of honor. It's our mother's sixpence. I'll go get it.

JENNIFER

Paige, what difference does it make?

RACHEL

It's fine, Jennifer. She's right. It's your family tradition. She should take care of it.

Rachel steps away as Paige receives more instructions.

PAIGE

Is it just loose in there?

JENNIFER

No, it's in mom's jewelry box.

PAIGE

Got it! Master bedroom closet, mom's jewelry box, square taped-up box. I'll be right back.

Paige gets Kevin's attention.

PAIGE

Dad, where are your keys?

KEVIN

Rachel drove.

Paige crosses the room and begrudgingly appeals to Rachel.

PAIGE

(Insincerely)

May I have your car key, please?

Rachel forces a pleasant smile.

RACHEL

I leave it inside. Just get in and drive.

Paige dramatically exits the room.

CHURCH SANCTUARY - CONTINUOUS

Bill is talking with Craig as he helps Anne slowly navigate the aisle and pews.

BILL

Thank God I decided to come home and change. It was like every plot to every adult film ever produced was going on in my bathroom.

ANNE

I can't believe you two find this so arousing.

The three take their seats in the pews.

BILL

It's not just us. Ask any man with a pulse and he'll tell you how erotic that scene was.

ANNE

Boys, I assure you, there was nothing erotic when she was helping me take my sports bra off. It was like trying to untangle two uncooperative jellyfish out of a fisherman's net.

BILL

Wait, you didn't tell me she took off your bra!

ANNE

(Appalled)

Bill, I wish you'd realize that the price for this fantasy of yours is what little dignity I have left.

BILL

There's no place for dignity in fantasy.

ANNE

(Agitated)

I am your wife!

Bill speaks through a laughing smile.

BILL

That's what makes this so hot.

RACHEL'S BEDROOM CLOSET - MOMENTS LATER

Paige enters the closet and begins searching quickly through the boxes stacked up on the floor. She comes to a heavily taped square box and breaks it open. She finds a small wooden box like the one described by Jennifer. She opens the box to find it's filled with handwritten letters.

She pauses a moment to read the top page. Her frenzy to find her mother's sixpence dulls as she continues to examine the papers. Each letter is addressed to "My love" and signed "Forever Yours, Jason." Every page contains details of an explicit love affair, and her anger grows more intense.

She stuffs the letters back into the box, gets up, and storms out of the closet.

CHURCH FAMILY GATHERING ROOM - MINUTES LATER

Rachel, Kevin, Jennifer, and the bridesmaids are congregated, waiting for Paige's return. Jennifer takes the opportunity to share a private moment with her father.

JENNIFER

Dad, I just want to tell you how happy I am, and it's all because of you. You got me through some rough times, and I don't think I could have made it without you. I love you so much.

Jennifer warmly embraces her father.

KEVIN

I wish your mom was here to see what a beautiful woman you've become.

Jennifer smiles through watery eyes.

JENNIFER

She is.

Kevin pulls out his handkerchief and dries the tears forming on her eyelids. The touching moment forces Rachel to wipe away her own tears. Mary enters the room.

MARY

How's everybody doing? You almost ready?

JENNIFER
We're just waiting for Paige. Are people getting restless?

MARY
This day is yours. They can wait.

Mary notices Rachel's glassy eyes and stands closer to her.

MARY
(Quietly)
Why Mrs. Easton, you never struck me as the type to get misty at weddings. That cardiac event softened you.

Rachel sniffs and turns her face toward the wall.

RACHEL
You make nothing better.

Paige storms into the room, carrying the wooden box in her hand.

JENNIFER
Did you find it?

Rachel's attention is drawn toward Jennifer's question. Synchronously, Paige hurls the wooden box at Rachel's head. The contents of the box scatter wildly as the box hits Rachel on her temple and sends her to the floor.

CHURCH PEWS - SIMULTANEOUSLY

Bill and Anne are seated in the pews waiting for the ceremony to begin. Anne hears the commotion from the back of the church. She sighs heavily and shakes her head.

ANNE
(Quietly)
Of course.

Anne slowly and gingerly starts to inch her way toward the source of the clamor.

BILL
Where are you going?

ANNE
With the history of this group, what are the chances that was an accident?

Bill closes his eyes while shaking his head.

BILL

You'd better hurry.

Anne painfully makes her way out of the pew.

CHURCH FAMILY GATHERING ROOM - SIMULTANEOUSLY

Rachel struggles to remain conscious as Mary bends down to give her aid.

KEVIN

Paige!

PAIGE

She's been cheating on you for years, dad! I found these hidden in a box in your closet!

Paige scoops several of the pages off the floor and throws them at Rachel.

PAIGE

She's been screwing some guy named Jason since before you even got married!

Mary looks to Kevin to intervene.

MARY

(Quietly)

Say something.

Kevin stands silent. Paige continues her attack as she hovers over Rachel.

PAIGE

I never trusted you! You're a liar and a whore! I want you out of this wedding and out of our lives!

KEVIN

That's enough, Paige!

Rachel uses assistance from Mary to get to her feet. She silently trades looks between a horrified Jennifer and a terrified Kevin.

PAIGE

Get out.

Rachel reaches up to her temple and draws back blood. After taking a moment to evaluate the situation, she unceremoniously walks out of the door. Mary flashes Kevin a look of disgust as she hurries to follow Rachel.

CHURCH VESTIBULE- CONTINUOUS

Anne is slowly making her way through the hall when she sees Rachel escape into the closest private space. Mary follows behind. Anne desperately, but not effectively, hurries to follow them.

CHURCH PRIEST QUARTERS - CONTINUOUS

Anne enters. Rachel is standing with her back to the room, near the Priest's desk. Mary tries to coax Rachel to turn toward her.

MARY
Please turn around!

RACHEL
Mary, just leave me alone.

Anne notices blood on Rachel's clothes and on the floor.

ANNE
What the hell happened?!

RACHEL
Jesus, Anne! Go back to your seat!

ANNE
Why is there blood on your clothes?

RACHEL
I popped a zit, okay. Will both of you just get out of here!

Anne wobbles over to Rachel and turns her around. The laceration on her temple is now swelling.

ANNE
Oh my God! What happened?!

MARY
That psychotic, spoiled brat found the love letters written to Kevin, and she thinks they were addressed to Rachel. Paige clocked her with a wooden box!

RACHEL
I'm fine.

ANNE

You are not fine!

MARY

Why did you let her do that?!

Rachel becomes more belligerent.

RACHEL

She came at me from behind, Mary! What was I supposed to do?! I don't have eyes in the back of my skull!

MARY

I'm talking about what she said!

Rachel spies the priest's stole hanging next to her. She grabs it, turns to a mirror on the wall, and begins using it as a blasphemous bandage.

ANNE

You need to have that looked at.

Rachel ignores Anne and continues in the mirror.

MARY

And Kevin just stood there! He didn't say a word!

ANNE

I'm serious, Rachel. At the very least, you have a concussion. You may even need stitches.

Rachel continues her self-diagnosis.

RACHEL

Anne, I'm fine.

MARY

Why didn't you say something?! Do something?! Of all the fights in your life, this was the most justified, and you walked away! Why?!

Rachel continues with her back to Mary and Anne.

RACHEL

I don't owe you an explanation, Mary.

MARY

God damn it, Rachel! I've been knocked around trying to pull you out of brawls! I've been embarrassed apologizing to bystanders! I've risked jail time making up countless cover stories! You DO owe me an explanation!

ANNE

Can we talk about this on the way to a hospital?

Rachel turns around and leans into Mary.

RACHEL

I've literally given you the blood from my veins, Mary! I find it comical that you think I owe you something!

Rachel pushes Mary away from her in anger.

MARY

You're unbelievable! You'll start a fight with a mindless goose, but when it's actually called for, you cower away!

ANNE

Back off, Mary!

Anne tries to calmly reason with Rachel.

ANNE

Rachel, you have a serious head injury! You need to be looked at by a doctor.

RACHEL

It's just a bump on the head.

Anne finally loses her patience.

ANNE

Of course! I forgot about ALL your first aid training! You know exactly what to do! Let me just take a look around here - I'm sure we'll have no problem finding a beer koozie and duct tape!

As the words leave Anne's mouth, she regrets them. Rachel's memory is jogged, and a quickening blend of enlightenment and fury spread across her face.

RACHEL

It was you.

Anne desperately looks to Mary for guidance.

ANNE
(Nervously)
No, it wasn't. I don't know what you're talking about. Let's go back to Mary taking the blood out of your veins.

Rachel processes the uncomfortable body language of both Anne and Mary.

RACHEL
Is there anything ELSE you two have been keeping from me?

The tension is broken by the door bursting open. Rachel, Mary, and Anne stand stunned as Jill and Robert tumble into the room, simultaneously undressing each other and passionately kissing. The couple falls onto a couch, in passion, while oblivious to the occupants in the room. Rachel is outraged when she identifies the amorous pair.

RACHEL
Are you fucking kidding me?!

Jill and Robert freeze at the sound of Rachel's voice. Rachel storms out of the room in disgust.

CHURCH PARKING LOT - CONTINUOUS

Rachel abandons her makeshift bandage on the ground as she abruptly walks to her car. Kevin emerges from the church and chases Rachel down.

KEVIN
Rachel! Wait!

Rachel continues on her path to the car.

KEVIN
Rachel! Please!

Rachel arrives at the car as Kevin catches up to her.

RACHEL
(Annoyed)
What do you want, Kevin?

Kevin takes a minute to catch his breath.

KEVIN

Are you okay?

RACHEL

Believe it or not, having a box thrown at my face was the least offensive sucker punch I've received in the last five minutes.

KEVIN

I'm sorry about Paige.

Rachel dishearteningly shrugs her shoulders.

RACHEL

Secrets have casualties.

An awkward moment passes while Kevin musters the courage to continue.

KEVIN

How did you...?

RACHEL

You suck at hiding things, Kevin. You're a wealthy man - safety deposit boxes are cheap.

Kevin hangs his head.

KEVIN

They should know.

Rachel takes a deep breath and sighs heavily.

RACHEL

Not today. This is Jennifer's wedding day. She shouldn't have to look back and remember it as the day her father came out.

Kevin lowers his head.

RACHEL

Wait for Paige's wedding day.

They share uncommon smiles with each other.

KEVIN

So, now what?

RACHEL

I think my public humiliation serves as the perfect exit strategy, don't you?

Kevin amicably nods.

KEVIN

I don't know how to thank you.

RACHEL

I'm sure my attorney will think of a few ways.

KEVIN

Anything you want.

Rachel opens her car door.

KEVIN

What are you going to do?

RACHEL

I have no idea.

KEVIN

You're pretty banged up. You sure you're going to be okay by yourself?

Rachel says nothing as she gets into her car and drives away.

RACHEL'S CAR - TEN MILES DOWN THE ROAD

Rachel is deep in thought, driving along a tree-lined country road. She checks her injury in the rearview mirror and returns her attention to the road.

A deer jumps out from the bushes and forces her to swerve dramatically across the road. She loses control and slams into a tree.

COUNTRY ROAD - MOMENTS LATER

The deer is in the middle of the road unharmed. Rachel's car is damaged but running. Rachel fights to maneuver around the deployed airbag. A voice speaks through the car's speakers.

EMS

Mrs. Easton, this is Emergency Monitoring Services. We have detected an airbag deployment in your vehicle. Do you require medical assistance?

Rachel's frustration grows as she continues to wrestle with the airbag.

RACHEL

No!

Rachel sees the deer staring at her from across the road.

RACHEL

Are all you woodland gremlins in it together? This must be hilarious for you!

EMS

No ma'am. Your safety is not a laughing matter.

RACHEL

I was talking to someone else!

EMS

Is there someone else in your vehicle, Mrs. Easton?

RACHEL

No! I'm talking to the giant rodent mocking me from across the road.

EMS

So, there IS someone with you?

Rachel is distracted by her continuing battle with the airbag, cursing the automobile's exemplary safety features.

RACHEL

No! There's no one!

EMS

I'm sorry, Mrs. Easton, can you repeat that?

RACHEL

I have no one!

Rachel stops her fight with the airbag and silently reflects on the words just spoken.

EMS

Do you have someone in your contacts you'd like me to call, Mrs. Easton?

Rachel remains in silent thought.

EMS

Mrs. Easton?

RACHEL'S DRIVEWAY - THREE HOURS LATER, EVENING

Mary and Jill help Anne as they slowly make their way past Rachel's damaged car and up to her front porch.

MARY

This isn't a good sign.

ANNE

At least she made it home.

JILL

I don't know what I'm going to say to her. I've never been so ashamed in my entire life.

MARY

You should be.

Jill is insulted and mocks Mary's previous advice with a northern accent.

JILL

What?! You told me to "just let things happen!"

MARY

And you decide to act on that in God's house?

JILL

At least I didn't give her a heart attack.

MARY

It wasn't a heart attack!

ANNE

Stop it, you two! We ALL did things we shouldn't have, and we ALL need to apologize! And I don't care if she verbally abuses us all night, we aren't leaving here until she understands how sorry we are.

The three agree as they arrive at the porch. Anne takes a deep breath and rings the doorbell. A great deal of commotion is heard from the inside, then silence. After some non-verbal debate, Mary knocks on the door.

The sound of the door unlocking prompts them all to step back. Rachel finishes tying her robe as she angrily opens the door.

RACHEL

What?!

The severity of Rachel's bruise is apparent as she steps into the porch light.

ANNE

Jesus! It looks like you have an eggplant on the side of your face.

Rachel quickly glances back inside the door and checks herself in an entry hall mirror.

RACHEL

It looks worse than it is. What do you want?

ANNE

We came to apologize.

RACHEL

Fine. Apology accepted. Go away.

Rachel tries to shoo them off her porch.

MARY

No, Rachel, you've done so much for us, and we were wrong to go through your personal things.

RACHEL

(Hastily)

It's fine. All's forgiven. Really.

JILL

I never should have let myself become involved with Robert. I won't be seeing him anymore.

RACHEL

Screw his brains out. Commit every carnal sin you can think of. I don't care.

Rachel pulls herself back inside and tries to shut the door. Anne raises her hand to prevent the door from closing.

ANNE

Are you sure you're okay? This is not the reaction we were expecting.

Mary looks past Rachel and into the house. She notices Caleb descending the stairs while pulling his shirt over his head.

MARY

Something tells me she's had a change of heart... and underwear.

Caleb walks up behind Rachel.

CALEB

Good evening, ladies. How was the wedding?

The women respond with wide-eyed silence. Caleb puts his hands on Rachel's shoulders and kisses her on the back of the head.

CALEB

Rachel, I'm getting you some fresh ice for your head.

Rachel directs a smile of self-satisfaction at her friends.

RACHEL

Anything else?

The women stand speechless as Rachel slowly pushes the door shut.

RACHEL

See you at bunco.

The door closes.

END OF ROUND 3

ROUND 4

Advancing to the Head Table

TEN MONTHS LATER

UPSCALE RESTAURANT - DAY

Rachel sits alone at a table. The ethereal atmosphere is complemented with a classical pianist in the corner and servers thoughtfully tending to guests. She sips the beautifully prepared drink in front of her. Her peaceful surroundings are interrupted by the MAITRE D' escorting Jill to the table.

Jill cheerfully takes a seat across from Rachel.

JILL
Thank you for meeting me here. I know this has all come at you pretty fast.

Jill speaks through her pageant-winning grin.

JILL
It's come at all of us pretty fast. I just can't believe how happy I am.

Jill allows the maître d' to take the napkin from the table and drape it across her lap.

JILL
(To the maître d')
Thank you.

MAITRE D'
You're welcome, madam. Ladies, your waiter will be here in a moment.

The maître d' leaves as Jill picks up a drink sitting in front of her. The large diamond ring on her engagement finger catches the light.

JILL
Rachel, you've been the absolute best friend in all of this. It means so much to have your support.

Rachel silently stares across the table at Jill.

JILL
Meeting Robert is the most wonderful thing that's ever happened to me. I never realized how considerate and thoughtful a man can be.

Rachel removes a cigarette from a sophisticated case and lights it.

JILL

After everything that's happened, you've really shown how kind and forgiving you can be. Robert and I are so impressed with the way you're handling everything.

Rachel remains quiet as she takes a long drag off her cigarette and blows the smoke in the air above her. The WAITER approaches the table.

WAITER

Are you ready to order?

JILL

(To the waiter)

I'll need another minute, thank you.

As the waiter leaves the table, Jill gleefully opens the menu and begins to peruse the selections. Rachel continues to smoke her cigarette while staring intently at Jill.

JILL

So many choices... I guess I should stick to something healthy since I'll have a wedding dress to fit into soon.

Rachel sits back, calmly snubs out her cigarette on her bread plate, and offers a snide grin. Jill puts down her menu and returns a sincere smile.

Rachel responds by lunging across the table and wrapping her hands around Jill's throat. The table settings crash to the ground as Rachel leans into Jill and topples her backward in her chair. Rachel never loosens her grip as the table turns over and both women tumble to the floor.

RACHEL'S BEDROOM - EARLY MORNING HOURS

Rachel's slumber is interrupted by her own violent gasp. The commotion stirs Caleb.

CALEB

(Half asleep)

Again?

Rachel continues to breathe heavily from the vivid memory of her dream.

RACHEL

Yeah.

Rachel sits up and kicks the covers off her legs. Caleb reaches out to Rachel.

CALEB

It was just a dream. Come back and lie down.

Rachel gets up and begins to put on her robe.

RACHEL

I can't.

Caleb looks over at the clock.

CALEB

It's barely five.

Rachel closes the door as she leaves the bedroom. Caleb grabs Rachel's pillow, pulls it over his head, and rolls back over.

ANNE'S PORCH - MOMENTS LATER

Rachel repeatedly rings the doorbell and knocks on the front door. Disheveled and groggy, Anne opens the door and stares at Rachel with bleary eyes.

ANNE

This is my day off, Rachel.

Rachel ignores Anne's reluctance to engage.

RACHEL

It happened again.

Rachel pushes past Anne and into the house, leaving Anne to address an empty porch.

ANNE

Come on in.

ANNE'S KITCHEN - MOMENTS LATER

Anne is preparing coffee at the counter. Rachel sits at the table with her face buried in her hands.

RACHEL

Every night. Every night I have a dream I'm killing her.
And it's never in a nice, gentle, "drink this pop and
antifreeze cocktail" kind of way either.

ANNE

I know I'm going to regret asking this, but why do you care?

Rachel lifts her face from her hands.

RACHEL

You're kidding, right? Don't you see? This is the perfect opportunity for Bobby to make my life miserable. He can use Jill as a way to move into the neighborhood, insert himself into my daily life, and methodically drive me insane.

Anne brings over coffee and sits down across from Rachel.

ANNE

OR - and this might just be the sleep deprivation talking - he loves Jill and you're not even a consideration.

Bill enters the kitchen in a bathrobe, his morning erection barely contained by his pajama bottoms.

BILL

Still dreaming about killing your future sister-in-law?

Rachel, seated at eye level of Bill's midsection, notices an opening in his robe.

RACHEL

Yes, but I didn't stab her to death, so you can put away your battle sword. And who said she's my future sister-in-law? Has Bobby talked to you? Are you hiding something from me?

ANNE

He knows nothing.

RACHEL

(Sarcastically)

Forgive me for thinking you might be keeping secrets.

Rachel holds her hand up to shield her eyes from Bill's crotch.

RACHEL

And please, cover that thing up. If you move any closer, you'll be stirring my coffee.

Embarrassed, Bill closes his robe and prepares his morning beverage.

BILL
Why are you over here, Rachel? Don't you have a naked man in your bed?

ANNE
He's right, you know. While you needlessly stress about this, you're wasting valuable bedroom hours.

RACHEL
Don't worry about Caleb, he can use the recovery time.

Rachel smirks as she suggestively raises her eyebrows.

ANNE
Please, allow for some mystery in your relationship.

RACHEL
The mystery is how an Irishman got his size shillelagh.

BILL
Don't you know? It's not the size, it's the way you swing it.

RACHEL
Well then, he could be a professional lumberjack.

Anne begins to lose her patience.

ANNE
Please! I beg of you. Can we at least wait until the sun comes up for this kind of discussion? Rachel, go home. Stop worrying about this.

Rachel takes a gulp of coffee and stands to leave.

RACHEL
Fine, but the second I see Jill lurking around a bridal magazine rack, I'm counting on you to dispose of all sharp objects and fashion her with a spiked collar.

ANNE
You have my word.

Rachel points at Bill's crotch.

RACHEL
(To Anne)
Give that thing some attention, will you.

Rachel walks out and Bill shouts after her.

BILL
How can she when the neighborhood mental patient is in my kitchen every morning?!

The front door slams shut.

BILL
I don't know what's worse, listening to her adventures in masturbation, or how she violated Caleb fourteen different ways in her butler's pantry.

Anne gets up and moves to Bill.

ANNE
Give her a break, she's been in a drought for fifteen years.

Anne moves to the counter and reaches into the cupboard to prepare breakfast. Bill comes up behind her, playfully draws back his robe, puts his hands on her waist, and sways his midsection against her backside.

BILL
It wouldn't be so bad if we were doing stuff like that.

Anne smiles as she toys with Bill's advances.

ANNE
We don't have a butler's pantry.

Bill steps back and abandons his attempts at arousal.

BILL
You know, I'm getting frustrated watching this neighborhood turn into the San Fernando Valley, while all we do is expand our Netflix queue.

Anne continues to focus on breakfast.

ANNE
And having sex in the kitchen will make you feel like we're keeping up?

Bill again approaches Anne from behind and puts his hands around her waist.

BILL

Yeah, it would. Don't you ever want something different than my uninspired moves?

Anne turns around.

ANNE

Hey, I like your uninspired moves.

BILL

And I like YOUR uninspired moves. I just think it wouldn't kill us to try something new.

Anne wraps her arms around Bill's neck as she plays along.

ANNE

(Facetiously)

Okay, so how deviant are you proposing? Do you want to install a sex swing in the basement or just dabble in some light sadomasochism?

Bill's interest is piqued.

BILL

Are those my only two choices or are you presenting a spectrum?

Anne smiles before kissing Bill. Jack enters the kitchen, sees his parents, and shields his eyes.

JACK

Impressionable child entering the room.

Jack takes a seat at the kitchen table. Anne breaks away from Bill and tends to Jack.

ANNE

Hi, honey, did we wake you?

Anne gently pats down Jack's bed head.

JACK

Mrs. Easton banging on the door did.

ANNE

I'm sorry about her.

JACK

No big deal. I had to get up anyway and study for a test.

BILL

What test?

JACK

Algebra. I'm so lost, I'm struggling to keep a "C."

BILL

I used to do pretty well in Algebra.

Anne chuckles.

ANNE

When?

BILL

(Jokingly overbearing)

Hush, woman!

Jack smiles at his parents' playful interaction.

BILL

Go get your notes. Let's see if we can figure it out.

JILL'S PORCH - LATER THAT WEEK, EVENING

Jill hurries to answer a knock at the door. Her ex-husband, John, stands alone on the front porch.

JILL

Hi. Come on in. The kids are gathering their things.

JILL'S LIVING ROOM - CONTINUOUS

John follows Jill into the living room and the obligatory small talk follows.

JOHN

How've you been?

JILL

Good. And you?

JOHN

Good.

A few silent moments pass.

JOHN

Wil tells me you're seeing someone.

JILL

Yes, I am.

JOHN

Is it serious?

JILL

(Confidently)

Yes.

John moves suggestively closer to Jill.

JOHN

Really? That's hard for me to hear. I've been holding out hope there's still a chance for us.

JILL

You got remarried a month after our divorce was final.

John shrugs off his new commitment.

JOHN

It's what she wanted. I never wanted our divorce.

Jill takes a step back from John.

JILL

Well, you could have prevented that.

John again moves closer to Jill and puts his hand on her waist.

JOHN

I think I've proven I'm willing to do anything to get you back, Jill. I was selfish. I admit that. If you forget about this guy and forgive me, we could go make up right now... in our bedroom.

With building disgust, Jill removes his hand.

JILL

What would Teresa say if she heard you refer to it as OUR bedroom?

John continues his suggestive manner.

JOHN

She couldn't say much. I mean, she did sleep with your husband, so she can't be surprised if you sleep with hers.

John smirks as Jill stands flabbergasted by his comment.

JILL

Even with all my pageant training, I can't think of a cordial way to respond to that, John.

A knock at the door rescues Jill from the uncomfortable situation.

JILL'S ENTRY HALL - CONTINUOUS

Jill opens the door and greets Robert with a relieved, affectionate smile.

JILL

(Quietly to Robert)

Thank goodness you're here.

Jill leads Robert by the hand, eager to use his introduction to silence John's advances.

JILL'S LIVING ROOM - CONTINUOUS

Jill presents Robert to John.

JILL

John, this is Robert Fitzpatrick. Robert, this is John Michaels.

The two men shake hands. Jill positions herself in a protective manner behind Robert.

JOHN

So, what do you do, Robert?

ROBERT

I'm with the Department of Justice.

JOHN

Really? I never thought Jill would settle for a federal employee's salary.

Jill scowls as Robert just patronizingly smiles at John's rudeness. The tension is broken by the happy sound of small children dragging big luggage down the stairs. Wil, Emma, and Grace tumble themselves and their travel bags down the stairs and into the living room.

JOHN

Think you guys have enough stuff?

WIL

I had to pack my baseballs and glove for the Reds game.

JOHN

Oh, I don't know if we'll be able to make it to a Reds game this weekend, buddy. Teresa has some other stuff planned for you.

Wil dramatically drops everything in his arms.

EMMA

Are we going shopping?

Grace enthusiastically jumps up and down while Wil rolls his eyes. Jill bends down to Wil.

JILL

I'm sure whatever you do will be fun.

WIL

Not if it's stupid shopping.

JILL

Wilber Jonathan Michaels, is that the attitude you should have?

WIL

(Dejectedly)

No, ma'am.

JILL

Now, y'all behave like the proper young gentleman and ladies I expect. All right?

WILL/GRACE/EMMA
(In chorus)
Yes, ma'am.

JILL
All right. Give me a kiss goodbye and go enjoy the time with your dad and Teresa.

The kids line up to say goodbye to their mother. Robert bends down and adds his farewells as they walk out of the door.

JOHN
It was nice meeting you, Robert.

Robert stands up straight to address John.

ROBERT
And you, John.

The two engage in another, more testosterone-driven, handshake.

JOHN
Fitzpatrick... what is that? Scottish?

ROBERT
Irish, actually.

John breaks the handshake, smiles back at Jill, and heads out of the door. Jill is happy to shut the door behind him.

ROBERT
You were married to that guy?

Jill turns to Robert and displays her frustration with a shrug of her shoulders.

JILL
I find it hard to believe myself.

Jill wraps her arms around Robert and kisses him passionately.

MARY'S FAMILY ROOM - ONE WEEK LATER, EVENING

Bunco is in its beginning stages, with Jill, Mary, and Anne casually sitting around a coffee table.

JILL
I wonder what's keeping Rachel.

Anne dramatically yawns.

MARY

Are we keeping you up?

ANNE

I'm sorry. She was at my house again this morning.

MARY

Again? You have to stop answering your door.

JILL

Who was at your house?

ANNE

Rachel. She's been having...

Anne looks up and sees Mary giving her a discreet shake of the head.

ANNE

...nightmares.

JILL

What does she expect you to do about it?

ANNE

You know Rachel, if she's having a bad night, everyone's having a bad night.

The front door opens, then slams shut.

MARY

Speaking of the nightmare...

Rachel enters the room and dramatically drops two pairs of handcuffs onto the table.

RACHEL

Anyone want these?

Just as quickly, Rachel pushes the handcuffs away from Jill.

RACHEL

(To Jill)

Except YOU.

Anne delicately picks up a pair.

MARY
Can't you ever enter a room like a normal person?

Anne studies the handcuffs.

ANNE
(Sarcastically)
And they say romance is dead.

RACHEL
Caleb's allergic to metal so they're useless. I was so disappointed, I kicked him out of bed... and did him on the floor.

Rachel laughs at herself.

ANNE
(Disgusted)
That's way more information than we needed.

Anne takes the cuffs in her hand and the pair on the table, then pushes them out of sight under the coffee table.

RACHEL
Just because you're a prude, doesn't mean someone else might not want them.

Jill bashfully smiles.

JILL
Robert has his own.

RACHEL
(Disgusted)
Well, thank you for killing this topic.

Rachel stomps into the kitchen in disgust. Anne leans over to Jill.

ANNE
Jill, are you serious or are you just trying to get to Rachel?

JILL
(Timidly)
A little of both.

Mary smirks at Jill.

MARY

Nothing makes a good Baptist girl blush like a bad Catholic boy.

Rachel re-enters the family room with a drink in hand.

RACHEL

I can't believe that I finally have something to offer to the sex conversation and you bring my brother into the discussion!

Rachel makes a puking gesture and sits down.

ANNE

Rachel, you should be happy for Jill.

RACHEL

I AM happy for Jill. I'm ridiculously, hysterically overjoyed for Jill. I just don't want to hear about it, know about it, or imagine it.

ANNE

But you can subject us to the details of your field trip to The Pleasure Chest?

RACHEL

Hey, I was interested in how the Orgasmatron 5000 worked and I thought you might want to know too.

MARY

But was the slideshow necessary?

Jill eagerly changes the subject.

JILL

I noticed a new car being delivered to you this morning.

RACHEL

Isn't it pretty? It's grotesquely overpriced, goes one hundred ninety, and has always been Bobby's dream car.

Jill shakes her head.

MARY

Speaking of Robert, how are things going between you two?

Rachel leans over, grabs a magazine from the coffee table, and buries her face in it.

JILL

Great! He's wonderful with the kids and they love having him around. Wil absolutely adores him.

MARY

Have you thought about any future plans?

Anne smacks Mary in the thigh, points to Rachel, and silently questions her motives.

JILL

I'd be lying if I said I didn't.

Rachel slaps the magazine closed and throws it back on the coffee table.

RACHEL

Are we playing bunco, or what?

ANNE

(Baffled)

We haven't played bunco in twelve years.

Rachel scoffs as she gets up and makes her way to the food.

MARY

Is John playing nice?

Jill rolls her eyes and shakes her head.

JILL

He's turned into someone I don't even recognize. If it weren't for the kids, I'd regret ever meeting him.

RACHEL

I'm still amazed that ambulatory tower of foreskins had the ability to squirt quality DNA.

JILL

He promises the kids things, then doesn't follow through. He rarely picks them up on time and almost always returns them early. I have no problem with that, but I hate that the kids are disappointed.

RACHEL

Get Kristine involved.

ANNE

Who's Kristine?

Rachel points to Jill.

RACHEL

She's our divorce attorney. Although, she didn't have to work too hard with me. Kevin just bent over and took it without much of a fight. Which, ironically, is what led to our divorce in the first place.

JILL

I'd rather not have to involve her. I'd just like John to realize how much he's missing on his own.

MARY

My parents divorced when I was young. Neither one really had an interest in parenting. Hence, my intense need for attention and inevitable descent into the acting profession.

ANNE

John will look back and regret this someday.

RACHEL

You need a conscience to feel regret.

JILL

Let's talk about something else. Mary, what's new with you?

MARY

Craig is taking the boys to visit his parents next week. I was conveniently left off the invitation.

RACHEL

Still bitter about the lake house?

MARY

The lake house, her last visit, my existence, take your pick. I'm fine with not having to go. It'll give me a chance to enjoy a few days of peace and quiet.

ANNE

At least your in-laws dislike you for being you.

MARY

That's a good thing?

ANNE

It's better than getting blamed for choices their precious son made.

JILL

John's parents loved me. I can only imagine what he told them caused our divorce.

MARY

Well, if things do progress between you and Robert, you'll win the intolerable in-law contest, hands down.

Mary smiles at Rachel and, in return, has a carrot stick thrown at her face.

RACHEL'S PORCH - ONE WEEK LATER, 5:30 PM

Jill, dressed for an evening out, rings the doorbell. Rachel opens the door while eating straight out of an ice cream container.

RACHEL

You didn't have to get all dressed up for me.

JILL

Rachel, can I ask a huge favor of you?

RACHEL

Sure. Come on in.

JILL

Actually, I need you to come over to my house. John is late picking up the kids, and Robert and I have dinner reservations. I called Mary, but she's taking Craig and the boys to the airport. Jack already had plans, and I can't reach Anne...

Rachel interrupts.

RACHEL

It's not a problem, Jill. Caleb is working late, and I have nothing to do but punish this pint of ice cream.

JILL

Oh, thank you so much. I know you and John don't get along and I hate to ask you to deal with him.

RACHEL

It's just loading the kids in his car. I'm fairly confident we can do THAT without incident. Let me go put this back in the freezer. I'll be over in a minute.

JILL

Oh, thank you so much.

JILL'S LIVING ROOM - MOMENTS LATER

Jill and Robert prepare to leave for the evening. Rachel stands behind Wil, Grace, and Emma as they all receive direction from Jill.

JILL

All right you three, I want you to be on your best behavior for Miss Rachel. Your dad will be here any minute so don't ask her to pull out any games or start any activities.

RACHEL

They'll be fine, Jill. Get out of here.

JILL

Mind your manners at your dad's house. I love y'all so much and I can't wait for Sunday.

Jill bends down to kiss each child goodbye. Robert adds his goodbyes, and both head out of the door. Rachel enthusiastically addresses the kids.

RACHEL

Okay, what's the ONE thing your mom never lets you do?

The kids answer in unison.

WIL/GRACE/EMMA

Jump on the bed!

Rachel motions upstairs.

RACHEL

Okay! Let's go jump on the bed!

JILL'S PORCH - 6:30 PM

Mary steps onto the front porch and hears a playful commotion coming from inside the house. Her knock at the door is answered by Rachel. She is covered in dramatic makeup and wearing an extravagant tiara.

MARY
Tell me that's not Jill's Miss South Carolina crown.

Rachel shrugs her shoulders.

RACHEL
She left it out.

Rachel leaves the door open and returns to the living room.

MARY
Yeah, in a glass case on her mantel.

JILL'S LIVING ROOM - CONTINUOUS

Mary enters Jill's living room and finds a sheet fort constructed over the couches and chairs. She hears laughter coming from inside and plays along.

MARY
Hey! Where is everybody?

RACHEL (INSIDE THE FORT)
Shhh. It's a hideous monster. Don't let her know we're in here.

Mary smiles and allows herself to be the subject of ridicule for the kids' amusement.

RACHEL
It sounds hungry. I better go make sure it doesn't try to get in.

Rachel crawls out of the fort and addresses Mary.

MARY
What's going on in there?

RACHEL
I can't divulge the sworn secrets of Fort GEW.

MARY

Gew?

RACHEL

Grace, Emma, and Wil.

Mary nods with a smile.

MARY

Aren't those Jill's good linens?

RACHEL

Maybe, I don't know. What are you doing here? I thought you had to take the boys to the airport.

MARY

I did. Jill left me a message saying she needed someone to watch the kids for a few minutes. I pulled in and saw all the lights on.

RACHEL

John's an hour and a half late. If he doesn't get here soon, I'm going to have to begin Jill's twenty-four-step bedtime routine.

MARY

I don't have anything to do. I'll stay and help you.

RACHEL

Thanks, but first you'll have to pass Fort GEW's rigorous initiation process.

Rachel crawls back into the sheet fort. Mary bends down and follows her inside.

RACHEL (INSIDE THE FORT)

It's okay, everybody. Turns out it's not a hideous monster. It's just a peri-menopausal member of The Screen Actors Guild.

TWO-LANE COUNTRY ROAD - SIMULTANEOUSLY

Robert and Jill are parked on the side of a desolate road with a flat tire. They wait for assistance on the opened back end of Robert's SUV.

ROBERT

I'm sorry we missed our reservations.

JILL

It's fine. We can go anytime.

ROBERT

I'm really sorry I didn't realize the jack was missing when I bought this car. Auto Club said it may take up to an hour for someone to get out here.

JILL

An hour, huh?

Jill rubs her arms to warm them. Robert quickly takes notice.

ROBERT

Oh, here.

Robert jumps off the rear of the car and takes off his jacket. He helps Jill put it around her shoulders.

JILL

Thanks.

ROBERT

This isn't how I pictured this evening.

Jill takes Robert's hand and pulls him close.

JILL

What do you mean? You wanted an evening that was just the two of us...

Jill looks around the empty road.

JILL

...and it IS just the two of us.

Jill smiles at Robert as he moves in to kiss her.

ROBERT

You make everything better.

JILL

I wouldn't be a southern woman if I didn't.

ROBERT

It's more than that.

Jill smiles and puts her hands in the pockets of his jacket. She feels a small item and begins to pull it out.

JILL

You'll probably need your key fob...

Jill opens her hand and reveals not a key fob, but a small ring-sized box. Robert holds his breath as Jill quickly figures out what she's holding. She does her best to cover up his spoiled surprise.

JILL

...or whatever this might be.

Robert takes the box out of Jill's hand and hangs his head.

ROBERT

(Dejected)

I was hoping to make tonight far more memorable, but everything has gone wrong.

Jill stands up, wraps her arms around Robert, and tries to lift his spirits.

JILL

I'm with you. So as far as I'm concerned, everything has gone right.

Robert smiles as he affectionately looks at Jill. He takes her hand and bends down onto one knee.

JILL'S UPSTAIRS BATHROOM - 8:30 PM

Rachel, covered in dramatic makeup, is in the bathroom while the twins wash their faces and brush their teeth. As each girl finishes, Rachel inspects their results.

RACHEL

Excellent, Emma. You got all of the eye shadow off your forehead and the lipstick is almost completely out of your ear.

EMMA

Can I wash your face?

RACHEL

You think you can clean this mess?

Rachel squeezes her eyes shut, hands Emma a washcloth, and lets her try to rub off her makeup.

EMMA
(Giggling)
It's not coming off.

RACHEL
Great. Now I'll have to live the rest of my life like this.

Emma giggles.

RACHEL
Grace, how are you coming?

Grace proudly presents herself with a smile.

GRACE
All clean.

RACHEL
Yes, you are. Well done, both of you. Now, you have five minutes to put on some pajamas and pick out a book.

Emma and Grace run out of the bathroom and into their room. Rachel fills the time by cleaning herself up.

INT. GRACE AND EMMA'S ROOM - CONTINUOUS

Grace and Emma finish putting on their pajamas and then go to their library to pick out a book. After some debate, a story is chosen and Grace hands Rachel their selection.

GRACE
Here. Can we read it in mommy's bed?

RACHEL
You know what? Let's stay in here. She may have plans for it later.

Rachel makes a puking gesture.

GRACE
Why do you always do that?

RACHEL
Because brothers are gross.

EMMA
Wil's not gross.

RACHEL

Well, HE'S not, but mine is.

EMMA

Who's your brother?

RACHEL

Bobby's my brother.

GRACE

Who's Bobby?

RACHEL

I can see I'm confusing you. The man you call Robert is my brother, Bobby.

EMMA

Why do you call him Bobby?

RACHEL

That's what I called him when we were growing up. When you get older, Wil might decide to become a pretentious egomaniac and use his full name, Wilber. But you'll always know him as Wil, right?

Emma and Grace are confused by Rachel's big words but nod in agreement.

RACHEL

Right. Now get into bed.

GRACE

What about prayers?

RACHEL

(Uncomfortably)

Oh, right. Do I leave you alone for that or...?

Grace and Emma kneel down by their bed. Emma pulls on Rachel's arm for her to join them. Rachel goes through the motions of getting on her knees, closing her eyes and clasping her fingers together in prayer.

GRACE/EMMA

Now I lay me down to sleep, I pray the Lord my soul to keep, watch and guard me through the night, and wake me with the morning light. God bless Mom, Dad, Wil, my sister, Teresa, and Robert.

GRACE

And Miss Rachel.

Rachel pops one eye open at Grace and smiles.

GRACE/EMMA

Amen.

Rachel and the girls stand.

RACHEL

Thanks. I don't think anyone has ever prayed for me before.

EMMA

Mom does all the time.

Rachel smiles at the girls and directs them to bed.

RACHEL

Okay, sleep time.

Grace and Emma obey and climb under the covers. Rachel checks out the chosen book's cover.

RACHEL

What's this story about? A rabies outbreak?

EMMA

No, it's Stellaluna.

GRACE

She's a baby bat.

Rachel acts frightened as she sits down and opens the book.

RACHEL

A baby bat, huh? I hope it doesn't end with her turning all the town children into vampires.

JILL'S UPSTAIRS HALLWAY - 9:00 PM

Rachel quietly shuts the door to the twin's bedroom and meets Mary in the hallway.

MARY
(Quietly)
I got Wil down. How'd you do with the girls?

RACHEL
(Quietly)
They're finally asleep. They negotiated three extra books out of me.

JILL'S ENTRY HALL - CONTINUOUS

As Mary and Rachel descend the stairs, they hear the front door being shaken, but remaining locked. Rachel moves to the front door to answer it.

RACHEL
Did you forget your keys, Jill?

Rachel opens the door wide and finds John trying to use his old key to get in.

JOHN
My key's not working.

RACHEL
Nor should it. This isn't your house anymore.

John surrenders by extending his arms to his sides.

JOHN
I'm here to get the kids.

Mary begins back up the staircase.

MARY
I'll get them.

Rachel stops Mary in her tracks.

RACHEL
Mary, don't.

Rachel turns back to John.

RACHEL
You should have been here four hours ago. They're sleeping now. You can come back in the morning and get them.

Mary watches the tension escalate from the stairs.

JOHN

I don't have time in the morning. Just give me my kids, Rachel.

RACHEL

What have you been doing all this time, John? Or should I ask, WHO have you been doing?

John sighs with annoyance.

JOHN

Why don't you go have another drink, Rachel?

RACHEL

(Patronizingly)

Ah, an alcohol consumption joke. Super creative, by the way. No, you see, I was asked to stay with the kids when you didn't show up. So, my only cocktail tonight has been a mixture of fruit punch and hot sauce that your son paid me a dollar to drink.

John tempers his anger and tries a kinder approach.

JOHN

Will you please get my kids?

From Jill's entry hall, a vehicle can be seen driving up and into the Hutchinson's driveway. Jack exits the vehicle and casually walks inside his house.

RACHEL

(Indignantly)

No.

John becomes insistent as he tries to push his way from the front porch to the entry hall. Rachel extends her arm and keeps him outside.

RACHEL

Come back in the morning.

John abandons kindness.

JOHN

I will NOT come back in the morning. They are MY kids, this is MY time with them, and I'm taking them now.

Headlights illuminate their heated conversation as a vehicle pulls into Jill's driveway. Jill and Robert quickly exit the vehicle. Jill hurries to the confrontation on her front porch.

JILL

What's going on?

JOHN

Jill, do something about this!

JILL

(Confused)

Rachel, where are the kids?

RACHEL

They're asleep. This omnidirectional semen sprinkler shows up hours late and wants me to wake them when he just as easily can come back in the morning!

JOHN

I'm getting tired of this, Jill!

Jill turns to Robert, who is patiently waiting for instructions.

JILL

Robert, will you help Mary wake up the kids and get them ready for John?

Robert moves past the confrontation and into the house. He and Mary disappear upstairs, leaving John, Jill, and Rachel alone on the porch.

JILL

Rachel, thank you for helping us out tonight. I'm sure John appreciates the fact that you gave up your evening to look after the kids until he could get here.

John ignores Jill's cue to be civil.

JOHN

I hear you're fucking a bartender now. I don't think you could embody any more Irish stereotypes if you tried.

JILL

John!

Rachel leans into John.

RACHEL

I could beat you senseless with a potato.

JILL

Rachel!

John leans closer into Rachel.

JOHN

Don't you come anywhere near me or my wife again.

RACHEL

How is Teresa? Has she relearned how to whistle yet?

Jill throws her hands up to separate them like two children on a playground.

JILL

Stop it! Both of you!

Jill places her left hand on John's chest. Rachel is too distracted to notice the new addition to Jill's ring finger.

JILL

John, come with me.

Jill takes John by the arm and leads him into the house. Rachel casually leans on the porch railing and begins to whistle, "All I Want For Christmas Is My Two Front Teeth."

JILL'S KITCHEN - CONTINUOUS

JOHN

You better figure out a way to control her!

JILL

John, when has anyone been able to control Rachel Easton?

JOHN

Rachel Easton? Rachel Fitzpatrick, you mean!

Jill's eyes widen.

JOHN

Yeah, Jill, I have an internet connection. I know who she is. I know who her brother is, and I know what happened in Chicago.

Jill looks down and twists the engagement diamond to her palm.

JILL
I don't know what you're talking about. I mean, yes, Robert is her brother, but what happened in Chicago was decades ago.

JOHN
You think a judge will see it that way?

JILL
What are you saying?

JOHN
I'm saying she's already killed one kid. Do you think I'm going to do nothing while you make her an aunt to ours?

JILL
Rachel has always been wonderful with the kids...

JOHN
Until she does something stupid.

John has a vengeful look in his eyes that Jill has not seen before. She stands silently as fear begins to rise.

JOHN
If you put our kids at risk by making her a permanent member of their family, I'll sue you for full custody.

JILL
FULL custody? John, you don't even take FULL advantage of the custody you have now.

JOHN
I'd rather have them under the care of a nanny than anywhere near that woman.

JILL
That's not fair, John. The children love Rachel. She has always been a generous and positive presence in their lives.

JOHN
Yeah, she buys them anything they want and encourages them to break our rules. Why wouldn't they love her?

JILL
(Defensively)
At least they can count on her when they need someone.

John takes a deep breath and lowers his voice.

JOHN
Have you even asked her what happened?

Jill says nothing.

JOHN
Or do you already know and you're just hoping it doesn't happen again?

John walks out of the kitchen with a look of satisfaction.

JILL'S ENTRY HALL - CONTINUOUS

Robert stands waiting with both sleeping twins in his arms while Mary holds Will. John enters the entry hall and takes Wil from Mary.

MARY
Their stuff is in your car.

JOHN
Thank you, Mary.

JILL'S DRIVEWAY - CONTINUOUS

John leads Robert out to his car, where he loads each child into their respective car seat. Jill joins Mary and Rachel on her porch.

RACHEL
I swear to God, Jill, I don't know why you ever let that gelatinous puddle of anal secretions stick his penis in you.

Jill's overwhelming concern leaves her unamused.

RACHEL
Then again, you let Bobby do it, so you're obviously not very discerning.

Mary notices Jill getting upset.

MARY

Enough, Rachel.

Rachel turns to face Jill, who is wiping tears from her face. She assumes the tears are from her comments.

RACHEL

Hey, it's your snatch. You can let anyone you want in there.

Jill doesn't have time to react before the looming sound of sirens and red lights grabs everyone's attention.

John pulls out of Jill's driveway and leaves the neighborhood.

The sirens grow louder and lights begin to bounce off nearby houses as paramedics, a fire truck, and an ambulance come to a halt in front of Anne's house. Mary, Rachel, Jill, and Robert stand silent in Jill's front yard as the first responders race into Anne's house.

MARY

Oh, no.

JILL'S FRONT YARD/STREET - 9:15 PM

Making their way down the driveway, they stare in dread as a stretcher is pulled out of the ambulance and rushed into the house. Rachel starts to move toward the Hutchinson's home when Robert grabs her arm and stops her.

ROBERT

No, Ellie. Don't get in their way.

They stand together silently waiting as the flashing lights continue their surreal light show. After a few long minutes, Jack emerges from the house. He anxiously wraps his fingers around the back of his head and walks down his driveway.

Mary and Rachel run across the street to Jack.

ANNE'S DRIVEWAY/STREET - CONTINUOUS

MARY

Jack! Are you okay?!

Mary holds Jack as he begins to cry.

RACHEL

Are you all right? What happened?

JACK

My dad...

Anne follows paramedics as they bring Bill out of the house on a stretcher. Bill is quickly loaded into the waiting ambulance. Mary stays with Jack while Jill joins Rachel in approaching Anne.

RACHEL

Anne, what happened?!

Anne is too distraught to answer. She climbs inside the ambulance at the urging of the paramedics and positions herself next to Bill. She pulls his unresponsive hand out from under the gurney straps and holds it next to her chest. The ambulance doors close, and the wail of sirens starts up as it speeds off down the street. Rachel and Jill return to Mary and Jack.

RACHEL

Let's go! Get in my car!

Rachel and Jill cross back over the street. Rachel starts to get into her car while Robert and Jill get into his. Mary tries to lead Jack across, but he refuses to move.

MARY

Jack, we have to get to the hospital.

Jack shakes his head vigorously.

MARY

Your mom needs you right now. We have to go!

JACK

No! I can't be near her!

Mary is confused by Jack's comment but doesn't have time for an explanation.

MARY

Fine. You don't have to be near her. Let's get to the hospital so you can be with your dad.

JACK

I can't.

Rachel looks back to see Mary negotiating with Jack. She steps away from her car and runs back over to them.

RACHEL

What's the problem?!

MARY

He can't be near his mom.

Rachel gets in Jack's face.

RACHEL

You can't be near your mom?!

Jack says nothing but continues to shake his head.

RACHEL

Get in the God damn car, Jack!

Rachel pulls Jack out of Mary's embrace and leads him over to her car. Mary throws her hands in the air at Rachel's unsympathetic treatment.

EMERGENCY ROOM WAITING AREA - 10:00 PM

Robert, Jill, and Mary stand nearby while Anne nervously paces the floor. Jack is as far away from his mom as he can be while still in the waiting room. Rachel is at the reception desk, demanding information. Anne quietly voices her frustration with Rachel.

ANNE

It's my husband. If they were going to tell anyone anything, it would be me.

JILL

She's just trying to be helpful.

ANNE

(Anxiously)

I know.

Rachel returns to the group.

RACHEL

Nothing new.

Rachel looks over and sees Jack sitting alone in the corner.

RACHEL

Hey, Jack!

Anne quickly moves to defend Jack's behavior.

ANNE

Rachel...

RACHEL

You know, your mom needs you right now, why don't you come over here with her!

Jack doesn't move.

ANNE

Rachel, he's fine. Just leave him be.

Rachel is disgusted by Jack's conduct toward his mother but abides by Anne's request.

MARY

Is there anything at all we can do to help?

ANNE

Actually, there is. Megan and I got into a fight this morning over something stupid, and she's not answering any of my calls or texts.

RACHEL

Do you want us to go up and get her?

ANNE

Would you?

MARY

We'll go right now. Jill, can you and Robert stay here with Anne and Jack?

JILL

Of course.

ANNE

Don't tell her how serious things are. Just tell her she needs to come home because her dad's not well.

Anne begins to tear up. Mary quickly moves in for a reassuring embrace.

MARY

Okay.

Rachel watches as Anne buries her head into Mary's shoulder and refuses to let her go. Mary closes her eyes as she comforts Anne with an equally intense embrace. After a few moments, Jill joins Mary and Anne. She pulls Anne away from Mary and takes over consoling her. Mary and Rachel move toward the exit.

RACHEL
Call us if you hear anything.

Jill and Anne sit down while Robert takes the opportunity to walk over to Jack.

ROBERT
Want to go for a walk?

JACK
No. Thanks.

ROBERT
Come on. I'll buy you something to drink.

JACK
I don't want to talk if that's what you're trying to get me to do.

ROBERT
Who said anything about talking? I'm suggesting we go get a pop, stretch our legs, burn off some energy.

Jack struggles with Robert's offer.

ROBERT
Come on.

Jack reluctantly gets up and walks away with Robert.

RACHEL'S CAR - 10:45 PM

Rachel and Mary drive to Megan's college apartment. Rhythmic windshield wipers clearing a light rain provide the only sound inside the car. With only a few miles to go, Rachel breaks the reflective silence.

RACHEL
Thank you.

MARY
For what?

RACHEL

For being there for Anne. You're good with that stuff and I'm not.

MARY

You mean human contact?

Rachel begrudgingly nods her head.

MARY

We all have our strengths. If it makes you feel better, I'd be useless in a fist fight.

Rachel changes the subject.

RACHEL

How soon is our next turn?

Mary consults her phone.

MARY

Left in half a mile.

COLLEGE APARTMENT COMPLEX - 10:50 PM

Rachel and Mary pull up to a rural, rowdy apartment complex in a small college town. Several students are in the parking lot and outside on their balconies, drinking and laughing with friends. Rachel and Mary get out of the car and try to get their bearings.

RACHEL

Do we know which apartment she's in?

MARY

Building 3, room 523.

RACHEL

Where do you suppose that is?

MARY

Let's ask someone.

Rachel and Mary approach a group of STUDENTS.

MARY

Hi. Can you tell us where Building 3 is?

STUDENT
Who are you looking for?

MARY
Megan Hutchinson.

STUDENT
Oh, she's in that building over there.

The student points Mary in the right direction.

MARY
Thank you.

Mary and Rachel make their way over to Megan's building.

MEGAN'S APARTMENT BUILDING - CONTINUOUS

Mary and Rachel walk up the stairwell to Megan's room. Rachel admires the casual party atmosphere of the apartment complex.

RACHEL
I never should have gone to a Catholic university.

MARY
I didn't know you went to college.

RACHEL
(Patronizingly)
I graduated and everything.

MARY
Really? What's your degree in?

RACHEL
Psychology.

Mary stops Rachel in her tracks.

MARY
You have a degree in psychology?

Rachel spins around.

RACHEL
You sound surprised.

Rachel returns to ascending the stairs.

MARY

I am! What college gave you a degree in psychology?

Rachel turns back to Mary to answer condescendingly.

RACHEL

Notre Dame.

Rachel continues upstairs. Mary's eyes widen and her mouth drops as she hurries behind Rachel.

Rachel and Mary arrive at Megan's apartment door.

MARY

Why haven't you ever told us you went to Notre Dame?

RACHEL

You know I'm a fan of their football team.

MARY

I just figured you identified with the Fighting Irish.

Rachel knocks on the door.

MARY

I hope she's here.

Twenty-year-old ALEXIS answers the door. Her failed career aspiration of social media influencer has left her with a sour attitude. Several other students are partying in the kitchen.

ALEXIS

Who are you?

MARY

We're friends of Megan. Is she here?

ALEXIS

I didn't know Megan was studying geriatrics.

Alexis drunkenly snorts. Her laughter is not reciprocated.

ALEXIS

She couldn't keep up with us at vodka pong. I think she's in her room.

Alexis opens the door wide, points to Megan's room, and stumbles back to her party guests. Rachel and Mary enter the apartment and knock on Megan's closed door.

RACHEL

Megan!

No response is heard from behind the door. Rachel checks the doorknob and finds it locked.

RACHEL

Call her.

Mary pulls out her phone and dials Megan's number.

MARY

It's ringing.

Seconds later, they hear Megan's phone ring behind the door. Both women put their ears against the closed door to confirm.

RACHEL

She's in there.

MARY

Maybe she didn't take her phone.

Rachel raises her eyebrows.

RACHEL

What's the likelihood of that?

Mary nods in agreement. Rachel steps back and pounds on the door.

RACHEL

Megan, it's Rachel Easton! There's an emer...

Mary hastily waves her fingers across her throat to stop Rachel from mentioning Bill's condition.

RACHEL

We need to talk to you!

The only sound heard is the commotion coming from the kitchen.

MARY

Megan! It's Mary Hueston. Honey, we need to talk to you! Will you please open the door?!

Frustration begins to set in.

RACHEL

Megan, open the door or I'll break it down!

Rachel pounds on the door again with more force.

RACHEL

Megan!

Rachel and Mary debate silently how to proceed.

MARY

Please open the door, Megan! I don't want Rachel twisting an ankle thinking she can break this door down.

Rachel motions for Mary to back up then takes a textbook police kick to the doorknob. The door remains firmly intact.

RACHEL

Damn it. I used to be really good at that.

Alexis angrily comes around the corner.

ALEXIS

Hey! What are you doing?! If you break that door, you're paying our security deposit!

Rachel's disgust for Alexis grows.

RACHEL

You can bill me.

Rachel musters all the force she can and successfully kicks the knob free of the door jam.

MEGAN'S BEDROOM - CONTINUOUS

Megan lays unconscious face up on her bed. Rachel and Mary rush to Megan while Alexis hovers by the door.

MARY

I'm calling an ambulance!

Mary pulls out her phone while Rachel struggles to wake Megan.

RACHEL

Megan!

Rachel grabs Megan's face to find a sign of life. The overpowering smell of alcohol quickly indicates the problem.

RACHEL

God damn it, Megan!

Rachel shakes Megan violently to try to arouse her. She remains completely unresponsive.

RACHEL

Not tonight.

Mary hands the phone to Alexis.

MARY

Talk to 9-1-1!

ALEXIS

I don't want cops here!

RACHEL

You don't have a choice!

Alexis takes the call into the other room. Mary turns her attention back to Rachel and Megan.

MARY

Is she breathing?

Rachel puts her ear to Megan's mouth while placing her hand on Megan's chest to check for breathing.

RACHEL

I can't tell.

Rachel grabs Megan's arm and puts it around her shoulder.

RACHEL

Help me!

Mary takes Megan's other arm and swings it over her shoulder. Rachel guides Mary to carry Megan into the bathroom and position her near the toilet.

RACHEL

Go get me the cheapest tequila you can find!

MARY

Where?!

RACHEL

Are you serious, Mary?! Just go shout for some off the balcony!

Mary runs out of the room on her quest for tequila. Rachel continues to try and revive Megan.

RACHEL

Where's that ambulance?!

Alexis comes into the bathroom while frantically giving answers into the phone.

ALEXIS

I don't know! We just found her passed out.

Alexis addresses Rachel.

ALEXIS

Is she responding to anything?

RACHEL

Nothing!

Alexis relays the information.

ALEXIS

No.

Mary returns with a bottle of tequila. Alexis takes her conversation out of the bathroom.

MARY

Here!

Rachel gets behind Megan and holds her up over the toilet.

RACHEL

Open it!

Mary takes the top off the bottle.

MARY

What are we doing? Giving her more to drink?

RACHEL

You don't think I have a little expertise here?! Pour it in my hand!

Mary pours a handful of liquor in Rachel's hand. Rachel takes the alcohol and rubs it all over Megan's face, including up her nose. Rachel then sticks her finger down Megan's throat. Her gag reflex kicks in and she violently throws up into the toilet. The release of vomit sparks some consciousness as she begins to cough violently. Mary leans in to assist Megan.

MARY

Megan? Megan, honey, look at me!

Megan struggles to lift her head, then quickly passes out again. Rachel lays her down on her side on the bathroom floor. Rachel and Mary let out sighs of relief.

RACHEL

She's breathing.

After a few moments, the PARAMEDICS come into the apartment and make their way into the bathroom. They quickly begin tending to Megan.

PARAMEDIC

Did she take anything?

RACHEL

I don't know.

PARAMEDIC

Go find out.

Rachel quickly stands up and hurries out of the room.

MEGAN'S APARTMENT FAMILY ROOM - CONTINUOUS

Alexis and her party guests are nervously watching the scene unfold. Rachel angrily approaches her.

RACHEL

Did she take anything?!

Alexis is hesitant to confess.

ALEXIS

I don't have to tell you anything.

Rachel grabs Alexis by the collar and jerks her close.

RACHEL

Give me a reason to kick your over-privileged ass! You know what she's taken! Tell me now!

ALEXIS

She only drank, okay! That's all! We offered her stuff, but she wouldn't take it!

RACHEL

Are you sure?!

ALEXIS

Yes, I'm sure! She's a boring wuss!

Rachel releases her grip on Alexis, causing her to stumble backward. The paramedics bring Megan out of her bedroom on a stretcher and carry her out of the apartment. Mary follows behind and tugs Rachel's arm to leave.

Rachel hesitates as she glares at Alexis.

RACHEL

If it turns out you're lying, I'm coming back here and beating the ever-loving shit out of you.

Mary rolls her eyes as she pulls Rachel out of the door, grabbing her phone from Alexis on the way.

MEGAN'S APARTMENT BUILDING - 11:15 PM

Mary and Rachel, along with the rest of the apartment complex residents, watch as paramedics load Megan into the back of an ambulance and drive away.

Mary begins to make a call.

RACHEL

Who are you calling?

MARY

Anne, of course.

Rachel grabs Mary's phone and ends the call.

MARY

What are you doing?!

Rachel holds Mary's phone behind her back.

RACHEL
You're not calling her.

Mary becomes irritated.

MARY
Give me my phone, Rachel.

RACHEL
She doesn't need THIS on top of everything else that's happened tonight. We can handle it.

Mary becomes angry at Rachel's proposal.

MARY
This is not ours to handle, Rachel! This is her daughter!

RACHEL
And her husband might be dying!

A crowd begins to circle them.

MARY
Her daughter might be dying!

RACHEL
She's just drunk.

Mary's frustration builds.

MARY
And you know this from all your years in medical school?!

RACHEL
No, I know this from all my years of being drunk.

MARY
We don't know what all happened here tonight! What if it's worse than that?!

RACHEL
Then you can call Anne while I beat the crap out of that roommate of hers.

Mary lunges and begins fighting Rachel for her phone. Rachel successfully avoids Mary's grasps then throws the phone into a nearby pond.

MARY

What the hell is wrong with you?! This is not up to us! You don't have kids, Rachel. We could fight about this all night and you'd never understand!

Rachel starts to walk toward her car, but Mary chases her down and shoves her from behind. The growing crowd encourages their confrontation.

Rachel turns around to face Mary.

MARY

(Angrily)

Give me your phone!

RACHEL

We're not calling her.

MARY

I'm not going to ask again.

Mary leans toward Rachel and enunciates each word.

MARY

GIVE. ME. YOUR. PHONE.

Rachel mocks Mary's speech pattern.

RACHEL

WE'RE. NOT. CALLING. HER.

Mary can't contain her rage. She tightens her fist, pulls it back, and lands a punch square on the bridge of Rachel's nose. Rachel stumbles backward and grabs her face.

The crowd erupts in cheers.

Mary fights through her shock and stands with a determined attitude. Rachel pulls her hands away from her face and inspects her blood-covered fingers.

MARY

Give it to me!

Rachel says nothing as she wipes the blood onto her pants. She removes her phone from her pocket and tauntingly offers it up. As Mary extends her hand to take the phone, Rachel reaches back and launches it into the air toward the pond. The women stand staring at each other as the crowd clamors for a fight. Mary steams with anger as Rachel contemptuously turns to leave.

The crowd yells louder and encourages them to continue.

Mary's entire body fills with fury as she listens to the crowd's incendiary chants. She drops her shoulder, charges Rachel, and tackles her to the ground. She positions herself on top of Rachel and unleashes a barrage of punches to her face.

Rachel doesn't fight back as much as shield herself from Mary's amateur blows. As the two rumble in the dirt, the cheering crowd tightens their circle around them. After a few moments of flying fists, the approach of red lights and sirens sends the crowd scattering.

Several POLICE OFFICERS make their way to Rachel and Mary fighting on the ground. Police struggle to separate and restrain them. Mud, grass - and the blood streaming from Rachel's nose - all camouflage the age of the two women.

Rachel wiggles loose enough to yell in Mary's face.

RACHEL

You're absolutely right, Mary. You ARE useless in a fist fight!

Rachel defiantly spits a mouthful of blood at Mary's feet.

Two officers fight to restrain Mary.

MARY

Yeah? Who's bleeding, MOUTH?!

The officers tighten their grip on the women before they can start up again.

POLICE OFFICER

Hey! Knock it off!

The police wrestle to handcuff both women, then escort them to the back of a waiting patrol car.

POLICE OFFICER

You should be ashamed of yourselves! Your parents are paying a fortune for you to come here and THIS is how you repay them!

The remaining crowd groans with disappointment.

EMERGENCY ROOM WAITING AREA - 12:30 AM

Jill and Anne sit together while Robert and Jack sit in a corner. The stress and fatigue are beginning to wear on Anne.

ANNE
Where are they? They should have been back by now.

JILL
I'll try calling them.

Jill steps away from Anne and pulls out her phone. She calls Mary's number and is instantly sent to voicemail.

MARY
(Recorded voice)
Hi. You've reached Mary Hueston. I'm not available right now, but if you leave me a message, I'll get back to you as soon as I can.

Jill tries Rachel's number. She's met with the same result.

RACHEL
(Recorded voice)
I probably didn't answer because I don't want to talk to you. Leave a message and I'll ignore that too.

Jill becomes concerned with her inability to reach either woman. She walks over to the corner where Robert is sitting with Jack.

JILL
Robert, can I talk to you for a minute.

ROBERT
Sure.

They step away from Jack to speak privately.

JILL
Rachel and Mary should have been back by now. Their phones are going straight to voicemail, and I'm starting to get worried.

ROBERT
Do you want me to make some calls?

JILL
Would you?

ROBERT

Of course.

Jill kisses Robert as he takes out his phone to make inquiries. She returns to try and engage Jack.

JILL

How are you doing, Jack? Is there anything I can get you?

Jack stares at the floor and silently shakes his head. Jill sits down and holds his hand.

JILL

I know you've been through a lot tonight, honey. If you need anything, just let one of us know.

Jack remains silent, keeping his head down. Jill's attention is drawn to the doctor coming out of the emergency room and approaching Anne. Jill watches as Anne stands and anxiously greets the doctor.

The doctor begins shaking his head in a consoling manner.

Anne buries her face into her palms.

JILL

Jack...

Jack looks up from the floor and sees his mother crying with the doctor. He gets up and runs out of the area. Jill hurries to Anne and consoles her with an embrace. Jill supports Anne in her arms as she guides her to nearby chairs. Jill says nothing as she continues to comfort her.

Robert cautiously approaches.

ROBERT

I'm so sorry, Anne.

Robert bends down, takes Anne's hand, and looks her in the eyes.

ROBERT

There's another problem.

JAIL CELL - 1:00 AM

Rachel and Mary sit in a small county holding cell. Both are still covered in grass and dirt. Mary has a bruise forming on her chin, while Rachel's eye is blackened, and dried blood has crusted under her nose.

BEAU, an older, intoxicated fellow inmate, takes a seat next to Rachel and smooths his flannel shirt. Rachel feels Beau's drunken stare.

RACHEL
Come here often?

BEAU
You smell good.

RACHEL
(Patronizingly)
Aww... thank you. I wish I could say the same.

BEAU
What are you in here for?

RACHEL
Insider trading. You?

BEAU
I threw a ‘possum out of my truck.

RACHEL
(Facetiously)
That's illegal in this county?

BEAU
It shouldn't be. Damn thing kept knocking over my whiskey bottle.

Rachel nods.

RACHEL
Sounds like the opossum was working with law enforcement. I'd use an entrapment defense.

The SHERIFF approaches the outside of the cell.

SHERIFF
Okay, ladies. Let's go.

BEAU

What about me?

SHERIFF

The opossum is pressing charges, Beau. It's best if you lie down and sleep it off.

Beau sighs with disappointment. Rachel and Mary quickly move to the door as the sheriff unlocks it. They refuse to make eye contact or speak with each other.

UNIVERSITY HOSPITAL WAITING ROOM - 1:30AM

Rachel and Mary rush into the hospital where Megan has been admitted. They proceed to the waiting area where Robert and Jill are watching Anne talk to the doctor. Jill intercepts Rachel and Mary before they can make their way to Anne.

JILL

What happened to you two?

RACHEL

It's a boring story. How's Bill?

JILL

(Gently)

He's gone.

Mary brings her hands to her mouth and begins to cry while Rachel's tough facade melts away.

RACHEL

What about Megan?

JILL

Anne's talking to the doctor now.

Rachel looks around.

RACHEL

Where's Jack?

JILL

He stayed behind with a friend.

Anne leaves her conversation with the doctor and joins the three women. She keeps her comments directed at Jill.

ANNE

She's stable. They're keeping her overnight.

JILL

Oh, thank God.

Anne turns to walk away.

RACHEL

Anne, I...

Anne whips around and confronts Rachel.

ANNE

NO! Do NOT talk to me! I have NO interest in anything you have to say.

Anne begins to walk away again but can't contain her anger. She turns back to get in Rachel's face.

ANNE

What the hell is wrong with you?! In the most twisted corners of my brain, I can't figure out what you were thinking.

Rachel silently takes Anne's abuse.

ANNE

You know, I'm the idiot! What part of your track record made me think you wouldn't make this situation worse?! How did I not realize asking you to pick up Megan would end up with her in the HOSPITAL and you two morons ARRESTED?!

Mary interjects.

MARY

Anne, let me explain.

Anne ignores Mary's appeal.

ANNE

(To Mary)

And YOU! I thought I could count on you to prevent this... fiasco grenade, from exploding her bad decisions all over everything!

Mary retreats as Anne furiously continues with Rachel.

ANNE

I will never forgive you for this, Rachel. I never want to see you again. Not in the neighborhood, not in my life. I'm through with you.

Anne begins to leave but returns for a final insult.

ANNE

If you're so hell-bent on destroying yourself, just go and do it for Christ's sake! Quit trying to take one of us with you.

Anne finishes her exit. Mary steps away to follow Anne.

JILL

Rachel... I'm sorry.

Rachel's face is blank, and her body deflated. She turns away from Jill and heads toward the exit. Robert chases her down.

ROBERT

Ellie...

Rachel reluctantly stops and turns toward Robert.

ROBERT

...a lot has happened tonight. Emotions are high and I wouldn't trust anything that's been said.

Rachel says nothing as she continues toward the door and walks out.

FUNERAL HOME OFFICE - THREE DAYS LATER

Anne feels very alone as she is faced with the countless decisions that no one ever wants to make. Megan is silent, still stinging with embarrassment from her incident, while Jack remains withdrawn and sullen.

FUNERAL DIRECTOR

This process is never easy, but it's particularly difficult when the deceased is someone so young. Did your husband communicate any final wishes?

ANNE

He never talked about it. The closest he got was joking about hanging a disco ball on the lid of his casket.

The funeral director compassionately smiles and tries to joke past the tears forming in Anne's eyes.

FUNERAL DIRECTOR
If that's something you'd like me to look into, I can.

Anne and Megan gently smile.

ANNE
No. He didn't even like dance music.

The funeral director smiles and treads gently.

FUNERAL DIRECTOR
Maybe that comment meant your husband preferred a burial service over cremation?

Anne looks at her kids for input but receives nothing.

ANNE
He didn't have strong religious feelings, so I don't think he had an opinion about either one.

FUNERAL DIRECTOR
Forgive me, Mrs. Hutchinson, but it's obvious this has all come quite unexpectedly. Since your family is still in a great deal of shock, and your husband didn't express any specific wishes, you may want to consider cremation. It will allow you all the time you need to make decisions you're comfortable with.

WAYNE and CAROLYN HUTCHINSON, Bill's ultra-religious parents, burst into the office.

WAYNE
Annie.

Anne and Megan stand up to face them while Jack remains seated. Carolyn opens her arms wide, moves past Anne, and embraces Megan.

ANNE
Wayne, Carolyn, I wasn't sure if you planned on coming.

Wayne, who is built much like his son, gives Anne a comforting bear hug.

CAROLYN
Of course, we planned on coming. We have to help you plan the service.

WAYNE
We need to make sure the traditions Billy grew up with are carried out at his memorial. You know, he was a devoted member of our congregation before he adopted your... secular lifestyle.

Anne drops her head and bites her lip.

CAROLYN
Have you decided on a casket?

Anne hesitates to answer the sensitive question in front of her children.

ANNE
Uh... Megan, Jack, why don't you take the car and go grab some lunch.

MEGAN
What about you?

ANNE
I'm fine. I'll get something later. Let your grandparents and I finalize these details, and I'll call you when we're done.

Megan tugs on Jack's jacket to cue their departure. With an excuse to escape, Jack eagerly jumps to his feet and leads Megan out of the door. Anne takes a deep breath and prepares for an uncomfortable afternoon.

MARY'S PORCH - NEXT DAY

A delivery man carries a box to Mary's porch. He rings the doorbell and sets the package down before leaving. Mary opens the door and picks up the box. She gives a thankful wave to the delivery man and takes the package inside.

MARY'S KITCHEN - MOMENTS LATER

Craig walks into his kitchen to find Mary opening the package.

CRAIG
Who was at the door?

MARY
Delivery guy.

Mary busts open the box, sifts through the packing material, and inspects the contents. Craig peeks over Mary's shoulder as she pulls out a top-of-the-line cell phone and two dice.

CRAIG

What's with the dice?

MARY

(Despondently)

It's... something we do.

CRAIG

Does this mean you're talking to Rachel again?

MARY

None of us are talking, except poor Jill. She's trying to play peacemaker with three unwilling participants.

CRAIG

Have you tried?

MARY

I don't know if I want to talk to Rachel, and Anne made it clear she doesn't want to talk to me. I'm afraid the situation may be beyond fixing.

Craig is aloof as he opens the refrigerator and digs around inside.

CRAIG

You're lucky your friends are still around to play these games with.

Mary addresses Craig, hidden by the refrigerator door.

MARY

(Annoyed)

Are you serious right now, Craig? Things couldn't be worse, and you're adding GUILT to this category five shitstorm?

Craig pops up from the fridge and closes the door.

CRAIG

If that's what it takes for you to realize how ridiculous you're acting.

MARY

How ridiculous I'M acting?

CRAIG

Yes, YOU. Do you expect Anne to cater to YOUR feelings right now? You still have your husband. Your kids still have their father.

A tearful frustration builds in Mary.

MARY

What am I supposed to do, Craig?! She won't talk to me!

CRAIG

When was the last time you tried?

Mary shakes her head as she remembers.

MARY

That night.

CRAIG

That night? That night she lost her husband AND sat in a hospital waiting for news on her daughter?

Mary backs off her previous stance.

CRAIG

You think, maybe, that wasn't the best time to cast judgment on her state of mind?

Mary thoughtfully hangs her head.

CRAIG

I'm sorry, I'm not sympathetic to your shitstorm. I was supposed to be playing golf with Bill on Friday. I'll be putting him in the ground instead. THAT'S a situation beyond fixing.

Craig walks out of the kitchen, leaving Mary alone.

ANNE'S PORCH - TEN MINUTES LATER

Mary stands with a blotchy face and watering eyes at Anne's front door. She takes a deep breath and knocks quietly. After a few moments of building anxiety, Megan answers the door.

MARY

Megan? How are you?

MEGAN
(Shamefully)
Better.

MARY
When did you, uh...?

MEGAN
Two days ago.

Mary smiles.

MARY
It's good to see you.

An awkward moment passes between them.

MARY
Is your mom here?

MEGAN
She's in the kitchen.

MARY
Would you mind asking her if she'll see me?

Megan shakes her head.

MEGAN
I don't have to ask.

Megan opens the door wide to welcome Mary into the house. As Mary steps over the threshold, Megan wraps her arms around her. They embrace tightly for several moments before Megan releases her grip. Mary smiles compassionately at Megan before proceeding into the kitchen.

ANNE'S KITCHEN - CONTINUOUS

Anne is sitting at her kitchen table with her back to Mary. Insurance paperwork, bills, and bank statements litter the area. Mary quietly comes into the room.

Anne hears her but doesn't take her eyes off the overwhelming stack of information in front of her.

ANNE

I had no idea our life was this complicated. I don't know where to begin. He has retirement accounts from jobs he left years ago. He always said he was going to consolidate them.

Mary addresses Anne's back.

MARY

I can try to help.

Anne drops her head into her hands and begins to cry. Mary moves to the chair next to her, sits down, and puts her arm around her.

MARY

I am so sorry. I'm sorry for that night with Megan, I'm sorry for not being there for you, but mostly I am so incredibly sorry for letting you down. Please forgive me.

Anne says nothing. She pulls her face out of her hands and falls onto Mary's shoulder. Mary begins to cry as they embrace.

RACHEL'S BACKYARD - CONTINUOUS

Rachel is walking aimlessly around her house when something catches her eye out a back window. Opening the back door, she sees Jack sitting on the steps of her pool. She approaches him and sits on the cement.

JACK

When I was little, you said I could use your pool any time I wanted.

RACHEL

You can.

Both stare at the center of the pool for several quiet moments before Jack interrupts the silence.

JACK

I hope you don't mind. I really don't want to talk.

RACHEL

I don't either. Consider me your goat.

Jack turns toward Rachel.

JACK

My goat?

Rachel shifts her attention to Jack.

RACHEL

Yeah, you know, like the ones at the racetrack.

JACK

I've never been to the racetrack.

RACHEL

You've never been to the racetrack? You're sixteen, I was going when I was ten.

Jack shrugs his shoulders.

RACHEL

Well, my sheltered friend, when you go to the paddock area and look in the stalls, you'll see goats paired up with some of the horses.

JACK

Why?

Rachel compassionately smiles.

RACHEL

Just so they aren't alone.

Both return their attention to the center of the pool. Jack takes a few reflective moments before speaking.

JACK

Are you religious?

Rachel sighs sympathetically.

RACHEL

(Gingerly)

Maybe this is a conversation for Mrs. Michaels.

JACK

(Angrily)

I don't believe in any of that crap.

Rachel is taken back by Jack's bluntness.

RACHEL
On second thought, I am the one you want to talk to.

JACK
My mom is having my dad's funeral at a church. He never went to church.

RACHEL
(Impartially)
Sometimes, in these situations, we find comfort in places we don't expect.

Jack rolls his eyes.

JACK
No one in my family has EVER taken comfort in church. It's my grandparents making her do it.

RACHEL
Your dad's parents?

Jack nods.

JACK
And my mom's making me speak at the funeral. I don't even want to go, and now I have to get up and give a speech.

Jack shakes his head.

JACK
I can't think about my dad right now, let alone talk about him.

Rachel feels Jack struggle with his emotions. She does her best to rescue him by changing the subject.

RACHEL
Hey, do you know how to drive a stick?

Jack is puzzled by the sudden shift in topics.

JACK
What?

RACHEL
A stick shift... do you know how to drive one?

Jack shakes his head.

RACHEL

Want to learn?

JACK

(Excitedly)

On your car?

RACHEL

Sure.

Rachel stands up.

JACK

But, it's like, worth more than my house. What if I wreck it?

RACHEL

Then you'll be like everyone else in this neighborhood.

Rachel starts for her garage and motions for Jack to follow her.

RACHEL

Come on.

Jack enthusiastically gets up and follows Rachel.

JILL'S KITCHEN - LATER

Jill is preparing several meals with the help of Grace and Emma. Wil and Robert enter the kitchen carrying baseball gloves and a ball.

JILL

Are you two going outside?

WIL

Yeah, Robert said he'd show me how to throw a curveball.

Jill smiles at Robert.

JILL

Try not to let it curve into a window.

ROBERT

We'll stay away from the house.

Robert kisses Jill. Grace and Emma giggle at their public display of affection. Robert playfully picks up both girls.

ROBERT
Are you two laughing at me?

Robert joyfully shakes the girls in his arms.

JILL
Don't damage my helpers!

Robert sets the girls back down next to their mother.

ROBERT
Oh, you girls are lucky your mom saved you!

The girls smile as they reposition themselves in their chairs. Robert and Wil head outside.

JILL'S BACKYARD - CONTINUOUS

Robert and Wil start throwing the baseball back and forth.

WIL
Will you take me to a Reds game?

ROBERT
Sure. I might even be able to get us a tour of the stadium.

WIL
You can do that?

ROBERT
Yeah, I know a couple of the people who run security down there. I could ask them to show us around.

WIL
That would be awesome! Can Charlie and Ethan come?

ROBERT
Sure, if their parents say it's okay.

The two continue to throw the baseball.

WIL
Are you going to marry my mom?

Robert catches the baseball and holds it in his glove.

ROBERT
Has she said something to you?

WIL
No.

Robert walks toward Wil.

ROBERT
How would you feel about that?

WIL
Good, I guess. I mean, my mom's really happy when you're around, and you're fun to play with.

Robert smiles as he bends down at eye level with Wil.

ROBERT
What about your sisters? How do you think they would feel?

WIL
They don't care about anything but their stupid dance classes.

ROBERT
Dance classes are as important to them as baseball is to you.

WIL
Yeah, but baseball isn't stupid.

Robert laughs.

ROBERT
Well, I wanted to make sure you were okay with this last week, but things didn't go as planned. Maybe now's the time you and I had a man-to-man talk.

Robert and Wil sit down on the lawn.

ANNE'S PORCH - LATER

Jill, Grace, and Emma wait on the porch with aluminum foil-covered casserole dishes in their hands. Jill's face lights up as the door opens and Mary stands in the doorway.

JILL

You're here!

Mary speaks through a smile.

MARY

Yes, I'm here.

JILL

Does that mean everything is okay?

MARY

Yes, everything is okay.

JILL

And Rachel?

Mary shakes her head as she opens the door wide and welcomes them all inside.

ANNE'S KITCHEN - CONTINUOUS

Anne gets up from the kitchen table and greets Jill and her girls with an embrace and a kiss on the cheek. Mary helps by taking the casserole dishes into the kitchen.

ANNE

Thank you so much. You didn't have to do all this.

JILL

It's the least we can do.

Megan walks into the kitchen and sees Grace and Emma.

MEGAN

Hi, girls!

The girls enthusiastically greet Megan.

JILL

Girls! Where are your manners?!

Megan allows Grace to climb on her back while she picks up Emma.

MEGAN

It's fine, Mrs. Michaels.

JILL

Grace, don't hang on Miss Megan.

ANNE

They're excited to see her. This house could use some happiness right now.

MEGAN

Do you mind if I take them upstairs and show them some new makeup?

The girls become giddy with excitement.

JILL

Do you two think you can remember how to behave at someone else's house?

Both girls nod, and Megan wastes no time taking them upstairs to her room. Jill, Mary, and Anne sit down at Anne's kitchen table.

JILL

How are you doing?

ANNE

I'm... losing my mind.

Anne nervously smiles.

ANNE

Bill's parents aren't making this process easy. They're insisting on a church funeral and a visitation. The kids don't want to do that, and I don't blame them. I think they're trying to save his soul now by doing all the ceremonial stuff that's important to them. I got so frustrated I actually picked up the phone to call him and complain. I started searching for his number before I realized what I was doing.

Anne drops her face into her hand and begins to cry.

ANNE

I can't believe he's gone.

Jill moves her chair closer to Anne and puts her arm around her.

JILL

We're here for you. Anything you EVER need, we're here.

Mary moves her chair closer and pulls Anne's hand away from her face.

MARY

You will get through this. You're one of the strongest women I've ever known. You ran a marathon for Christ's sake.

JILL

You've raised two amazing kids who think the world of you.

ANNE

I don't know about that. Megan's one mistake away from getting kicked out of school.

Mary smiles.

MARY

You just described my entire college experience.

Anne gently laughs.

ANNE

And Jack...

Anne can't finish her sentence before she lowers her head back into her hand.

MARY

Anne, I don't know if this is the right time to point it out, but Bill's heart attack, as tragic as it was, probably saved Megan's life.

Anne lifts her head to give Mary her full attention.

MARY

She was struggling to breathe when we found her. And if we weren't up there to get her, I don't want to think what might have happened.

Anne furrows her brow as she processes this new information.

ANNE

What are you talking about? When was she struggling to breathe?

Mary's face pinches with confusion.

MARY
Didn't you have this conversation with Megan?

ANNE
She said she was playing a drinking game with her roommates, and the next thing she remembers is Rachel trying to make her drink tequila.

Mary drops her shoulders in frustration.

MARY
Oh my God, Anne. No wonder you're so angry with her.

ANNE
Isn't that what happened?

MARY
Technically yes, but no. There's so much more to it.

Mary repositions herself to the edge of her chair.

MARY
We got to Megan's apartment and she was locked in her room. Rachel had to break the door down so we could get to her. We found her passed out, and we weren't sure if she was breathing. Rachel rubbed tequila in her face just so she'd throw up. Rachel absolutely did NOT give her anything to drink.

Anne becomes distressed at the revelation.

ANNE
Then, why were you arrested?

MARY
Because she wouldn't let me call you. She knew you were distracted with everything happening here, and she was trying to protect you from having to deal with another crisis. I felt we had to tell you, and we got into a huge fight over it. She destroyed my phone to prevent me from calling. Then she went and destroyed her own. I was so angry I punched her.

Jill's eyes bulge out with astonishment.

JILL

I'm sorry, Mary, did you say you PUNCHED her?

MARY

Yeah, and when that didn't work, I tackled her to the ground.

Jill and Anne let out a shocked chuckle.

ANNE

You PUNCHED and TACKLED Rachel Easton?

Jill and Anne look at each other with disbelief.

MARY

Yeah. I've never been so terrified in my entire life.

Jill and Anne begin laughing.

MARY

When the campus police showed up, we were covered in mud, so they figured we were drunk students. They pulled us apart and arrested both of us.

Mary's description of the ridiculous scene sends all three women into several moments of cathartic laughter.

Anne's guilt creeps in as she realizes she's allowed herself to forget the reality of her situation. Jill and Mary watch her laughter turn to tears.

Anne's sobs dramatically build. Mary and Jill become concerned as they watch Anne get up from the kitchen table and walk over to a shelf filled with family pictures. Anne swings from grief to anger as she sweeps her hands across the shelf, knocking every picture to the ground. She turns back to the kitchen table and violently pushes all of the financial documents to the floor.

Mary and Jill jump up and away from the table.

ANNE

God damn it, Bill!

Mary grabs Anne as she begins to uncontrollably sob.

MARY

Stop it, Anne! Not in your house! You can freak out all you want with us, but you have to be strong in front of Megan and Jack!

Anne begins to calm down.

ANNE

Jack... how am I supposed to be strong for him after what I did?

MARY

(Bewildered)

What did you do?

Megan frantically enters the kitchen.

MEGAN

What was that?!

Mary releases her grip. Anne remains silent as she shamefully sits back down at the table.

MARY

Nothing, honey. I tripped and bumped the shelf. A few pictures fell, that's all.

Megan reluctantly accepts Mary's explanation and goes back upstairs.

ANNE

(Quietly)

I can't...

Mary sits back down, holds Anne's tear-soaked face, and looks at her compassionately.

MARY

That's not an option.

Anne succumbs to exhaustion.

MARY

We will do everything we can to get you through this.

Anne takes Mary's hand as she continues to cradle her face. Mary lets go of Anne's face and brings both women's hands to the table.

ANNE

What am I going to do about Rachel? I said the cruelest things to her. How can I ever apologize enough?

Jill sits down next to Anne and places her hand on top of theirs.

JILL

Honey, if Rachel understands one thing, it's speaking without thinking.

Mary stares sympathetically into Anne's eyes.

MARY

You churned her in a box of shit, and she got over it. She'll get over this.

RACHEL'S BEDROOM - VERY EARLY HOURS OF NEXT DAY

Rachel wakes to the sound of someone aggressively pounding on her front door. She jumps out of bed, puts on her robe, and heads downstairs.

RACHEL'S PORCH/FRONT YARD - CONTINUOUS

Rachel is greeted by a POLICE OFFICER, Jack, and her car parked askew on the street.

POLICE OFFICER

Is that your vehicle?

Rachel strains her eyes through the darkness.

RACHEL

Yes.

POLICE OFFICER

Did you give this young man permission to drive it?

Jack stands with his eyes shamefully lowered. Rachel quickly realizes her car has been on an unauthorized adventure. She does her best to mask her disappointment and lies to protect Jack.

RACHEL

Yeah, he had my permission.

POLICE OFFICER

Do you know how irresponsible it is to give a boy his age access to a car like this?

Rachel doesn't appreciate the lecture.

RACHEL

Was he doing something wrong, officer?

She inspects her car and realizes a goat is in the passenger seat. She tries to look at Jack, but he evades eye contact.

POLICE OFFICER

He was speeding down Route 4 at one hundred twenty miles an hour. Then I had to follow him all the way over here before he pulled over.

Rachel can't help but be impressed with her car's performance.

POLICE OFFICER

He's being arrested for reckless driving and failure to yield to an officer.

Rachel moves closer to the officer and takes him aside.

RACHEL

(Quietly)

Look, officer, this young man just lost his father and is having a rough time. Any chance you could let him off with a warning?

The officer sighs sympathetically and weighs his options.

POLICE OFFICER

I guess I don't have to arrest him, but I do have to cite him.

RACHEL

I appreciate that.

The police officer walks to his car, completes a ticket, and presents it to Jack. He gets in his car and leaves Rachel and Jack in the front yard.

RACHEL

Jack.

Jack reluctantly looks up at Rachel.

RACHEL

Next time... just ask.

Jack remorsefully nods and turns to walk home. Headlights illuminate the driveway as Caleb drives up and parks his truck. He gets out and walks to Rachel.

CALEB

What's going on?

Caleb notices the unexpected passenger in Rachel's car.

CALEB
What's that in your car?

Rachel sighs with frustration.

RACHEL
A metaphor.

Caleb looks closer at the inside of her vehicle.

CALEB
Well, the metaphor is eating your upholstery.

JACK'S BEDROOM - MOMENTS LATER

Jack quietly enters his bedroom with his speeding ticket in hand. He flips on his light and falls backwards into his bed. Anne quickly enters.

ANNE
Where have you been?

Jack says nothing causing Anne to become aggravated.

ANNE
Jack, I'm talking to you.

Jack sits up on his bed.

JACK
Driving.

ANNE
Driving what? The car has been here all night.

Anne sees the ticket in his hand. She reaches out and grabs the citation.

ANNE
What's this?

Anne looks over the ticket.

ANNE
(Exasperated)
How were you going a hundred and twenty?

JACK

Mrs. Easton's car.

ANNE

Mrs. Easton? Why would she let you drive that car?!

Jack jumps up off of the bed and gets in Anne's face.

JACK

She didn't, I just took it.

ANNE

You just TOOK it?! On top of everything else, I have to worry about you stealing cars now?!

Anne shakes her head in desperation.

ANNE

What are we going to do, Jack? We have to figure out a way to get through this.

Jack walks across his room and digs through his dresser.

JACK

You can NOT make me get up and speak in front of a bunch of people I don't care about!

ANNE

That's what your grandparents want, Jack, not me.

Jack turns around with pajamas in hand.

JACK

The same grandparents who keep asking if I have a girlfriend?

Jack slams the dresser drawer shut. Anne brings her hands to her face, drags them to her chin, and locks her fingers as she pleads.

ANNE

Please, Jack. I don't have the strength to fight them. Please do me this favor and help me get through this. Once it's over, we can figure out everything else together.

Jack walks into his bathroom.

JACK
(Disgusted)
Don't you think you're out of favors, mom?

Jack slams his bathroom door. Anne sighs heavily at the ceiling.

CHURCH - LATER THAT AFTERNOON

Anne and Megan are greeting family members and friends. Jack hovers near the two but doesn't engage in the formalities. Wayne and Carolyn are close by, receiving condolences from their fellow church members. Jill and Robert, along with Mary and Craig, stand near Anne and her family.

John Michaels walks in with Teresa at his side and takes a seat in the pews.

Kevin Easton enters, greets Anne, and sits down.

Caleb and Rachel enter the back of the congregation. Rachel hesitates to move to the pews before Caleb takes her hand and guides her to the back row. She sits down and accidentally makes eye contact with Anne.

The BISHOP approaches Anne and quietly lets her know the service is about to begin. Anne nods, gathers Megan and Jack, and sits down.

The bishop moves toward the pulpit and signals the attendees to take their seats. Anne leans over to Megan and whispers in her ear. Megan nods, gets up, and walks back toward Rachel.

Rachel defensively stiffens as Megan approaches and bends down to speak.

MEGAN
My mom would like to invite you to sit with the family.

Rachel looks past Megan and sees Anne turned around and smiling. She looks to Caleb.

CALEB
Go.

Rachel gets up and follows Megan down to the family's seating area. Megan rejoins her mother's side while Rachel sits down behind them next to Bill's parents. Wayne tries to stop Rachel from sitting down.

WAYNE
This area is reserved for family.

Anne abruptly turns around.

ANNE

She IS family, Wayne.

Rachel gently smiles as she takes her seat. Carolyn leans over her husband to address Rachel.

CAROLYN

Did you know Billy well?

RACHEL

Very well. I had to keep him from stirring my coffee in the morning.

Anne hears the exchange and smothers a much-needed laugh.

The bishop takes the pulpit.

BISHOP

Today is a day none of us ever want to think about. A day parents lose a son, a wife loses a husband, children lose a father, and we all lose a friend...

CHURCH - LATER IN THE CEREMONY

The bishop finishes up his remarks.

BISHOP

Brothers and sisters, we do not want you to be uninformed about those who sleep in death, so that you do not grieve like the rest of mankind, who have no hope.

Jack sits disinterested with his arms folded.

BISHOP

For we believe that Jesus died and rose again, and so we believe that God will bring with Jesus those who have fallen asleep in him.

The bishop closes his Bible.

BISHOP

I would now like to invite his children, Megan and Jackson, up so they can say a few words about their father.

Bill's children reluctantly stand and walk up to the pulpit. Megan steps up and takes out prepared remarks. Her voice trembles as she greets the congregation.

MEGAN

Thank you all for coming.

Megan tries to level out her shaky voice by clearing her throat, then reads from her prepared remarks.

MEGAN

I was so lucky to have my dad. He was such a funny and loving guy. He hated being angry and he never yelled at us unless my mom told him to.

The congregation softly laughs.

MEGAN

When I left for college, he used to send me random texts with thoughts that would pop into his head. He wasn't very good with remembering things, so he'd send them at all hours. It would always startle me to hear my text notification go off in the middle of the night. I'd worry it was something horrible but instead I'd read, "never pass up an opportunity to go to the bathroom" or "be nice to flight attendants because they control the snack cart."

The congregation again laughs softly.

MEGAN

I'm going to miss getting those texts. I'm going to miss all the little things he did. The way he used to make faces behind mom's back. The way he always hit the trash cans when he pulled into the garage. How he burned his tongue on his coffee every morning.

Megan begins to cry as she looks at her mom.

MEGAN

I'll miss watching him make my mom laugh.

Megan watches her mom's face fill with tears. Grief overcomes her and she abruptly folds up her speech.

MEGAN

I'll miss everything about him every day for the rest of my life.

Megan wipes her eyes as she steps down and takes the seat next to her mother. Jack becomes increasingly uncomfortable as he hovers in the background. The bishop motions for him to step up and speak. Jack reluctantly walks up to the pulpit.

JACK

It's very hard for me to sit here and listen to this. I don't believe in any of it.

Anne watches Jack's contempt build. She closes her eyes and tries to wish her way out of the unfolding scene.

JACK

My dad died because his heart quit, not because God decided to take him. I hate that I have to stand up here and pretend like these meaningless Bible verses provide me with some sort of comfort.

An uncomfortable tension hangs over the congregation as the bishop steps in.

BISHOP

We know this is a difficult time for you, son. Why don't you share with us the last thing you remember doing with your dad?

Jack becomes very agitated as he broods over the bishop's suggestion. After a moment of awkward fidgeting, he leans into the pulpit microphone and releases all the frustration he's been harboring.

JACK

The last thing I did with my dad was pull him off my mom!

Anne drops her forehead into her palm as a wave of whispers ripples through the mourners.

JACK

Yeah, he was on top of her when his heart stopped, and he was crushing her! I came home just in time to pull him off and uncuff her from the bedpost! You want to talk about God having a reason for putting me through that?! A benevolent deity would have let him finish so he could climb off her himself!

The bishop tries to push Jack away from the pulpit, but his outburst is unstoppable. Craig motions to Robert for help as he stands up and begins making his way out of the pew.

JACK

There, Nana and Papa, I honored my father! Are you happy now?! Oh, and if I wasn't gay before, this would have sent me straight to the registration window!

Craig and Robert forcefully escort Jack off the altar and into a side room.

Rachel whispers to Wayne.

RACHEL

And I thought my family fucked me up.

Wayne cringes with disgust as he gathers up Carolyn and leads the way to the exit. Megan stands up and hurries to accompany Jack.

Anne sits alone with her head buried in her hands.

The bishop tries to salvage some dignity in the moment and approaches the pulpit.

BISHOP

That... uh... concludes the services for this afternoon. Please join us at the reception next door.

Anne sits motionless as the rest of the congregation quickly moves toward the doors. Rachel leans forward and pats Anne on the shoulder.

RACHEL

(Quietly to Anne)

Don't get mad, but I think I MAY have offended your in-laws.

Rachel leaves the pew and joins Jill and Mary at the back of the now-empty room. As they wait patiently for Anne, Mary awkwardly tries to engage in civil discussion.

MARY

How's your nose?

RACHEL

Fine.

The battle to minimize the excruciating silence rages on.

MARY

Thank you for the phone.

RACHEL

I owed you one.

Jill struggles with their uncomfortable interaction.

JILL

Listen y'all, can we just start talking again? We've lost Bill, and now Jack's in the middle of a nervous breakdown. We need each other right now.

Rachel doesn't let go of her grudge.

RACHEL

She started it.

MARY

Rachel, what was I supposed to do? You were being totally unreasonable.

RACHEL

And sucker punching me was reasonable?

Mary becomes defensive.

MARY

You sucker punch people all the time!

RACHEL

That's different. I don't like those people.

Jill loses her patience over their behavior.

JILL

Enough! I can't believe y'all are acting like this. My children are more mature than you.

Rachel and Mary back off as Jill continues to chastise them.

JILL

From what I understand, neither one of you did the right thing that night. Rachel, you should have let Mary call Anne. Mary, you shouldn't have beaten up Rachel.

Rachel is insulted by Jill's characterization of events.

RACHEL

Who said she beat me up? She didn't beat me up.

JILL

It doesn't matter! The point is, y'all were both wrong and y'all both need to apologize!

A moment passes as they both contemplate how to proceed.

RACHEL
(Reluctantly)
I should have let you call Anne.

MARY
(Antagonistically)
I shouldn't have beaten you up.

Rachel becomes more insulted at the second characterization. Her eyes bulge in anger as she reaches to grab Mary. Jill throws up her hands to separate them. Her engagement ring catches Rachel's attention.

JILL
Anne was right, y'all ARE morons.

Rachel grabs Jill's left hand and shakes it at her.

RACHEL
What the hell is this?!

Mary gasps.

MARY
Oh my God! When did that happen?

Jill pulls her hand out of Rachel's grasp.

JILL
Last week. With everything that's happened, it's been the last thing on my mind.

Rachel shakes her head with a disgusted look on her face.

RACHEL
So, it's Bobby.

JILL
Of course, it's Robert, who else?

RACHEL
O.J. Simpson, Jeffrey Epstein, Rasputin... anyone but him.

MARY
Rachel! Be happy for her!

Rachel struggles to be civil.

RACHEL

Fine. Mazel tov. I hope he disclosed the male pattern baldness and lazy testicle that runs in our family.

MARY

Lazy testicle?

RACHEL

Yeah. You've heard of a lazy eye? Well, it's like that except between his legs and much weirder looking.

Mary looks to Jill for confirmation. Jill subtly shakes her head and denies the condition.

SIDE ROOM OF CHURCH - CONTINUOUS

Megan and Robert hover near the door while Craig tries to comfort Jack.

CRAIG

It's okay, Jack. You've been under more pressure than anyone could possibly imagine.

Jack sits silently while occasionally wiping a tear from his eye.

CRAIG

Your dad would want you to forgive him for putting you through that.

A knock at the door cues Megan to open it. Caleb walks in.

CALEB

Hi. Do you mind if I have a word with him?

Craig looks to Jack for some guidance. He doesn't get an objection, so he gets up and heads for the door.

CRAIG

(Quietly to Caleb)

Good luck.

Craig, Robert, and Megan leave the room.

CALEB

Hi, Jack. I don't know if we've officially met. I'm Caleb.

Caleb extends his hand to Jack and he half-heartedly shakes it.

Caleb sits down next to Jack.

CALEB
Man, just seeing your folks is bad enough, but what happened to you just sucks.

Jack appreciates Caleb's candor.

CALEB
I work behind the bar sometimes, so I've heard some pretty outrageous stories.

Jack shows interest in conversation for the first time.

JACK
Nothing like mine, though.

CALEB
I don't want to hurt your feelings, but you wouldn't even crack my top ten.

JACK
(Sarcastically)
Right.

CALEB
Okay, I'll let you be the judge. Here's number ten on my list. A guy came in and just starting ordering shot after shot. After about a dozen in an hour, I tell him I can't serve him anymore. He grabs me by the shirt and tells me he just walked in on his wife cheating, so I have to keep serving him. I tell him I sympathize, but the law doesn't allow me to keep serving intoxicated people. He looks at me dead in the eyes and tells me, the person his wife was cheating with, was his mother.

Jack smiles with shock.

CALEB
I kept pouring and paid for his cab.

Jack's mood lightens and they share a laugh.

JACK
What are the other nine?

CHURCH - CONTINUOUS

Anne finally musters the courage to stand and make her way out of the pew. She turns around and finds the only people left in the church are her friends.

ANNE

See why I don't go to church?

Jill and Mary smile at Anne's attempt at humor. She shares hugs with Mary and Jill before facing Rachel.

ANNE

Rachel, I don't know the words that would adequately express how truly sorry I am. Megan was confused. I should have considered the condition she was in. I should have let you explain, and I shouldn't have said those horrible things to you.

Jill and Mary smile as they watch the reconciliation.

ANNE

And I had no idea what you did for Megan until Mary told me. I can never thank you enough for everything you did that night.

Anne hesitates as she leans toward Rachel. Awkwardness builds between them before Anne ignores Rachel's uncomfortable body language and wraps her arms tightly around her. Rachel's eyes begin to tear as she hugs Anne back.

Feeling vulnerable, Rachel quickly releases Anne, steps away, and wipes her eyes.

RACHEL

I'm glad she's all right.

Anne and Rachel exchange smiles to signal their rift is over.

The side room door opens, with Jack and Caleb casually exiting the room.

RACHEL

You should probably go check on Jack.

Relieved to see Jack in a better state of mind, Robert and Craig head for the door. As the last people exit, Anne, Megan, and Jack remain together inside the church. Anne stands teary-eyed in front of Jack while Megan positions herself between them.

ANNE

I'm sorry. I'm sorry for everything. Please know, if there was any other way that night, I wouldn't have put you through that. And as for your grandparents... I should have stood up to them. I should have done this in a way that would have made us all feel better, not pressured and uncomfortable. Please forgive me.

Jack looks directly into Anne's eyes for the first time since the night of Bill's death.

JACK

I'm sorry I came out to everyone without talking to you first. You probably wanted to tell people in your own way.

Anne laughs through her tears.

ANNE

Jack, you just detailed the most humiliating event of my life to hundreds of strangers. I don't care how my friends found out you're gay.

Anne and Jack smile.

MEGAN

(Facetiously)

And I was worried MY bad decisions would be the talk of the funeral.

They laugh together.

ANNE

It's just the three of us now. Let's try to have one crisis at a time from now on, okay?

They all embrace.

CHURCH MULTI-PURPOSE ROOM - CONTINUOUS

Family and friends mingle at the post-service reception. John and Teresa Michaels approach Rachel and Caleb. John lifts his hand and waves it at the fading bruise under Rachel's eye.

JOHN

I see you're still making quality life choices.

Rachel lifts her hand and waves it up and down Teresa.

RACHEL

As are you.

Teresa glares at Rachel as she and John continue walking through the crowd.

CALEB

Who was that?

RACHEL

Remember the guy I thought Jill shot a couple years ago?

Caleb nods.

CALEB

And the woman?

RACHEL

Remember the teeth you pulled out of my hair?

Caleb smiles devilishly.

CALEB

(Casually)

I love you.

Rachel stands stunned as Caleb kisses her.

CALEB

I'm getting something to drink. Can I get you anything?

Rachel's stunned expression doesn't change as she gently shakes her head. Caleb leaves as Mary approaches.

MARY

Okay, in all seriousness, I'm very sorry for the other night. If it matters at all, I know you weren't fighting back. If you were, I would have been unconscious after the first punch.

Rachel remains totally preoccupied with Caleb's words. Mary is puzzled by Rachel's glazed-over appearance.

MARY

Rachel?

Rachel pulls her attention to Mary.

RACHEL

What?

MARY

(Sincerely)

I'm apologizing.

RACHEL

For what?

MARY

(Surprised)

For what? For our collegiate cage match, that's what.

RACHEL

Oh, that. Forget about it.

MARY

Forget about it?! Are you all right? Did that beating knock some humility into you?

Rachel glares at Mary.

MARY

I'm kidding, I'm kidding.

Mary holds up her hands in surrender as she walks away.

Jill and Robert hold hands quietly in a corner of the room. Robert receives a call.

ROBERT

Fitzpatrick.

Robert lets go of Jill's hand and checks his watch.

ROBERT

I can be there in ten minutes.

Robert ends his call and turns to Jill.

ROBERT

I'm so sorry, Jill. There's something that needs my immediate attention. Can you have one of the girls give you a ride home?

JILL

Of course. Will I see you later?

ROBERT

I hope so.

Robert kisses Jill goodbye and quickly leaves the reception. Jill takes out her phone and thumbs through her contacts. She is interrupted when John and Teresa approach. She lowers her phone and tries to appear pleasant.

JOHN

Teresa, I'll meet you at the car. I have to discuss something with Jill.

Teresa does her best to make Jill jealous by seductively whispering in John's ear.

TERESA

Don't keep me waiting.

She kisses John on the cheek before she leaves. Jill smiles to keep from laughing at Teresa's transparent behavior.

JOHN

I spoke with Wil. He's really excited about you and Robert getting married.

Jill awkwardly covers up her engagement ring by placing her phone over her left hand.

JOHN

So, you're okay with losing the kids?

John reaches into his coat pocket, removes a folded piece of paper, and hands it to Jill. She refuses to take it.

JOHN

Did you think I was kidding?

Jill unwillingly takes the paper from John and opens it. She sees the words "Summons To Appear" on the top of the paper and immediately refolds it.

JILL

You are the worst person I have ever known.

John smiles, taking the insult as a compliment.

JILL

You're hardly interested in the time you have with them now. Why are you really doing this?

John leans closer to Jill and lowers his voice.

JOHN

Are you kidding me? Rachel Easton... in front of the world... forced to detail her career-ending screw-up.

John grins broadly.

JOHN

It'll be worth every penny in legal fees.

Jill breathes deeply, trying to contain her anger.

JILL

So that's what this is all about? An opportunity for you to get back at Rachel.

JOHN

(Smugly)

Yeah, it is. That, and keeping you single.

JILL

These are our children, John. Do you know what this will do to them? Are you seriously going to sacrifice them to fulfill your insane revenge fantasy?

JOHN

We all need some childhood trauma to work through. Besides, unlike a federal employee, I can afford their therapy.

Jill's rage builds and she struggles to keep her poise.

JILL

You are SO cruel and SO vindictive. I'm surprised you had the decency to wait until the end of Bill's funeral to give me this.

JOHN

(Indifferently)

To be honest, I never really cared for the guy. He always struck me as a corpulent boy scout who'd probably end up dying on the toilet. If you think about it, since he croaked on top of Anne, I was right.

John turns to walk away but stops and returns.

JOHN

Oh, and you might want to get Mary away from the buffet. I heard this caterer charges by the pound.

John continues on his way.

CHURCH MULTI-PURPOSE ROOM - CONTINUOUS

Anne, Megan, and Jack enter the room and begin receiving condolences from guests. Wayne and Carolyn hastily approach Anne.

WAYNE

We were just told Billy isn't having a proper burial.

ANNE

Yes, Wayne. The kids and I just aren't ready to make these kinds of decisions. I've asked that Bill be cremated so we can take our time deciding what helps us heal.

WAYNE

This is outrageous. I can't believe you're going to allow Billy to be destroyed so YOU can feel better.

ANNE

(Defiantly)

I'm sorry you feel that way. I would hope as Megan and Jack's grandparents, you would want what's easiest on them.

CAROLYN

This isn't about what's easiest. It's about eternity.

ANNE

No, it's about figuring out how to go on without someone we all loved very much.

Anne steps in front of her children and into Wayne's personal space.

ANNE

Wayne, you need to accept that Bill didn't subscribe to this. These are your beliefs, not his. He wouldn't have wanted this kind of ceremony, and he certainly wouldn't have allowed you to bully Jack into getting up there today. We're all going to have to deal with losing Bill in our own way, and I hope you'll respect what I decide he would have wanted from this point forward.

Wayne pinches his face with disgust as he takes Carolyn by the arm and escorts her away. Anne faces her children.

MEGAN
I'm sorry they're being like this, mom.

ANNE
I'm sorry too, but it's not their feelings I'm worried about anymore.

Anne pulls both her kids close.

RACHEL'S KITCHEN - AFTER THE FUNERAL

Rachel and Caleb enter her kitchen through the garage entrance. Rachel is guarded and quiet. Caleb goes straight for the refrigerator, opens the door, and begins searching inside. Caleb finds an energy drink and pulls it out of the fridge.

CALEB
I'm closing the bar tonight, and this genetically modified liquid cocaine is the only thing that gets me through.

Caleb notices Rachel's muted mood.

CALEB
Hey, are you okay? You were quiet all the way back.

RACHEL
(Aloof)
I'm fine.

CALEB
Are you sure? Because I hate to leave you alone tonight if something's wrong.

RACHEL
Nothing's wrong, I've just been thinking.

Caleb shows genuine concern.

CALEB
About what happened at the funeral?

RACHEL
About what was SAID at the funeral.

CALEB
What Jack said? By next week, no one's going to remember.

RACHEL

Not what Jack said, what YOU said.

CALEB

You've been thinking about what I said to Jack?

Rachel closes her eyes in frustration.

RACHEL

God, you're making this difficult. No, what YOU said to ME.

Caleb playfully acts dumb.

CALEB

What did I say to you?

Rachel throws up her arms and moves away from him.

RACHEL

If you don't remember, it's not worth talking about.

Caleb moves to Rachel and puts his hands on her waist.

CALEB

Oh, are you talking about when I said I love you?

Rachel becomes very uncomfortable and avoids eye contact.

RACHEL

Yeah, that.

Caleb toys with Rachel's discomfort.

CALEB

What didn't you understand? I'd use smaller words, but I don't think there are any. Is it easier if I draw you pictures or break out in interpretive dance?

Rachel rolls her eyes with an embarrassed smile.

CALEB

This past year has been the most fun of my life. I think about you constantly, I can't wait to spend time with you, and I feel incomplete when you're not around. Does that help you understand?

Caleb takes Rachel's hands and playfully maneuvers his head to force eye contact.

CALEB

Now, I know you have a tendency to be a little bit... emotionally constipated, so I have no expectation of hearing it from you until you're ready. I'm going to warn you though, I'm pretty adorable, so you'll eventually give in.

Caleb kisses Rachel.

CALEB

I gotta go.

As Caleb leaves the room, Rachel cannot suppress the smile slowly creeping across her face.

JILL'S KITCHEN - LATER THAT EVENING

Jill sits at her kitchen table, lost in thought. Her attention shifts toward the front door as she hears keys in the lock and the turn of the knob. Robert enters the kitchen and finds Jill.

ROBERT

You're still up?

Jill directs her puffy eyes and tear-soaked cheeks toward Robert.

ROBERT

What's wrong? Are the kids okay?

Robert pulls out a chair and sits down next to Jill.

JILL

They're fine.

ROBERT

Why are you upset?

JILL

(Cautiously)

If I asked you something, would you answer me truthfully without any questions?

ROBERT

Of course.

Robert takes Jill's hand and listens intently.

JILL

Was Rachel responsible for that boy dying in Chicago?

Robert lets go of Jill's hand, sits back in his chair, and takes a deep breath.

ROBERT

Why in the world are you bringing that up?

JILL

You said you wouldn't ask any questions.

Robert looks down at the floor.

ROBERT

Jill, you're asking about a very complicated incident. I don't think you want to hear what I have to say.

JILL

I know I don't, but I have to know.

Robert looks up and carefully formulates his response.

ROBERT

Yes. Ellie disobeyed orders... and a boy died.

Jill sinks her face into her hands.

ROBERT

But that doesn't mean she caused it.

Jill becomes impatient and abruptly draws her hands down.

JILL

What DOES it mean?

Robert becomes flustered in his attempts to evade disclosure.

ROBERT

It means I don't know! Hell, she doesn't even know! I told you it was complicated. It was over twenty years ago. I can't think of any reason why you'd want to...

Jill leans into Robert and interrupts.

JILL

John's suing for full custody of the kids. He's using the incident in Chicago to say Rachel's dangerously irresponsible and he doesn't want her a part of their family.

Robert pulls his head back and scoffs.

ROBERT

That's ridiculous.

JILL

I agree, but right now I'm only concerned with what a judge might think.

Robert uncomfortably weighs Jill's request.

JILL

Please. Tell me what happened.

Robert reluctantly gives in.

ROBERT

She thought she was responding to a routine domestic violence call, but it was more serious than that. An armed suspect was on a balcony, threatening a young boy. A second unit arrived, and the decision was made to call in hostage negotiation. The suspect became more agitated and Ellie didn't think they'd get there in time. She entered the building... and...

Robert hesitates to finish.

JILL

And?

ROBERT

(Somberly)

The suspect killed the boy and then himself.

Jill swallows hard as tears begin to roll down her cheeks.

ROBERT

The whole situation was...

Robert begins to choke up as the memory becomes too overwhelming. He shakes off his emotions and continues with the factual retelling of events.

ROBERT

A witness claimed Ellie threatened the suspect with a gun, but she couldn't have.

JILL

How do you know?

Robert takes a deep breath.

ROBERT

Because she handed me her weapon.

Robert recognizes Jill's puzzled reaction and continues to explain.

ROBERT

I was the second unit.

Jill stands up and nervously paces the floor for several moments.

JILL

That's why she hates you.

Robert nods.

ROBERT

She doesn't think I did enough to defend her.

JILL

Did you?

ROBERT

I thought I did.

Jill continues to pace as she processes the information and thinks to herself.

JILL

What if she had the opportunity to tell her side of the story...

Robert interrupts.

ROBERT

She won't talk about it.

Jill reformulates her train of thought.

JILL

Maybe she needs...

Robert shakes his head vigorously and interrupts again.

ROBERT

She doesn't.

Jill becomes annoyed at Robert's unwillingness to consider her suggestions.

JILL

You don't know, Robert.

ROBERT

Yes, I do, Jill.

JILL

How can you be so sure? It's been years since you've really talked to her. Things change. She might see it as a chance to clear her name.

Robert loses his patience for subtlety.

ROBERT

You're right, I haven't talked to her in years, and things do change. But you should know, the last time she was forced to talk about this, I found her with her service revolver under her chin.

Jill covers her mouth as she retreats in shock. Robert stands up from the table and goes to Jill.

ROBERT

I'm sorry. I shouldn't have told you that. It's just that... this destroyed her. You can't have any expectation she'll be willing to talk about it.

Jill drops her hands from her face and holds them tightly against her chest.

JILL

I won't.

Jill begins to twist her engagement ring around her finger as she walks away from Robert and turns her back on him. She stands for several moments, contemplating her future.

JILL

There's only one thing I want more than to spend the rest of my life with you...

Jill turns back around and places her engagement ring in Robert's hand.

ANNE'S LIVING ROOM - TWO WEEKS LATER, EVENING

Although scheduled, the setting is not bunco. There are no fancy foods or beverages. No elaborate table settings decorate the room. It's just the four women quietly sitting and providing comfort to one another. Mary places a consoling hand on Anne's back as they share the couch. Rachel and Jill sit in chairs across from them. The women defer to Anne to direct the conversation.

ANNE
Megan moved into a new apartment.

MARY
Good. New surroundings will help.

ANNE
She's coming home on the weekends until the semester ends.

JILL
The girls will love having her home.

Anne flashes a brief smile to Jill.

ANNE
Oh, and I've been offered a teaching position.

MARY
Really? Do you think you'll take it?

ANNE
I do. It'll allow me a better schedule for Jack.

RACHEL
How's he doing?

ANNE
Better. He's able to make eye contact with me so that's encouraging.

The women sympathetically smile. Anne's attention drifts away.

ANNE
So many times, I wished for peace and quiet in this house. Now I have it, and it's the worst thing I've ever known.

Jill attempts to lighten the discussion.

JILL

I don't think I ever heard how you and Bill met.

Anne smiles as she remembers.

ANNE

We were in college. We were both taking a class we didn't need. He sat in the row behind me. I thought he was cute and from the few times we spoke, he seemed to have a good sense of humor. He actually had a crush on the girl sitting next to me.

MARY

Did he really?

ANNE

Yeah, but she had a boyfriend. Another girl moved in on him, but I could see he wasn't interested. I would interrupt her attempts at conversation with questions about the class. I think he knew what I was doing and appreciated it.

Jill smiles as Anne continues.

ANNE

We got to talking and eventually we decided to go to a school play together. The only tickets we could get were singles on opposite sides of the theater. I had no idea what the play was about because I spent the entire night sneaking looks at him across the aisle. Turned out, he was doing the same to me. We started going out, and we really haven't spent much time apart since.

Anne stifles her emerging tears.

ANNE

I don't know how I'll ever get used to him not being here. All day I'm surrounded by things that remind me he's gone. Even at night... I unconsciously reach across the bed for him, but all I feel is his undisturbed side of the sheets.

Anne wipes the tears from her eyes and drops her head onto Mary's shoulder.

JILL

What can we do?

Anne thinks while she takes several deep breaths.

ANNE

Would you think I'm an awful person if I asked you to take Bill's clothes to the donation center?

JILL

Not at all.

MARY

Why would you even ask that?

Anne lifts her head off of Mary.

ANNE

My mother told me I need to be mindful of appearances. After everything that happened at the funeral, people will be scrutinizing my every move.

Anne thinks for a moment as she wipes her tears.

ANNE

She never fails to make a situation worse.

MARY

With all due respect, Anne... your mother is at best, inappropriate, but more likely, just a bitch.

Anne gently laughs.

MARY

Don't listen to her. She's never gone through anything like this, and she has no right to make you feel self-conscious. You handle this whatever way makes it easier for you and the kids. Besides, I think Rachel can deal with anyone who has a problem with the way you handle things.

RACHEL

Just give me names.

Anne smiles and begins to cry.

ANNE

You know, right after Jack's... speech, I could physically feel everyone in that room scramble to distance themselves from me. I felt so toxic and so alone. Bill's gone. Megan was busy nursing Jack's meltdown. My parents, my brother, my in-laws, they all left me in that church. I had no idea what to do next. Where do I go? How am I going to do this all by myself? What makes me think I can survive this? Then, and only because I knew it had to happen eventually, I stood up and turned around...

Anne thoughtfully looks at each of her friends.

ANNE

...and there you were.

Mary takes Anne's hand and holds it tight.

MARY

Here we are.

Mary smiles sympathetically.

ANNE

I don't know what I'd do without you.

Jill leans forward and places her right hand on top of theirs.

JILL

You'll never need to find out.

Rachel gets up and heads into the kitchen.

RACHEL

Unless you punch me in the face. Mary used up this group's freebie.

The women welcome Rachel's levity with tender laughter.

ANNE'S BEDROOM - THE NEXT DAY

Jill, Rachel, and Mary are boxing up Bill's clothing in Anne's closet. Mary replaces a pile of men's shirts stacked neatly on a shelf with two dice.

MARY

I can't believe we're packing up Bill's things. I keep expecting him to come around the corner with a box of donuts.

Rachel finds Bill's bathrobe hanging on the back of the closet door. She privately reminisces as she removes the robe and folds it neatly into a box.

MARY

(Holding back tears)

Can someone start a happy conversation?

Mary looks to Jill, who is unusually quiet.

MARY

Jill, have you and Robert thought about any details of your wedding?

Jill sighs deeply, then speaks with a heavy heart.

JILL

There isn't going to be a wedding.

Both Mary and Rachel stop what they're doing.

MARY

(Shocked)

What? Why?

Jill avoids eye contact as she continues to remove clothes from hangers and pack them into a box.

JILL

I... I thought about it, and I don't want to get married, that's all.

Mary and Rachel share a look of bewilderment with each other.

MARY

Don't want to? When did you decide this?

Jill sneaks a look at Mary as she continues her packing.

JILL

It's just... too hard.

Mary and Rachel stand motionless, staring at Jill in confusion. Mary nudges Rachel, encouraging her to engage in conversation.

RACHEL

Look, if you're really worried, that lazy testicle thing can skip a generation.

Jill half-heartedly smiles and continues to avoid eye contact.

MARY

I can't believe you don't want to get married.

Jill stops what she's doing and looks at Mary with tearing eyes.

JILL

Well, I don't.

MARY

Jill, you're about to burst into tears. Forgive me, but I don't believe you.

Jill wipes the forming tears from her eyes.

RACHEL

Did he do something? Do I need to kick his ass?

Jill tries to regain her composure.

JILL

Of course not.

MARY

Then what happened?

Jill grabs a full box and starts out of the closet.

JILL

Anne's going to be back soon. I'd like to have this done for her before she gets home.

Mary silently encourages Rachel to follow Jill.

ANNE'S UPSTAIRS HALLWAY - CONTINUOUS

Rachel catches up to Jill.

RACHEL

Jill.

Jill reluctantly turns around.

RACHEL

Look, I have my issues with Bobby, but I have no doubt he'd be a great husband and father. It's really all he's ever wanted to be.

Jill smiles sadly.

JILL

I know.

Jill continues down the hall.

CELLULAR PHONE RETAIL STORE - LATER THAT AFTERNOON

Rachel waits patiently as the SALES REPRESENTATIVE brings out her new phone.

SALES REPRESENTATIVE

Here you go, Mrs. Easton, fresh off the truck.

Rachel takes the phone out of the special, limited-edition box and inspects it.

RACHEL

What do I have to do?

SALES REPRESENTATIVE

Nothing. I've transferred your contacts and content. Any texts or messages you received while your number was out of commission should be waiting for you.

Rachel inspects the phone and begins sifting through her messages.

RACHEL

(Under her breath)

Delete... delete... delete... delete... delete... delete... delete...

She comes across an unexpected voicemail notification. With an inquisitive expression, she holds her phone to her ear and listens to the message.

SALES REPRESENTATIVE

You're very lucky to be getting one of these, Mrs. Easton. This model has very limited quantities, and the manufacturer has strict distribution controls over it.

Rachel clenches her teeth with rage as she continues to listen to the message.

SALES REPRESENTATIVE

Of course, the price tag keeps most people out of consideration. I'm just excited I got to see one in person.

Rachel pulls the phone away from her ear and slams it against a nearby display case repeatedly. The glass on the front of the phone cracks so severely that pieces of it fall to the floor. Rachel tempers her anger as she looks around and sees she has drawn the attention of everyone in the store. She calmly shows what's left of the phone to the sales representative.

RACHEL

This one's broken.

RACHEL'S BACKYARD - LATER THAT EVENING

Rachel sits in the dark of her backyard. She thoughtfully smokes a cigarette with a drink in front of her. Mary enters from her side yard.

MARY

Rachel?!

Rachel says nothing as she continues to sit in deep contemplation.

MARY

Rachel?!

Mary approaches Rachel and sits down next to her.

MARY

What are you doing out here in the dark? Caleb can't reach you, and he's worried.

Mary takes out her phone and texts a message to Caleb.

RACHEL

I'm... having trouble with my new phone.

MARY

Well, I told him you're fine.

Mary finishes up her text.

MARY

It's sweet how he worries about you. I think you should keep him.

Mary gets up to return home when Rachel interrupts her exit.

RACHEL

Can I ask you a question?

Mary stops and returns to her seat.

MARY

Sure.

RACHEL

What was going through your head that night?

MARY

What night?

Rachel can't believe Mary's obtuseness.

RACHEL

(Sarcastically)

The night you first tried anal.

Mary doesn't read Rachel's snarky tone as she begins to reminisce.

MARY

It was our honeymoon. Craig and I had been drinking all day, and we had done just about everything else we could have sexually...

Rachel shakes her head as she interrupts.

RACHEL

This sounds like a charming story, Mary, but that's NOT what I'm talking about.

Mary stops talking but still doesn't understand Rachel's question.

RACHEL

I was talking about the night at Megan's apartment.

Mary realizes her mistake and tries to mask her embarrassment.

MARY

I thought we agreed to add that to the list of things we never talk about.

Mary takes a drink from Rachel's glass.

RACHEL

I'm not asking to rehash it. I'm asking if you considered the consequences of what you were doing.

Mary becomes suspect of Rachel.

MARY

This is ginger ale. What's going on with you? First, you're out here in the dark with only pop in your glass, and now you're asking me questions about consequences? I didn't think that word was in your vocabulary.

Rachel becomes uncomfortable.

RACHEL

Just... tell me.

Mary sits thoughtfully for a moment.

MARY

Honestly, consequences never entered my mind.

RACHEL

But what if things didn't go well? Weren't you worried about yourself?

Mary shrugs her shoulders.

MARY

I know I should have been. I mean... I'm familiar with your work, but at that moment, whatever was going to happen to me didn't matter. The only thing I was concerned about was Anne.

Rachel thoughtfully nods as she turns her attention back to the darkness of her backyard. The goat strolls onto Rachel's patio and takes Mary by surprise.

MARY

Rachel? Why do you have a goat in your backyard?

The goat obnoxiously bleats in answer.

LAWYER'S OFFICE - ONE WEEK LATER

KRISTINE MARSHALL, a flawlessly manicured, veteran jurist, works diligently behind her desk as knocks rap on her door.

KRISTINE

Yes.

Kristine looks up from her desk as Rachel enters.

KRISTINE

Rachel? Did we have an appointment today?

RACHEL

No. I'm here to talk to you about the Michaels divorce.

KRISTINE

The Michaels divorce? You know I can't discuss that with you.

Rachel sits down in a chair across from Kristine and places her horribly damaged cell phone on the desk.

RACHEL

You'll want to talk to me after you hear this.

KRISTINE

What is it?

Kristine gently picks up the shattered remains of Rachel's cellular device.

RACHEL

(Reluctantly)

A conversation between Jill and John. She must have accidentally dialed my number, and my voicemail recorded the whole thing. After you listen to it, I'm sure you'll want to ask me some questions.

Kristine navigates what's left of the phone well enough to play back the voicemail. She holds the phone close to her ear and listens intently. Rachel watches Kristine listen to the message.

RACHEL

(Restlessly)

I'll do whatever I have to.

Kristine brings the phone down to her desk. Bits of broken screen fall from her ear.

KRISTINE

(Appalled)

He said this at a funeral?

Rachel shrugs her shoulders.

RACHEL
I don't know where he said it.

KRISTINE
Does Jill know you have this?

Rachel shakes her head.

RACHEL
I don't know.

Kristine takes the phone, walks to her door, and summons her assistant, NINA.

KRISTINE
Nina, would you come here for a minute.

Nina enters the doorway and takes Rachel's phone from Kristine.

KRISTINE
Take this. Make an audio copy of the voicemail and prepare a transcript.

NINA
Yes, Ms. Marshall.

Nina leaves the doorway and Kristine returns to her desk.

KRISTINE
Thank you for bringing this to me. Jill won't have to worry about any further custody litigation.

Rachel is perplexed.

RACHEL
What? Don't you need me to testify or something?

KRISTINE
Testify about what?

Rachel makes a series of befuddled facial expressions.

RACHEL
You heard the conversation.

KRISTINE
Yes, I did. Did you?

RACHEL

Yeah! He's using ME as an excuse to get the kids.

KRISTINE

And then he continued. Didn't you listen to the entire conversation?

Rachel tries to recall.

RACHEL

I guess not. My phone had a slight... malfunction.

Kristine smiles.

KRISTINE

You won't need to testify. After John's attorney hears him on that recording, he's not going to want to pursue this.

RACHEL

What's on it?

KRISTINE

Let's just say John can never try to impeach your character without putting his own in question.

Rachel sits motionless in astonishment. Nina enters the office and lays Rachel's phone on the desk.

NINA

Here you go, Ms. Marshall.

KRISTINE

Thank you, Nina. Would you close the door on your way out?

Nina pulls the door shut as she leaves the room. Kristine becomes stern and authoritative.

KRISTINE

Rachel, if half the things I've heard about you are only ten percent accurate, I would be remiss if I didn't advise you NOT to listen to the rest of this message. Delete it, immediately. This is over. Jill won. There's no need for you to give John Michaels any more of your attention.

Kristine picks up Rachel's phone, stands, and opens the door. Rachel takes the cue.

KRISTINE
Thank you for bringing this to my attention. Jill's lucky to have a friend like you.

Kristine presents the phone to Rachel, who gingerly takes it back.

KRISTINE
Enjoy the rest of your day, Rachel.

Rachel anxiously smiles and exits the office.

BACK ALLEY BAR - ONE WEEK LATER, EVENING

Jill enters and scans the bar for anyone familiar. LISA, the hostess, greets Jill.

LISA
Hi. Can I help you with something?

JILL
Yes, I'm meeting some friends here, but it looks like I may be the first one.

LISA
You're friends with Caleb's girlfriend, aren't you?

Jill is taken back by Lisa's description.

JILL
I'm sorry. I'm not used to hearing that word when referring to her.

Their conversation is interrupted when Rachel emerges from the kitchen area while actively buttoning up her shirt. Rachel makes eye contact with Jill and tries to avoid any questions.

RACHEL
Jill! You're here. Let's go wait for the others.

Jill knowingly smirks as she follows Rachel to their table.

BACK ALLEY BAR BACK ROOM - CONTINUOUS

Rachel and Jill take their seats at what has become their regular table. Caleb quickly approaches with water and menus.

JILL

Thank you, Caleb. It's nice to see you.

Jill takes a menu and opens it.

CALEB

Nice to see you too, Jill. Can I get you anything from the bar?

Jill keeps her attention on her open menu.

JILL

Caleb, honey, your shirt is inside out.

Caleb looks down at his inverted collar and excuses himself.

JILL

I hope y'all didn't desecrate any food preparation areas.

Rachel smiles and opens her menu.

RACHEL

I'll stop you from ordering anything potentially contaminated.

Rachel and Jill continue their conversation behind their open menus.

JILL

John withdrew his petition.

RACHEL

Good.

Jill drops her menu.

JILL

I can't thank you enough for what you were willing to do.

Rachel continues using her menu as a shield.

RACHEL

Don't mention it. Literally.

Jill sighs as her thankful smile is deliberately ignored.

Rachel finally lowers her menu when Mary and Anne enter the room and sit down.

MARY
Sorry we're late.

ANNE
It's my fault.

RACHEL
Fasten yourself to another piece of furniture?

JILL/MARY
(Outraged)
Rachel!

RACHEL
What?! I've waited a month!

Jill and Mary shake their heads with disgust over Rachel's comment.

ANNE
It's okay. I know it's been killing her holding it in this long.

As the women situate themselves around the table, Mary notices Jill's ring finger.

MARY
You're wearing your engagement ring! Is the wedding back on?

Jill radiates happiness.

JILL
Yes, the wedding is back on.

ANNE
Was it off? What'd I miss?

RACHEL
Robert came clean about his clown fetish, and Jill wasn't sure if she could fill those big red shoes.

Anne and Mary dismissively shake their heads.

JILL
(To Rachel)
Did you just call him Robert?

Rachel lets out a surrendering sigh.

RACHEL

Yeah, I should probably get used to it. I don't want to confuse the kids.

Jill smiles broadly.

JILL

Thanks.

Anne lifts her glass of water for a toast.

ANNE

Well, congratulations. May you have many years of happiness together.

The women lift their glasses and toast to Jill.

MARY

This calls for a celebration. Order accordingly, ladies, because we're getting dessert!

Rachel follows through with her warning and silently advises Jill against ordering dessert.

JOHN MICHAELS' DRIVEWAY - NEXT MORNING

John exits his front door with his car keys in hand. He stops in his tracks as he looks into his luxury sedan and discovers the car's interior is completely destroyed.

John watches powerlessly as the goat continues to devour his upholstery.

END OF BUNCO